SOLUTIONS
MANUAL

SOLUTIONS MANUAL

for use with

macroeconomics
eighth edition

N. GREGORY MANKIW

Nora Underwood
University of Central Florida

WORTH PUBLISHERS

Solutions Manual
by Nora Underwood
for use with
Mankiw: **Macroeconomics,** Eighth Edition

© 2013, 2010, 2007, 2003, 2000, 1997, 1994 by Worth Publishers

ISBN 13: 978-1-4641-0510-4
ISBN 10: 1-4641-0510-3

Second printing 2013
Printed in the United States of America.

Worth Publishers
41 Madison Avenue
New York, NY 10010
www.worthpublishers.com

Contents

Preface

The best way to learn any skill is to practice it. Listening to lectures and reading textbooks are important in learning to think like an economist, but alone they are insufficient for thoroughly understanding and applying the skills of economic reasoning.

Each chapter of **Macroeconomics, Eighth Edition** by N. Gregory Mankiw contains "Questions for Review" and "Problems and Applications." These give your students opportunities to practice and hone their skills in economic reasoning—to consolidate their understanding of the concepts and analytic tools in the chapter and to apply these tools to new situations.

To make the most of this opportunity, however, students need feedback. This manual provides answers to all of the questions and complete solutions to all of the problems in the text so that you can decide what feedback to give your students from this source. If students find a problem difficult, seeing an example of clear reasoning is enormously helpful. The solutions illustrate the logical application of concepts and analytic tools.

In addition to the textbook questions and problems, the answers to selected questions from the **Student Guide and Workbook** by Roger T. Kaufman are included. In order for these questions to be used for homework or exams, their answers appear only in this **Solutions Manual** for instructors.

I have put every effort into providing clear and complete solutions, as well as finding and correcting any typographical errors. I would like to thank and acknowledge the authors of previous editions of the solutions manual (Paula DeMasi, Jason Furman, and John Fernald) as my work has built upon what was done in past editions. I would also like to thank Lukia Kliossis, Edgar Bonilla, and Stacey Alexander of Worth Publishers for their assistance, patience, and commitment to getting all the details right.

Nora Underwood

Answers to Textbook Questions
and Problems

Questions for Review

1. Microeconomics is the study of how individual firms and households make decisions, and how they interact with one another. Microeconomic models of firms and households are based on principles of optimization—firms and households do the best they can given the constraints they face. For example, households choose which goods to purchase in order to maximize their utility, whereas firms decide how much to produce in order to maximize profits. In contrast, macroeconomics is the study of the economy as a whole; it focuses on issues such as how total output, total employment, and the overall price level are determined. These economy-wide variables are based on the interaction of many households and many firms; therefore, microeconomics forms the basis for macroeconomics.

2. Economists build models as a means of summarizing the relationships among economic variables. Models are useful because they abstract from the many details in the economy and allow one to focus on the most important economic connections.

3. A market-clearing model is one in which prices adjust to equilibrate supply and demand. Market-clearing models are useful in situations where prices are flexible. Yet in many situations, flexible prices may not be a realistic assumption. For example, labor contracts often set wages for up to three years. Or, firms such as magazine publishers change their prices only every three to four years. Most macroeconomists believe that price flexibility is a reasonable assumption for studying long-run issues. Over the long run, prices respond to changes in demand or supply, even though in the short run they may be slow to adjust.

Problems and Applications

1. Most of the macroeconomic issues that have been in the news lately (early 2012) are related to the after-effects of the "great recession" that officially lasted from December 2007 to June 2009. Although the recession technically ended over two and a half years ago, the unemployment rate is still above 8% and GDP growth has been sluggish. Discussion continues to focus on policy options to stimulate growth and employment. The Federal Reserve has limited options since the target federal funds rate has been near zero since 2008. European countries are also struggling and there is some debate about whether the European Union will continue to exist as is, or whether it might move forward with a smaller number of member countries.

2. Many philosophers of science believe that the defining characteristic of a science is the use of the scientific method of inquiry to establish stable relationships. Scientists examine data, often provided by controlled experiments, to support or disprove a hypothesis. Economists are more limited in their use of experiments. They cannot conduct controlled experiments on the economy; they must rely on the natural course of developments in the economy to collect data. To the extent that economists use the scientific method of inquiry, that is, developing hypotheses and testing them, economics has the characteristics of a science.

3. We can use a simple variant of the supply-and-demand model for pizza to answer this question. Assume that the quantity of ice cream demanded depends not only on the price of ice cream and income, but also on the price of frozen yogurt:

$$Q^d = D(P_{IC}, P_{FY}, Y).$$

We expect that demand for ice cream rises when the price of frozen yogurt rises, because ice cream and frozen yogurt are substitutes. That is, when the price of frozen yogurt goes up, I consume less of it and, instead, fulfill more of my frozen dessert urges through the consumption of ice cream.

The next part of the model is the supply function for ice cream, $Q^s = S(P_{IC})$. Finally, in equilibrium, supply must equal demand, so that $Q^s = Q^d$. Y and P_{FY} are the exogenous variables, and Q and P_{IC} are the endogenous variables. Figure 1-1 uses this model to show that a fall in the price of frozen yogurt results in an inward shift of the demand curve for ice cream. The new equilibrium has a lower price and quantity of ice cream.

Figure 1-1

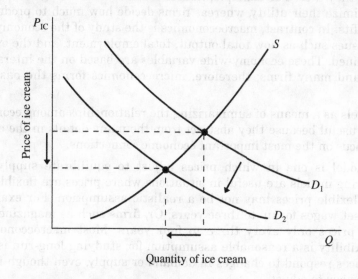

4. The price of haircuts changes rather infrequently. From casual observation, hairstylists tend to charge the same price over a one- or two-year period irrespective of the demand for haircuts or the supply of cutters. A market-clearing model for analyzing the market for haircuts has the unrealistic assumption of flexible prices. Such an assumption is unrealistic in the short run when we observe that prices are inflexible. Over the long run, however, the price of haircuts does tend to adjust; a market-clearing model is therefore appropriate.

Questions for Review

1. GDP measures the total income earned from the production of the new final goods and services in the economy, and it measures the total expenditures on the new final goods and services produced in the economy. GDP can measure two things at once because the total expenditures on the new final goods and services by the buyers must be equal to the income earned by the sellers of the new final goods and services. As the circular flow diagram in the text illustrates, these are alternative, equivalent ways of measuring the flow of dollars in the economy.

2. The consumer price index measures the overall level of prices in the economy. It tells us the price of a fixed basket of goods relative to the price of the same basket in the base year. The GDP deflator is the ratio of nominal GDP to real GDP in a given year. The GDP deflator measures the prices of all goods and services produced, whereas the CPI only measures prices of goods and services bought by consumers. The GDP deflator includes only domestically produced goods, whereas the CPI includes domestic and foreign goods bought by consumers. Finally, the CPI is a Laspeyres index that assigns fixed weights to the prices of different goods, whereas the GDP deflator is a Paasche index that assigns changing weights to the prices of different goods. In practice, the two price indices tend to move together and do not often diverge.

3. The Bureau of Labor Statistics classifies each person into one of the following three categories: employed, unemployed, or not in the labor force. The unemployment rate, which is the percentage of the labor force that is unemployed, is computed as follows:

$$\text{Unemployment Rate} = \frac{\text{Number of Unemployed}}{\text{Labor Force}} \times 100.$$

Note that the labor force is the number of people employed plus the number of people unemployed.

4. Every month, the Bureau of Labor Statistics (BLS) undertakes two surveys to measure employment. First, the BLS surveys about 60,000 households and thereby obtains an estimate of the share of people who say they are working. The BLS multiplies this share by an estimate of the population to estimate the number of people working. Second, the BLS surveys about 160,000 business establishments and asks how many people they employ. Each survey is imperfect; so the two measures of employment are not identical.

Problems and Applications

1. A large number of economic statistics are released regularly. These include the following:

    Gross Domestic Product—the market value of all final goods and services produced in a year.

    The Unemployment Rate—the percentage of the civilian labor force who do not have a job.

    Corporate Profits—the income of corporations after payments to workers and creditors. It gives an indication of the general financial health of the corporate sector.

The Consumer Price Index (CPI)—a measure of the average price that consumers pay for the goods they buy; changes in the CPI are a measure of inflation.

The Trade Balance—the difference between the value of goods exported abroad and the value of goods imported from abroad.

In looking at the economic statistics, most people want to see a low and stable inflation rate of about 2–3 percent, a low and stable unemployment rate of about 5 percent, and GDP growth in the 3–4-percent range. This indicates the economy is "healthy" and performing at its long-run average level. In early 2012, the unemployment rate fell to 8.3 percent, its lowest level in three years. In addition, the percentage of the working-age population that was in the labor force fell to its lowest level in 29 years. Inflation remains at about 2 percent. GDP growth was 2.8 percent (annualized rate) in the fourth quarter of 2011, up from 1.8 percent the previous quarter. The federal funds rate remained near zero, where it has been since 2008.

2. Value added by each person is the value of the good produced minus the amount the person paid for the materials needed to make the good. Therefore, the value added by the farmer is $1.00 ($1 − 0 = $1). The value added by the miller is $2: she sells the flour to the baker for $3 but paid $1 for the flour. The value added by the baker is $3: she sells the bread to the engineer for $6 but paid the miller $3 for the flour. GDP is the total value added, or $1 + $2 + $3 = $6. Note that GDP equals the value of the final good (the bread).

3. When a woman marries her butler, GDP falls by the amount of the butler's salary. This happens because measured total income, and therefore measured GDP, falls by the amount of the butler's loss in salary. If GDP truly measured the value of all goods and services, then the marriage would not affect GDP since the total amount of economic activity is unchanged. Actual GDP, however, is an imperfect measure of economic activity because the value of some goods and services is left out. Once the butler's work becomes part of his household chores, his services are no longer counted in GDP. As this example illustrates, GDP does not include the value of any output produced in the home. Similarly, GDP does not include other goods and services, such as the imputed rent on durable goods (e.g., cars and refrigerators) and any illegal trade.

4. a.   The airplane sold to the Air Force counts as government purchases because the Air Force is part of the government.
   b.   The airplane sold to American Airlines counts as investment because it is a capital good sold to a private firm.
   c.   The airplane sold to Air France counts as an export because it is sold to a foreigner.
   d.   The airplane sold to Amelia Earhart counts as consumption because it is sold to a private individual.
   e.   The airplane built to be sold next year counts as investment. In particular, the airplane is counted as inventory investment, which is where goods that are produced in one year and sold in another year are counted.

5. Data on parts (a) to (g) can be downloaded from the Bureau of Economic Analysis (www.bea.doc.gov—follow the links to Gross Dometic Product). Most of the data (not necessarily the earliest year) can also be found in the *Economic Report of the President.* By dividing each component (a) to (g) by nominal GDP and multiplying by 100, we obtain the following percentages:

	1950	1980	2005	2012
a. Personal consumption expenditures	65.5%	63.0%	70.0%	71.1%
b. Gross private domestic investment	18.4%	17.2%	16.9%	13.1%
c. Government consumption purchases	15.9%	20.3%	18.9%	19.7%
d. Net exports	0.2%	−0.5%	−5.8%	−3.8%
e. National defense purchases	6.7%	6.0%	4.7%	5.3%
f. State and local purchases	7.0%	11.6%	11.9%	11.7%
g. Imports	3.9%	10.5%	16.2%	17.7%

(Note: These data were downloaded February 8, 2012, from the BEA Web site.)

Among other things, we observe the following trends in the economy over the period 1950–2012:

(a) Personal consumption expenditures have been around two-thirds of GDP, although the share increased markedly between 1980 and 2005.

(b) The share of GDP going to gross private domestic investment fell slightly from 1950 to 2005. It fell sharply from 2005 to 2012 due to the 2007–2009 recession.

(c) The share going to government consumption purchases rose sharply from 1950 to 1980.

(d) Net exports, which were positive in 1950, have been negative since that time.

(e) The share going to national defense purchases has fallen slightly.

(f) The share going to state and local purchases rose from 1950 to 1980.

(g) Imports have grown rapidly relative to GDP.

6. a.   i.   Nominal GDP is the total value of goods and services measured at current prices. Therefore,

$$\text{Nominal GDP}_{2000} = (P_{cars}^{2000} \times Q_{cars}^{2000}) + (P_{bread}^{2000} \times Q_{bread}^{2000})$$
$$= (\$50,000 \times 100) + (\$10 \times 500,000)$$
$$= \$5,000,000 + \$5,000,000$$
$$= \$10,000,000.$$
$$\text{Nominal GDP}_{2010} = (P_{cars}^{2010} \times Q_{cars}^{2010}) + (P_{bread}^{2010} \times Q_{bread}^{2010})$$
$$= (\$60,000 \times 120) + (\$20 \times 400,000)$$
$$= \$7,200,000 + \$8,000,000$$
$$= \$15,200,000.$$

ii.   Real GDP is the total value of goods and services measured at constant prices. Therefore, to calculate real GDP in 2010 (with base year 2000), multiply the quantities purchased in the year 2010 by the 2000 prices:

$$\text{Real GDP}_{2010} = (P_{cars}^{2000} \times Q_{cars}^{2010}) + (P_{bread}^{2000} \times Q_{bread}^{2010})$$
$$= (\$50,000 \times 120) + (\$10 \times 400,000)$$
$$= \$6,000,000 + \$4,000,000$$
$$= \$10,000,000.$$

Real GDP for 2000 is calculated by multiplying the quantities in 2000 by the prices in 2000. Since the base year is 2000, real GDP$_{2000}$ equals nominal GDP$_{2000}$, which is \$10,000,000. Hence, real GDP stayed the same between 2000 and 2010.

iii.   The implicit price deflator for GDP compares the current prices of all goods and services produced to the prices of the same goods and services in a base year. It is calculated as follows:

$$\text{Implicit Price Deflator}_{2010} = \frac{\text{Nominal GDP}_{2010}}{\text{Real GDP}_{2010}}.$$

Using the values for Nominal GDP$_{2010}$ and real GDP$_{2010}$ calculated above:

$$\text{Implicit Price Deflator}_{2010} = \frac{\$15,200,000}{\$10,000,000}$$
$$= 1.52.$$

This calculation reveals that prices of the goods produced in the year 2010 increased by 52 percent compared to the prices that the goods in the economy sold for in 2000. (Because 2000 is the base year, the value for the implicit price deflator for the year 2000 is 1.0 because nominal and real GDP are the same for the base year.)

iv.   The consumer price index (CPI) measures the level of prices in the economy. The CPI is called a fixed-weight index because it uses a fixed basket of goods over time to weight prices. If the base year is 2000, the CPI in 2010 is an average of prices in 2010, but weighted by the composition of goods produced in 2000. The CPI$_{2010}$ is calculated as follows:

$$\text{CPI}_{2010} = \frac{(P_{\text{cars}}^{2010} \times Q_{\text{cars}}^{2000}) + (P_{\text{bread}}^{2010} \times Q_{\text{bread}}^{2000})}{(P_{\text{cars}}^{2000} \times Q_{\text{cars}}^{2000}) + (P_{\text{bread}}^{2000} \times Q_{\text{bread}}^{2000})}$$

$$= \frac{(\$60,000 \times 100) + (\$20 \times 500,000)}{(\$50,000 \times 100) + (\$10 \times 500,000)}$$

$$= \frac{\$16,000,000}{\$10,000,000}$$

$$= 1.6.$$

This calculation shows that the price of goods purchased in 2010 increased by 60 percent compared to the prices these goods would have sold for in 2000. The CPI for 2000, the base year, equals 1.0.

b.   The implicit price deflator is a Paasche index because it is computed with a changing basket of goods; the CPI is a Laspeyres index because it is computed with a fixed basket of goods. From (6.a.iii), the implicit price deflator for the year 2010 is 1.52, which indicates that prices rose by 52 percent from what they were in the year 2000. From (6.a.iv.), the CPI for the year 2010 is 1.6, which indicates that prices rose by 60 percent from what they were in the year 2000.

If prices of all goods rose by, say, 50 percent, then one could say unambiguously that the price level rose by 50 percent. Yet, in our example, relative prices have changed. The price of cars rose by 20 percent; the price of bread rose by 100 percent, making bread relatively more expensive.

As the discrepancy between the CPI and the implicit price deflator illustrates, the change in the price level depends on how the goods' prices are weighted. The CPI weights the price of goods by the quantities purchased in the year 2000. The implicit price deflator weights the price of goods by the quantities purchased in the year 2010. The quantity of bread consumed was higher in 2000 than in 2010, so the CPI places a higher weight on bread. Since the price of bread increased relatively more than the price of cars, the CPI shows a larger increase in the price level.

c.   There is no clear-cut answer to this question. Ideally, one wants a measure of the price level that accurately captures the cost of living. As a good becomes relatively more expensive, people buy less of it and more of other goods. In this example, consumers bought less bread and more cars. An index with fixed weights, such as the CPI, overestimates the change in the cost of living because it does not take into account that people can substitute less expensive goods for the ones that become more expensive. On the other hand, an index with changing weights, such as the GDP deflator, underestimates the change in the cost of living because it does not take into account that these induced substitutions make people less well off.

7. a.   The consumer price index uses the consumption bundle in year 1 to figure out how much weight to put on the price of a given good:

$$\text{CPI}^2 = \frac{(\$2 \times 10) + (\$1 \times 0)}{(\$1 \times 10) + (\$2 \times 0)}$$

$$= \frac{(P_{\text{red}}^2 \times Q_{\text{red}}^1) + (P_{\text{green}}^2 \times Q_{\text{green}}^1)}{(P_{\text{red}}^1 \times Q_{\text{red}}^1) + (P_{\text{green}}^1 \times Q_{\text{green}}^1)}$$

$$= 2.$$

According to the CPI, prices have doubled.

b. Nominal spending is the total value of output produced in each year. In year 1 and year 2, Abby buys 10 apples for $1 each, so her nominal spending remains constant at $10. For example,

$$\text{Nominal Spending}_2 = (P^2_{red} \times Q^2_{red}) + (P^2_{green} \times Q^2_{green})$$

$$= (\$2 \times 0) + (\$1 \times 10)$$

$$= \$10.$$

c. Real spending is the total value of output produced in each year valued at the prices prevailing in year 1. In year 1, the base year, her real spending equals her nominal spending of $10. In year 2, she consumes 10 green apples that are each valued at their year 1 price of $2, so her real spending is $20. That is,

$$\text{Real Spending}_2 = (P^1_{red} \times Q^2_{red}) + (P^1_{green} \times Q^2_{green})$$

$$= (\$1 \times 0) + (\$2 \times 10)$$

$$= \$20.$$

Hence, Abby's real spending rises from $10 to $20.

d. The implicit price deflator is calculated by dividing Abby's nominal spending in year 2 by her real spending that year:

$$\text{Implicit Price Deflator}_2 = \frac{\text{Nominal Spending}_2}{\text{Real Spending}_2}$$

$$= \frac{\$10}{\$20}$$

$$= 0.5.$$

Thus, the implicit price deflator suggests that prices have fallen by half. The reason for this is that the deflator estimates how much Abby values her apples using prices prevailing in year 1. From this perspective green apples appear very valuable. In year 2, when Abby consumes 10 green apples, it appears that her consumption has increased because the deflator values green apples more highly than red apples. The only way she could still be spending $10 on a higher consumption bundle is if the price of the good she was consuming fell.

e. If Abby thinks of red apples and green apples as perfect substitutes, then the cost of living in this economy has not changed—in either year it costs $10 to consume 10 apples. According to the CPI, however, the cost of living has doubled. This is because the CPI only takes into account the fact that the red apple price has doubled; the CPI ignores the fall in the price of green apples because they were not in the consumption bundle in year 1. In contrast to the CPI, the implicit price deflator estimates the cost of living has been cut in half. Thus, the CPI, a Laspeyres index, overstates the increase in the cost of living and the deflator, a Paasche index, understates it.

8. a. Real GDP falls because Disney does not produce any services while it is closed. This corresponds to a decrease in economic well-being because the income of workers and shareholders of Disney falls (the income side of the national accounts), and people's consumption of Disney falls (the expenditure side of the national accounts).

b. Real GDP rises because the original capital and labor in farm production now produce more wheat. This corresponds to an increase in the economic well-being of society, since people can now consume more wheat. (If people do not want to consume more wheat, then farmers and farmland can be shifted to producing other goods that society values.)

c.   Real GDP falls because with fewer workers on the job, firms produce less. This accurately reflects a fall in economic well-being.

d.   Real GDP falls because the firms that lay off workers produce less. This decreases economic well-being because workers' incomes fall (the income side), and there are fewer goods for people to buy (the expenditure side).

e.   Real GDP is likely to fall, as firms shift toward production methods that produce fewer goods but emit less pollution. Economic well-being, however, may rise. The economy now produces less measured output but more clean air; clean air is not traded in markets and, thus, does not show up in measured GDP, but is nevertheless a good that people value.

f.   Real GDP rises because the high-school students go from an activity in which they are not producing market goods and services to one in which they are. Economic well-being, however, may decrease. In ideal national accounts, attending school would show up as investment because it presumably increases the future productivity of the worker. Actual national accounts do not measure this type of investment. Note also that future GDP may be lower than it would be if the students stayed in school, since the future work force will be less educated.

g.   Measured real GDP falls because fathers spend less time producing market goods and services. The actual production of goods and services need not have fallen, however. Measured production (what the fathers are paid to do) falls, but unmeasured production of child-rearing services rises.

9.   As Senator Robert Kennedy pointed out, GDP is an imperfect measure of economic performance or well-being. In addition to the left-out items that Kennedy cited, GDP also ignores the imputed rent on durable goods such as cars, refrigerators, and lawnmowers; many services and products produced as part of household activity, such as cooking and cleaning; and the value of goods produced and sold in illegal activities, such as the drug trade. These imperfections in the measurement of GDP do not necessarily reduce its usefulness. As long as these measurement problems stay constant over time, then GDP is useful in comparing economic activity from year to year. Moreover, a large GDP allows us to afford better medical care for our children, newer books for their education, and more toys for their play. Finally, countries with higher levels of GDP tend to have higher levels of life expectancy, better access to clean water and sanitation, and higher levels of education. GDP is therefore a useful measure for comparing the level of growth and development across countries.

CHAPTER 3 National Income: Where It Comes From and Where It Goes

Questions for Review

1. The factors of production and the production technology determine the amount of output an economy can produce. The factors of production are the inputs used to produce goods and services: the most important factors are capital and labor. The production technology determines how much output can be produced from any given amounts of these inputs. An increase in one of the factors of production or an improvement in technology leads to an increase in the economy's output.

2. When a firm decides how much of a factor of production to hire or demand, it considers how this decision affects profits. For example, hiring an extra unit of labor increases output and therefore increases revenue; the firm compares this additional revenue to the additional cost from the higher wage bill. The additional revenue the firm receives depends on the marginal product of labor (MPL) and the price of the good produced (P). An additional unit of labor produces MPL units of additional output, which sells for P dollars per unit. Therefore, the additional revenue to the firm is $P \times MPL$. The cost of hiring the additional unit of labor is the wage W. Thus, this hiring decision has the following effect on profits:

$$\Delta\text{Profit} = \Delta\text{Revenue} - \Delta\text{Cost}$$
$$= (P \times MPL) - W.$$

If the additional revenue, $P \times MPL$, exceeds the cost (W) of hiring the additional unit of labor, then profit increases. The firm will hire labor until it is no longer profitable to do so—that is, until the MPL falls to the point where the change in profit is zero. In the equation above, the firm hires labor until Δprofit = 0, which is when $(P \times MPL) = W$.

This condition can be rewritten as:

$$MPL = W/P.$$

Therefore, a competitive profit-maximizing firm hires labor until the marginal product of labor equals the real wage. The same logic applies to the firm's decision regarding how much capital to hire: the firm will hire capital until the marginal product of capital equals the real rental price.

3. A production function has constant returns to scale if an equal percentage increase in all factors of production causes an increase in output of the same percentage. For example, if a firm increases its use of capital and labor by 50 percent, and output increases by 50 percent, then the production function has constant returns to scale.

   If the production function has constant returns to scale, then total income (or equivalently, total output) in an economy of competitive profit-maximizing firms is divided between the return to labor, $MPL \times L$, and the return to capital, $MPK \times K$. That is, under constant returns to scale, economic profit is zero.

4. A Cobb–Douglas production function function has the form $F(K,L) = AK^{\alpha}L^{1-\alpha}$. The text showed that the parameter α gives capital's share of income. (Since income equals output for the overall economy, it is also capital's share of output.) So if capital earns one-fourth of total income, then $a = 0.25$. Hence, $F(K,L) = AK^{0.25}L^{0.75}$.

5. Consumption depends positively on disposable income—the amount of income after all taxes have been paid. The higher disposable income is, the greater consumption is.

   The quantity of investment goods demanded depends negatively on the real interest rate. For an investment to be profitable, its return must be greater than its cost. Because the real interest rate measures the cost of funds, a higher real interest rate makes it more costly to invest, so the demand for investment goods falls.

6. Government purchases are a measure of the dollar value of goods and services purchased directly by the government. For example, the government buys missiles and tanks, builds roads, and provides services such as air traffic control. All of these activities are part of GDP. Transfer payments are government payments to individuals that are not in exchange for goods or services. They are the opposite of taxes: taxes reduce household disposable income, whereas transfer payments increase it. Examples of transfer payments include Social Security payments to the elderly, unemployment insurance, and veterans' benefits.

7. Consumption, investment, and government purchases determine demand for the economy's output, whereas the factors of production and the production function determine the supply of output. The real interest rate adjusts to ensure that the demand for the economy's goods equals the supply. At the equilibrium interest rate, the demand for goods and services equals the supply.

8. When the government increases taxes, disposable income falls, and therefore consumption falls as well. The decrease in consumption equals the amount that taxes increase multiplied by the marginal propensity to consume (*MPC*). The higher the *MPC* is, the greater is the negative effect of the tax increase on consumption. Because output is fixed by the factors of production and the production technology, and government purchases have not changed, the decrease in consumption must be offset by an increase in investment. For investment to rise, the real interest rate must fall. Therefore, a tax increase leads to a decrease in consumption, an increase in investment, and a fall in the real interest rate.

Problems and Applications

1. a. According to the neoclassical theory of distribution, the real wage equals the marginal product of labor. Because of diminishing returns to labor, an increase in the labor force causes the marginal product of labor to fall. Hence, the real wage falls.

   Given a Cobb–Douglas production function, the increase in the labor force will increase the marginal product of capital and will increase the real rental price of capital. With more workers, the capital will be used more intensively and will be more productive.

   b. The real rental price equals the marginal product of capital. If an earthquake destroys some of the capital stock (yet miraculously does not kill anyone and lower the labor force), the marginal product of capital rises and, hence, the real rental price rises.

   Given a Cobb–Douglas production function, the decrease in the capital stock will decrease the marginal product of labor and will decrease the real wage. With less capital, each worker becomes less productive.

   c. If a technological advance improves the production function, this is likely to increase the marginal products of both capital and labor. Hence, the real wage and the real rental price both increase.

   d. High inflation that doubles the nominal wage and the price level will have no impact on the real wage. Similarly, high inflation that doubles the nominal rental price of capital and the price level will have no impact on the real rental price of capital.

2. a. To find the amount of output produced, substitute the given values for labor and land into the production function:

$$Y = 100^{0.5}100^{0.5} = 100.$$

   b. According to the text, the formulas for the marginal product of labor and the marginal product of capital (land) are:

$$MPL = (1 - \alpha)AK^\alpha L^{-\alpha}$$

$$MPK = \alpha AK^{\alpha - 1}L^{1 - \alpha}$$

In this problem, α is 0.5 and A is 1. Substitute in the given values for labor and land to find the marginal product of labor is 0.5 and marginal product of capital (land) is 0.5. We know that the real wage equals the marginal product of labor and the real rental price of land equals the marginal product of capital (land).

c. Labor's share of the output is given by the marginal product of labor times the quantity of labor, or 50.

d. The new level of output is 70.71.

e. The new wage is 0.71. The new rental price of land is 0.35.

f. Labor now receives 71.

3. A production function has decreasing returns to scale if an equal percentage increase in all factors of production leads to a smaller percentage increase in output. For example, if we double the amounts of capital and labor, and output less than doubles, then the production function has decreasing returns to scale. This may happen if there is a fixed factor such as land in the production function, and this fixed factor becomes scarce as the economy grows larger.

A production function has increasing returns to scale if an equal percentage increase in all factors of production leads to a larger percentage increase in output. For example, if doubling inputs of capital and labor more than doubles output, then the production function has increasing returns to scale. This may happen if specialization of labor becomes greater as the population grows. For example, if only one worker builds a car, then it takes him a long time because he has to learn many different skills, and he must constantly change tasks and tools. But if many workers build a car, then each one can specialize in a particular task and become very fast at it.

4. a. A Cobb–Douglas production function has the form $Y = AK^{\alpha}L^{1-\alpha}$. The text showed that the marginal products for the Cobb–Douglas production function are:

$$MPL = (1 - \alpha)Y/L.$$

$$MPK = \alpha Y/K.$$

Competitive profit-maximizing firms hire labor until its marginal product equals the real wage, and hire capital until its marginal product equals the real rental rate. Using these facts and the above marginal products for the Cobb–Douglas production function, we find:

$$W/P = MPL = (1 - \alpha)Y/L.$$

$$R/P = MPK = \alpha Y/K.$$

Rewriting this:

$$(W/P)L = MPL \times L = (1 - \alpha)Y.$$

$$(R/P)K = MPK \times K = \alpha Y.$$

Note that the terms $(W/P)L$ and $(R/P)K$ are the wage bill and total return to capital, respectively. Given that the value of $\alpha = 0.3$, then the above formulas indicate that labor receives 70 percent of total output (or income), which is $(1 - 0.3)$, and capital receives 30 percent of total output (or income).

b. To determine what happens to total output when the labor force increases by 10 percent, consider the formula for the Cobb–Douglas production function:

$$Y = AK^{\alpha}L^{1-\alpha}.$$

Let Y_1 equal the initial value of output and Y_2 equal final output. We know that $\alpha = 0.3$. We also know that labor L increases by 10 percent:

$$Y_1 = AK^{0.3}L^{0.7}.$$

$$Y_2 = AK^{0.3}(1.1L)^{0.7}.$$

Note that we multiplied L by 1.1 to reflect the 10-percent increase in the labor force.

To calculate the percentage change in output, divide Y_2 by Y_1:

$$\frac{Y_2}{Y_1} = \frac{AK^{0.3}(1.1L)^{0.7}}{AK^{0.3}L^{0.7}}$$

$$= (1.1)^{0.7}$$

$$= 1.069.$$

That is, output increases by 6.9 percent.

To determine how the increase in the labor force affects the rental price of capital, consider the formula for the real rental price of capital R/P:

$$R/P = MPK = \alpha AK^{\alpha-1}L^{1-\alpha}.$$

We know that $\alpha = 0.3$. We also know that labor (L) increases by 10 percent. Let $(R/P)_1$ equal the initial value of the rental price of capital, and $(R/P)_2$ equal the final rental price of capital after the labor force increases by 10 percent. To find $(R/P)_2$, multiply L by 1.1 to reflect the 10-percent increase in the labor force:

$$(R/P)_1 = 0.3AK^{-0.7}L^{0.7}.$$

$$(R/P)_2 = 0.3AK^{-0.7}(1.1L)^{0.7}.$$

The rental price increases by the ratio

$$\frac{(R/P)_2}{(R/P)_1} = \frac{0.3AK^{-0.7}(1.1L)^{0.7}}{0.3AK^{-0.7}L^{0.7}}$$

$$= (1.1)^{0.7}$$

$$= 1.069.$$

So the rental price increases by 6.9 percent.

To determine how the increase in the labor force affects the real wage, consider the formula for the real wage W/P:

$$W/P = MPL = (1-\alpha)AK^{\alpha}L^{-\alpha}.$$

We know that $\alpha = 0.3$. We also know that labor (L) increases by 10 percent. Let $(W/P)_1$ equal the initial value of the real wage and $(W/P)_2$ equal the final value of the real wage. To find $(W/P)_2$, multiply L by 1.1 to reflect the 10-percent increase in the labor force:

$$(W/P)_1 = (1-0.3)AK^{0.3}L^{-0.3}.$$

$$(W/P)_2 = (1-0.3)AK^{0.3}(1.1L)^{-0.3}.$$

To calculate the percentage change in the real wage, divide $(W/P)_2$ by $(W/P)_1$:

$$\frac{(W/P)_2}{(W/P)_1} = \frac{(1-0.3)AK^{0.3}(1.1L)^{-0.3}}{(1-0.3)AK^{0.3}L^{-0.3}}$$

$$= (1.1)^{-0.3}$$

$$= 0.972.$$

That is, the real wage falls by 2.8 percent.

c.   We can use the same logic as in part (b) to set

$$Y_1 = AK^{0.3}L^{0.7}.$$

$$Y_2 = A(1.1K)^{0.3}L^{0.7}.$$

Therefore, we have:

$$\frac{Y_2}{Y_1} = \frac{A(1.1K)^{0.3}L^{0.7}}{AK^{0.3}L^{0.7}}$$

$$= (1.1)^{0.3}$$

$$= 1.029.$$

This equation shows that output increases by about 3 percent. Notice that $\alpha < 0.5$ means that proportional increases to capital will increase output by less than the same proportional increase to labor.

Again using the same logic as in part (b) for the change in the real rental price of capital:

$$\frac{(R/P)_2}{(R/P)_1} = \frac{0.3A(1.1K)^{-0.7}L^{0.7}}{0.3AK^{-0.7}L^{0.7}}$$

$$= (1.1)^{-0.7}$$

$$= 0.935.$$

The real rental price of capital falls by 6.5 percent because there are diminishing returns to capital; that is, when capital increases, its marginal product falls.

Finally, the change in the real wage is:

$$\frac{(W/P)_2}{(W/P)_1} = \frac{0.7A(1.1K)^{0.3}L^{-0.3}}{0.7AK^{0.3}L^{-0.3}}$$

$$(1.1)^{0.3}$$

$$= 1.029.$$

Hence, real wages increase by 2.9 percent because the added capital increases the marginal productivity of the existing workers. (Notice that the wage and output have both increased by the same amount, leaving the labor share unchanged—a feature of Cobb–Douglas technologies.)

d. Using the same formula, we find that the change in output is:

$$\frac{Y_2}{Y_1} = \frac{(1.1A)K^{0.3}L^{0.7}}{AK^{0.3}L^{0.7}}$$

$$= 1.1.$$

This equation shows that output increases by 10 percent. Similarly, the rental price of capital and the real wage also increase by 10 percent:

$$\frac{(R/P)_2}{(R/P)_1} = \frac{0.3(1.1A)K^{-0.7}L^{0.7}}{0.3AK^{-0.7}L^{0.7}}$$

$$= 1.1.$$

$$\frac{(W/P)_2}{(W/P)_1} = \frac{0.7(1.1A)K^{0.3}L^{-0.3}}{0.7AK^{0.3}L^{-0.3}}$$

$$= 1.1.$$

5. Labor income is defined as

$$\frac{W}{P} \times L = \frac{WL}{P}.$$

Labor's share of income is defined as

$$\left(\frac{WL}{P}\right) / Y = \frac{WL}{PY}.$$

If this ratio is about constant at, say, a value of 0.7, then it must be the case that $W/P = 0.7*Y/L$. This means that the real wage is roughly proportional to labor productivity. Hence, any trend in labor productivity must be matched by an equal trend in real wages—otherwise, labor's share would deviate from 0.7. Thus, the first fact (a constant labor share) implies the second fact (the trend in real wages closely tracks the trend in labor productivity)

6. a. According to the neoclassical theory, technical progress that increases the marginal product of farmers causes their real wage to rise.

b.   The real wage for farmers is measured as units of farm output per worker. The real wage is W/P_F, and this is equal to (\$/worker)/(\$/unit of farm output).

c.   If the marginal productivity of barbers is unchanged, then their real wage is unchanged.

d.   The real wage for barbers is measured as haircuts per worker. The real wage is W/P_B, and this is equal to (\$/worker)/(\$/haircut).

e.   If workers can move freely between being farmers and being barbers, then they must be paid the same wage W in each sector.

f.   If the nominal wage W is the same in both sectors, but the real wage in terms of farm goods is greater than the real wage in terms of haircuts, then the price of haircuts must have risen relative to the price of farm goods. We know that $W/P = MPL$ so that $W = P \times MPL$. This means that $P_F MPL_F = P_H MPL_B$, given that the nominal wages are the same. Since the marginal product of labor for barbers has not changed and the marginal product of labor for farmers has risen, the price of a haircut must have risen relative to the price of the farm output. If we put it in growth-rate terms, then the growth of the farm price + the growth of the marginal product of the farm labor = the growth of the haircut price.

g.   Both groups benefit from technological progress in farming.

7. a.   The marginal product of labor MPL is found by differentiating the production function with respect to labor:

$$MPL = \frac{dY}{dL}$$

$$= \frac{1}{3} K^{1/3} H^{1/3} L^{-2/3}.$$

An increase in human capital will increase the marginal product of labor because more human capital makes all the existing labor more productive.

b.   The marginal product of human capital MPH is found by differentiating the production function with respect to human capital:

$$MPH = \frac{dY}{dH}$$

$$= \frac{1}{3} K^{1/3} L^{1/3} H^{-2/3}.$$

An increase in human capital will decrease the marginal product of human capital because there are diminishing returns.

c.   The labor share of output is the proportion of output that goes to labor. The total amount of output that goes to labor is the real wage (which, under perfect competition, equals the marginal product of labor) times the quantity of labor. This quantity is divided by the total amount of output to compute the labor share:

$$\text{Labor Share} = \frac{(\frac{1}{3} K^{1/3} H^{1/3} L^{-2/3}) L}{K^{1/3} H^{1/3} L^{1/3}}$$

$$= \frac{1}{3}.$$

We can use the same logic to find the human capital share:

$$\text{Human Capital Share} = \frac{(\frac{1}{3} K^{1/3} L^{1/3} H^{-2/3}) H}{K^{1/3} H^{1/3} L^{1/3}}$$

$$= \frac{1}{3},$$

so labor gets one-third of the output, and human capital gets one-third of the output. Since workers own their human capital (we hope!), it will appear that labor gets two-thirds of output.

d.   The ratio of the skilled wage to the unskilled wage is:

$$\frac{W_{skilled}}{W_{unskilled}} = \frac{MPL + MPH}{MPL}$$

$$= \frac{\frac{1}{3}K^{1/3}L^{-2/3}H^{1/3} + \frac{1}{3}K^{1/3}L^{1/3}H^{-2/3}}{\frac{1}{3}K^{1/3}L^{-2/3}H^{1/3}}$$

$$= 1 + \frac{L}{H}.$$

Notice that the ratio is always greater than 1 because skilled workers get paid more than unskilled workers. Also, when H increases this ratio falls because the diminishing returns to human capital lower its return, while at the same time increasing the marginal product of unskilled workers.

e.   If more college scholarships increase H, then it does lead to a more egalitarian society. The policy lowers the returns to education, decreasing the gap between the wages of more and less educated workers. More importantly, the policy even raises the absolute wage of unskilled workers because their marginal product rises when the number of skilled workers rises.

8. The effect of a government tax increase of $100 billion on (a) public saving, (b) private saving, and (c) national saving can be analyzed by using the following relationships:

$$\text{National Saving} = [\text{Private Saving}] + [\text{Public Saving}]$$
$$= [Y - T - C(Y - T)] + [T - G]$$
$$= Y - C(Y - T) - G.$$

a.   **Public Saving**—The tax increase causes a 1-for-1 increase in public saving. T increases by $100 billion and, therefore, public saving increases by $100 billion.

b.   **Private Saving**—The increase in taxes decreases disposable income, $Y - T$, by $100 billion. Since the marginal propensity to consume (MPC) is 0.6, consumption falls by $0.6 \times \$100$ billion, or $60 billion. Hence,

$$\Delta\text{Private Saving} = -\$100b - 0.6(-\$100b) = -\$40b.$$

Private saving falls $40 billion.

c.   **National Saving**—Because national saving is the sum of private and public saving, we can conclude that the $100 billion tax increase leads to a $60 billion increase in national saving.

Another way to see this is by using the third equation for national saving expressed above, that national saving equals $Y - C(Y - T) - G$. The $100 billion tax increase reduces disposable income and causes consumption to fall by $60 billion. Since neither G nor Y changes, national saving thus rises by $60 billion.

d.   **Investment**—To determine the effect of the tax increase on investment, recall the national accounts identity:

$$Y = C(Y - T) + I(r) + G.$$

Rearranging, we find

$$Y - C(Y - T) - G = I(r).$$

The left-hand side of this equation is national saving, so the equation just says that national saving equals investment. Since national saving increases by $60 billion, investment must also increase by $60 billion.

How does this increase in investment take place? We know that investment depends on the real interest rate. For investment to rise, the real interest rate must fall. Figure 3-1 illustrates saving and investment as a function of the real interest rate.

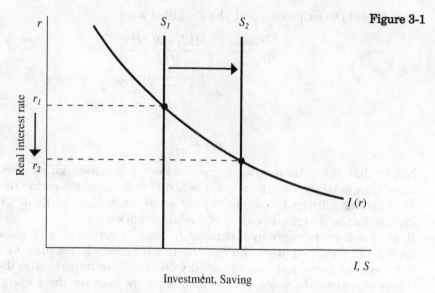

Figure 3-1

The tax increase causes national saving to rise, so the supply curve for loanable funds shifts to the right. The equilibrium real interest rate falls, and investment rises.

9. If consumers increase the amount that they consume today, then private saving and, therefore, national saving will fall. We know this from the definition of national saving:

$$\text{National Saving} = [\text{Private Saving}] + [\text{Public Saving}]$$
$$= [Y - T - C(Y - T)] + [T - G].$$

An increase in consumption decreases private saving, so national saving falls.

Figure 3-2 illustrates saving and investment as a function of the real interest rate. If national saving decreases, the supply curve for loanable funds shifts to the left, thereby raising the real interest rate and reducing investment.

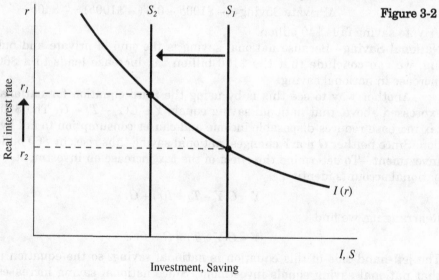

Figure 3-2

10. a. Private saving is the amount of disposable income, $Y - T$, that is not consumed:

$$S^{\text{private}} = Y - T - C$$
$$= 5,000 - 1,000 - (250 + 0.75(5,000 - 1,000))$$
$$= 750.$$

Public saving is the amount of taxes the government has left over after it makes its purchases:

$$S^{\text{public}} = T - G$$
$$= 1,000 - 1,000$$
$$= 0.$$

Total saving is the sum of private saving and public saving:

$$S = S^{\text{private}} + S^{\text{public}}$$
$$= 750 + 0$$
$$= 750.$$

b.   The equilibrium interest rate is the value of r that clears the market for loanable funds. We already know that national saving is 750, so we just need to set it equal to investment:

$$S = I$$
$$750 = 1,000 - 50r$$

Solving this equation for r, we find:

$$r = 5\%.$$

c.   When the government increases its spending, private saving remains the same as before (notice that G does not appear in the S^{private} above) while government saving decreases. Putting the new G into the equations above:

$$S^{\text{private}} = 750$$

$$S^{\text{public}} = T - G$$
$$= 1,000 - 1,250$$
$$= -250.$$

Thus,

$$S = S^{\text{private}} + S^{\text{public}}$$
$$= 750 + (-250)$$
$$= 500.$$

d.   Once again the equilibrium interest rate clears the market for loanable funds:

$$S = I$$
$$500 = 1,000 - 50r$$

Solving this equation for r, we find:

$$r = 10\%.$$

11.   To determine the effect on investment of an equal increase in both taxes and government spending, consider the national income accounts identity for national saving:

$$\text{National Saving} = [\text{Private Saving}] + [\text{Public Saving}]$$
$$= [Y - T - C(Y - T)] + [T - G].$$

We know that Y is fixed by the factors of production. We also know that the change in consumption equals the marginal propensity to consume (MPC) times the change in disposable income. This tells us that

$$\Delta\text{National Saving} = [-\Delta T - (MPC \times (-\Delta T))] + [\Delta T - \Delta G]$$
$$= [-\Delta T + (MPC \times \Delta T)] + 0$$
$$= (MPC - 1)\,\Delta T.$$

The above expression tells us that the impact on saving of an equal increase in T and G depends on the size of the marginal propensity to consume. The closer the MPC is to 1, the smaller is the fall in saving. For example, if the MPC equals 1, then the fall in consumption equals the rise in government purchases, so national saving $[Y - C(Y - T) - G]$ is unchanged. The closer the MPC is to 0 (and therefore the larger is the amount saved rather than spent for a one-dollar change in disposable income), the greater is the impact on saving. Because we assume that the *MPC* is less than 1, we expect that national saving falls in response to an equal increase in taxes and government spending.

The reduction in saving means that the supply of loanable funds curve shifts to the left in Figure 3-3. The real interest rate rises, and investment falls.

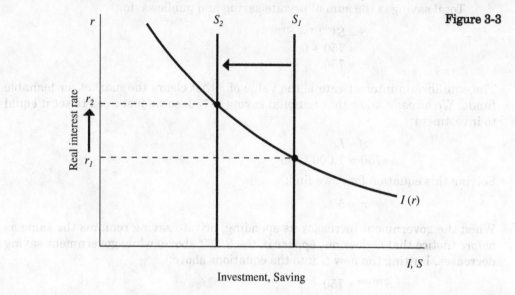

Figure 3-3

12. a. The demand curve for business investment shifts out to the right because the subsidy increases the number of profitable investment opportunities for any given interest rate. The demand curve for residential investment remains unchanged.

b. The total demand curve for investment in the economy shifts out to the right since it represents the sum of business investment, which shifts out to the right, and residential investment, which is unchanged. As a result the real interest rate rises as in Figure 3-4.

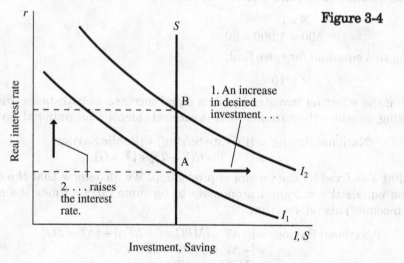

Figure 3-4

c. The total quantity of investment does not change because it is constrained by the inelastic supply of savings. The investment tax credit leads to a rise in business investment, but an offsetting fall in residential investment. That is, the higher interest rate means that residential investment falls (a movement along the curve), whereas the rightward shift of the business investment curve leads business investment to rise by an equal amount. Figure 3-5 shows this change. Note that $I_1^B + I_1^R = I_2^B + I_2^R = \bar{S}$

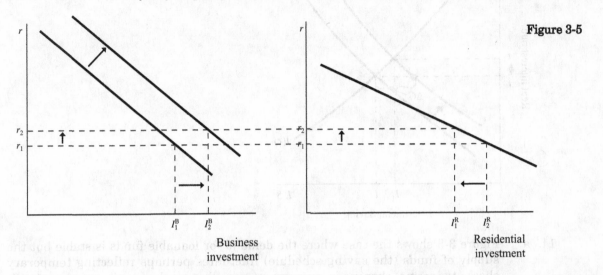

Business investment

Residential investment

Figure 3-5

13. In this chapter, we concluded that an increase in government expenditures reduces national saving and raises the interest rate; it therefore crowds out investment by the full amount of the increase in government expenditure. Similarly, a tax cut increases disposable income and hence consumption; this increase in consumption translates into a fall in national saving—again, it crowds out investment by the full amount of the increase in consumption.

If consumption depends on the interest rate, then these conclusions about fiscal policy are modified somewhat. If consumption depends on the interest rate, then so does saving. The higher the interest rate, the greater the return to saving. Hence, it seems reasonable to think that an increase in the interest rate might increase saving and reduce consumption. Figure 3-6 shows saving as an increasing function of the interest rate.

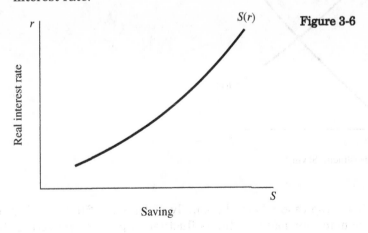

Figure 3-6

Consider what happens when government purchases increase. At any given level of the interest rate, national saving falls by the change in government purchases, as shown in Figure 3-7. The figure shows that if the saving function slopes upward, investment falls by less than the amount that government purchases rises by; this happens because consumption falls and saving increases in response to the higher interest rate. Hence, the more responsive consumption is to the interest rate, the less government purchases crowd out investment.

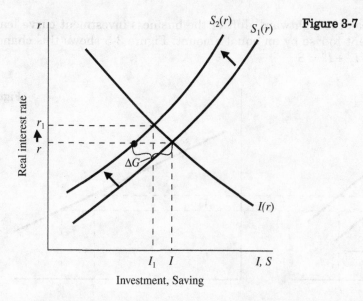

Figure 3-7

14. a. Figure 3-8 shows the case where the demand for loanable funds is stable but the supply of funds (the saving schedule) fluctuates perhaps reflecting temporary shocks to income, changes in government spending, or changes in consumer confidence. In this case, when interest rates fall, investment rises; when interest rates rise, investment falls. We would expect a negative correlation between investment and interest rates.

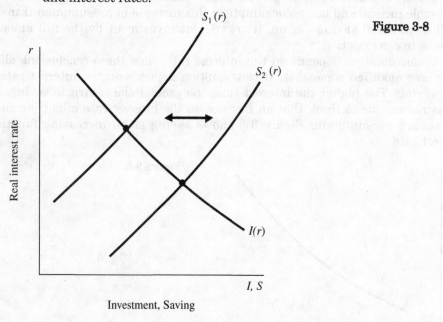

Figure 3-8

   b. Figure 3-9 shows the case where the supply of loanable funds (saving) is stable, whereas the demand for loanable funds fluctuates, perhaps reflecting changes in firms' expectations about the marginal product of capital. We would now find a positive correlation between investment and the interest rate—when demand for funds rises, this pushes up the interest rate, so we see investment increase and the real interest rate increase at the same time.

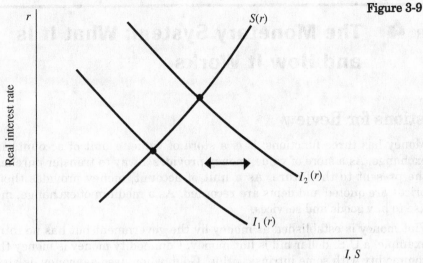

Figure 3-9

c.   If both curves shift, we might generate a scatter plot as in Figure 3-10, where the economy fluctuates among points A, B, C, and D. Depending on how often the economy is at each of these points, we might find little clear relationship between investment and interest rates.

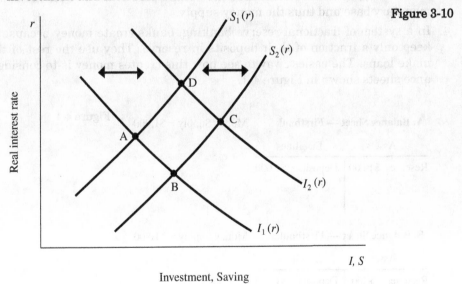

Figure 3-10

d.   Situation (c) seems fairly reasonable—both the supply of and demand for loanable funds fluctuate over time in response to changes in the economy.

CHAPTER **4** The Monetary System: What It Is and How It Works

Questions for Review

1. Money has three functions: it is a store of value, a unit of account, and a medium of exchange. As a store of value, money provides a way to transfer purchasing power from the present to the future. As a unit of account, money provides the terms in which prices are quoted and debts are recorded. As a medium of exchange, money is what we use to buy goods and services.

2. Fiat money is established as money by the government but has no intrinsic value. For example, a U.S. dollar bill is fiat money. Commodity money is money that is based on a commodity with some intrinsic value. Gold, when used as money, is an example of commodity money.

3. Open market operations are the purchase and sale of government bonds by the Federal Reserve. If the Fed buys government bonds from the public, then the dollars it pays for the bonds increase the monetary base and thus the money supply. If the Fed sells government bonds to the public, then the dollars paid to the Fed for the bonds decrease the monetary base and thus the money supply.

4. In a system of fractional-reserve banking, banks create money because they ordinarily keep only a fraction of their deposits in reserve. They use the rest of their deposits to make loans. The easiest way to see how this creates money is to consider the bank balance sheets shown in Figure 4-1.

A. Balance Sheet — Firstbank   Money Supply = $1,000   **Figure 4-1**

Assets	Liabilities
Reserves $1,000	Deposits $1,000

B. Balance Sheet — Firstbank   Money Supply = $1,800

Assets	Liabilities
Reserves $200	Deposits $1,000
Loans $800	

C. Balance Sheet — Secondbank   Money Supply = $2440

Assets	Liabilities
Reserves $160	Deposits $800
Loans $640	

Suppose that people deposit the economy's supply of currency of $1,000 into Firstbank, as in Figure 4-1(A). Although the money supply is still $1,000, it is now in the form of demand deposits rather than currency. If the bank holds 100 percent of these deposits in reserve, then the bank has no influence on the money supply. Yet under a system of fractional-reserve banking, the bank need not keep all of its deposits in reserve; it must have enough reserves on hand so that reserves are available whenever depositors want to make withdrawals, but it makes loans with the rest of its deposits. If Firstbank has a reserve–deposit ratio of 20 percent, then it keeps $200 of the $1,000 in reserve and lends out the remaining $800. Figure 4-1(B) shows the balance sheet of Firstbank after $800 in loans have been made. By making these loans, Firstbank increases the money supply by $800. There are still $1,000 in demand deposits, but now borrowers also hold an additional $800 in currency. The total money supply equals $1,800.

Money creation does not stop with Firstbank. If the borrowers deposit their $800 of currency in Secondbank, then Secondbank can use these deposits to make loans. If Secondbank also has a reserve–deposit ratio of 20 percent, then it keeps $160 of the $800 in reserves and lends out the remaining $640. By lending out this money, Secondbank increases the money supply by $640, as in Figure 4-1(C). The total money supply is now $2,440.

This process of money creation continues with each deposit and subsequent loans made. The text demonstrated that each dollar of reserves generates ($1/$rr$) of money, where rr is the reserve–deposit ratio. In this example, rr = 0.20, so the $1,000 originally deposited in Firstbank generates $5,000 of money.

5. The Fed influences the money supply through open-market operations, reserve requirements, and the discount rate. *Open-market operations* are the purchases and sales of government bonds by the Fed. If the Fed buys government bonds, the dollars it pays for the bonds increase the monetary base and, therefore, the money supply. If the Fed sells government bonds, the dollars it receives for the bonds reduce the monetary base and therefore the money supply. *Reserve requirements* are regulations imposed by the Fed that require banks to maintain a minimum reserve–deposit ratio. A decrease in the reserve requirements lowers the reserve–deposit ratio, which allows banks to make more loans on a given amount of deposits and, therefore, increases the money multiplier and the money supply. The *discount rate* is the interest rate that the Fed charges banks to borrow money. Banks borrow from the Fed if their reserves fall below the reserve requirements. A decrease in the discount rate makes it less expensive for banks to borrow reserves. Therefore, banks will be likely to borrow more from the Fed; this increases the monetary base and therefore the money supply.

6. To understand why a banking crisis might lead to a decrease in the money supply, first consider what determines the money supply. The model of the money supply we developed shows that

$$M = m \times B.$$

The money supply M depends on the money multiplier m and the monetary base B. The money multiplier can also be expressed in terms of the reserve–deposit ratio rr and the currency–deposit ratio cr. This expression becomes

$$M = \left[\frac{(cr + 1)}{(cr + rr)} \right] B.$$

This equation shows that the money supply depends on the currency–deposit ratio, the reserve–deposit ratio, and the monetary base.

A banking crisis that involved a considerable number of bank failures might change the behavior of depositors and bankers and alter the currency–deposit ratio and the reserve–deposit ratio. Suppose that the number of bank failures reduced public confidence in the banking system. People would then prefer to hold their money in currency (and perhaps stuff it in their mattresses) rather than deposit it in banks. This change in the behavior of depositors would cause massive withdrawals of deposits and, therefore, increase the currency–deposit ratio. In addition, the banking crisis would change the behavior of banks. Fearing massive withdrawals of deposits, banks would become more cautious and increase the amount of money they held in reserves, thereby increasing the reserve–deposit ratio. As the preceding formula for the money multiplier indicates, increases in both the currency–deposit ratio and the reserve–deposit ratio result in a decrease in the money multiplier and, therefore, a fall in the money supply.

Problems and Applications

1. Money functions as a store of value, a medium of exchange, and a unit of account.

    a. A credit card can serve as a medium of exchange because it is accepted in exchange for goods and services. A credit card is, arguably, a (negative) store of value because you can accumulate debt with it. A credit card is not a unit of account—a car, for example, does not cost 5 VISA cards.

    b. A Rembrandt painting is a store of value only.

    c. A subway token, within the subway system, satisfies all three functions of money. Yet outside the subway system, it is not widely used as a unit of account or a medium of exchange, so it is not a form of money.

2. a. When the Fed buys bonds, the dollars that it pays to the public for the bonds increase the monetary base, and this in turn increases the money supply. The money multiplier is not affected, assuming no change in the reserve–deposit ratio or the currency–deposit ratio.

    b. When the Fed increases the interest rate it pays banks for holding reserves, this gives banks an incentive to hold more reserves relative to deposits. The increase in the reserve deposit ratio will decrease the money multiplier. The decline in the money multiplier will lead to a decrease in the money supply. Since banks are holding more reserves (because they are making fewer loans), the monetary base will increase.

    c. If the Fed reduces its lending to banks through the Term Auction Facility, then the monetary base will decrease, and this in turn will decrease the money supply. The money multiplier is not affected, assuming no change in the reserve–deposit ratio or the currency–deposit ratio.

    d. If consumers lose confidence in ATMs and prefer to hold more cash, then the currency–deposit ratio will increase, and this will reduce the money multiplier. The money supply will fall because banks have fewer reserves to lend. The monetary base will increase because people are holding more currency, but will decrease because banks are holding fewer reserves. The net effect on the monetary base is zero.

    e. If the Fed drops newly minted $100 bills from a helicopter, then this will increase the monetary base and the money supply. If any of the currency ends up in the bank, then there will be a further increase in the money supply. If people end up holding more currency relative to deposits, then the money multiplier would fall.

3. a. If all money is held as currency, then the money supply is equal to the monetary base. The money supply will be $1,000.

    b. If all money is held as deposits, but banks hold 100 percent of deposits on reserve, then there are no loans. The money supply will be $1,000.

    c. If all money is held as deposits and banks hold 20 percent of deposits on reserve, then the reserve–deposit ratio is 0.20. The currency–deposit ratio is 0, and the money multiplier will be 1/0.2, or 5. The money supply will be $5,000.

    d. If people hold an equal amount of currency and deposits, then the currency–deposit ratio is 1. The reserve–deposit ratio is 0.2 and the money multiplier is $(1 + 1)/(1 + 0.2) = 1.67$. The money supply will be $1,666.67.

    e. The money supply is proportional to the monetary base and is given by $M = m \times B$, where M is the money supply, m is the money multiplier, and B is the monetary base. Since m is a constant number defined by the currency–deposit ratio and the reserve–deposit ratio, a 10-percent increase in the monetary base B will lead to a 10-percent increase in the money supply M.

4. The model of the money supply developed in Chapter 4 shows that

$$M = mB.$$

The money supply M depends on the money multiplier m and the monetary base B. The money multiplier can also be expressed in terms of the reserve–deposit ratio rr and the currency–deposit ratio cr. Rewriting the money supply equation:

$$M = \left[\frac{(cr + 1)}{(cr + rr)} \right] B.$$

This equation shows that the money supply depends on the currency–deposit ratio, the reserve–deposit ratio, and the monetary base.

To answer parts (a) through (c), we use the values for the money supply, the monetary base, the money multiplier, the reserve–deposit ratio, and the currency–deposit ratio from Table 4-2:

	August 1929	March 1933
Money supply	26.5	19.0
Monetary base	7.1	8.4
Money multiplier	3.7	2.3
Reserve–deposit ratio	0.14	0.21
Currency–deposit ratio	0.17	0.41

a. To determine what would happen to the money supply if the currency–deposit ratio had risen but the reserve–deposit ratio had remained the same, we need to recalculate the money multiplier and then plug this value into the money supply equation $M = mB$. To recalculate the money multiplier, use the 1933 value of the currency–deposit ratio and the 1929 value of the reserve–deposit ratio:

$$m = (cr_{1933} + 1)/(cr_{1933} + rr_{1929})$$
$$m = (0.41 + 1)/(0.41 + 0.14)$$
$$m = 2.56.$$

To determine the money supply under these conditions in 1933:

$$M_{1933} = mB_{1933}.$$

Plugging in the value for m just calculated and the 1933 value for B:

$$M_{1933} = 2.56 \times 8.4$$

$$M_{1933} = 21.504.$$

Therefore, under these circumstances, the money supply would have fallen from its 1929 level of 26.5 to 21.504 in 1933.

b. To determine what would have happened to the money supply if the reserve–deposit ratio had risen but the currency–deposit ratio had remained the same, we need to recalculate the money multiplier and then plug this value into the money supply equation $M = mB$. To recalculate the money multiplier, use the 1933 value of the reserve–deposit ratio and the 1929 value of the currency–deposit ratio:

$$m = (cr_{1929} + 1)/(cr_{1929} + rr_{1933})$$
$$m = (0.17 + 1)/(0.17 + 0.21)$$
$$m = 3.09.$$

To determine the money supply under these conditions in 1933:

$$M_{1933} = mB_{1933}.$$

Plugging in the value for m just calculated and the 1933 value for B:

$$M_{1933} = 3.09 \times 8.4$$
$$M_{1933} = 25.96.$$

Therefore, under these circumstances, the money supply would have fallen from its 1929 level of 26.5 to 25.96 in 1933.

c. From the calculations in parts (a) and (b), it is clear that the decline in the currency–deposit ratio was most responsible for the drop in the money multiplier and, therefore, the money supply.

5. a. The introduction of a tax on checks makes people more reluctant to use checking accounts as a means of exchange. Therefore, they hold more cash for transactions purposes, raising the currency–deposit ratio cr.

b. The money supply falls because the money multiplier, $\frac{cr+1}{cr+rr}$, is decreasing in cr.

Intuitively, the higher the currency–deposit ratio, the lower the proportion of the monetary base that is held by banks in the form of reserves and, hence, the less money banks can create.

c. The check tax was not a good policy to implement in the middle of the Great Depression because it did result in a decrease in the money supply as people preferred to pay in currency rather than write a check. Banks had fewer reserves and were able to make fewer loans.

6. The leverage ratio is the ratio of a bank's total assets to its bank capital. If the leverage ratio is 10, this means that for each dollar of capital contributed by the bank owners, the bank has $10 of assets, and therefore $9 of deposits and debts. The balance sheet below has a leverage ratio of 10: total assets are $1,200 and capital is $120.

Assets		Liabilities and Owner's Equity	
Reserves	$200	Deposits	$800
Loans	$600	Debt	$280
Securities	$400	Capital (Owner's Equity)	$120

If the value of the bank's assets rises by 5 percent and deposits and debt do not change, then owner's equity will also rise by 5 percent. Since the sum of the entries on each side of the balance sheet must be the same, a 5-percent rise in the asset value must be balanced by a 5-percent rise in the right-hand-side value. To reduce the bank's capital to zero, assets must decline in value by $120, which is 10 percent of the current asset value.

Questions for Review

1. The quantity equation is an identity that expresses the link between the number of transactions that people make and how much money they hold. We write it as

$$\text{Money} \times \text{Velocity} = \text{Price} \times \text{Transactions}$$
$$M \times V = P \times T.$$

The right-hand side of the quantity equation tells us about the total number of transactions that occur during a given period of time, say, a year. T represents the total number of transactions. P represents the price of a typical transaction. Hence, the product $P \times T$ represents the number of dollars exchanged in a year.

The left-hand side of the quantity equation tells us about the money used to make these transactions. M represents the quantity of money in the economy. V represents the transactions velocity of money—the rate at which money circulates in the economy.

Because the number of transactions is difficult to measure, economists usually use a slightly different version of the quantity equation, in which the total output of the economy Y replaces the number of transactions T:

$$\text{Money} \times \text{Velocity} = \text{Price} \times \text{Output}$$
$$M \times V = P \times Y.$$

P now represents the price of one unit of output, so that $P \times Y$ is the dollar value of output—nominal GDP. V represents the income velocity of money—the number of times a dollar bill becomes a part of someone's income.

2. If we assume that velocity in the quantity equation is constant, then we can view the quantity equation as a theory of nominal GDP. The quantity equation with fixed velocity states that

$$MV = PY.$$

If velocity V is constant, then a change in the quantity of money (M) causes a proportionate change in nominal GDP (PY). If we assume further that output is fixed by the factors of production and the production technology, then we can conclude that the quantity of money determines the price level. This is called the *quantity theory of money*.

3. The holders of money pay the inflation tax. As prices rise, the real value of the money that people hold falls—that is, a given amount of money buys fewer goods and services since prices are higher.

4. The Fisher equation expresses the relationship between nominal and real interest rates. It says that the nominal interest rate i equals the real interest rate r plus the inflation rate π:

$$i = r + \pi.$$

This tells us that the nominal interest rate can change either because the real interest rate changes or the inflation rate changes. The real interest rate is assumed to be unaffected by inflation; as discussed in Chapter 3, it adjusts to equilibrate saving and investment. There is thus a one-to-one relationship between the inflation rate and the nominal interest rate: if inflation increases by 1 percent, then the nominal interest rate also increases by 1 percent. This one-to-one relationship is called the **Fisher effect**.

If inflation increases from 6 to 8 percent, then the Fisher effect implies that the nominal interest rate increases by 2 percentage points, while the real interest rate remains constant.

5. The costs of expected inflation include the following:
   a. **Shoeleather costs.** Higher inflation means higher nominal interest rates, which mean that people want to hold lower real money balances. If people hold lower money balances, they must make more frequent trips to the bank to withdraw money. This is inconvenient (and it causes shoes to wear out more quickly).
   b. **Menu costs.** Higher inflation induces firms to change their posted prices more often. This may be costly if they must reprint their menus and catalogs.
   c. **Greater variability in relative prices.** If firms change their prices infrequently, then inflation causes greater variability in relative prices. Since free-market economies rely on relative prices to allocate resources efficiently, inflation leads to microeconomic inefficiencies.
   d. **Altered tax liabilities.** Many provisions of the tax code do not take into account the effect of inflation. Hence, inflation can alter individuals' and firms' tax liabilities, often in ways that lawmakers did not intend.
   e. **The inconvenience of a changing price level.** It is inconvenient to live in a world with a changing price level. Money is the yardstick with which we measure economic transactions. Money is a less useful measure when its value is always changing.

   There is an additional cost to unexpected inflation:

   f. **Arbitrary redistributions of wealth.** Unexpected inflation arbitrarily redistributes wealth among individuals. For example, if inflation is higher than expected, debtors gain and creditors lose. Also, people with fixed pensions are hurt because their dollars buy fewer goods.

6. Hyperinflation is always a reflection of monetary policy. That is, the price level cannot grow rapidly unless the supply of money also grows rapidly; and hyperinflations do not end unless the government drastically reduces money growth. This explanation, however, begs a central question: Why does the government start and then stop printing lots of money? The answer almost always lies in fiscal policy: When the government has a large budget deficit (possibly due to a recent war or some other major event) that it cannot fund by borrowing, it resorts to printing money to pay its bills. And only when this fiscal problem is alleviated—by reducing government spending and collecting more taxes—can the government hope to slow its rate of money growth.

7. *Real variables* are measured in physical units, and *nominal variables* are measured in terms of money. Real variables have been adjusted for inflation and are often measured in terms of constant dollars, while nominal variables are measured in terms of current dollars. For example, real GDP is measured in terms of constant base-year dollars, while nominal GDP is measured in current dollars. An increase in real GDP means we have produced a larger total quantity of goods and services, valued in base-year dollars. As another example, the real interest rate measures the increase in your purchasing power, the quantity of goods and services you can buy with your dollars, while the nominal interest rate measures the increase in the amount of current dollars you possess. The interest rate you are quoted by your bank, say 3 percent, is a nominal rate. If the inflation rate is 3 percent, then the real interest rate is 5 percent, meaning your purchasing power has only increased by 5 percent and not 8 percent. The quantity of dollars you possess has increased by 8 percent but you can only afford to buy 5 percent more goods and services with these dollars.

Problems and Applications

1. The real interest rate is the difference between the nominal interest rate and the inflation rate. The nominal interest rate is 11 percent, but we need to solve for the inflation rate. We do this with the quantity equation expressed in percentage-change form:

   % Change in M + % Change in V = % Change in P + % Change in Y.

   Rearranging this equation tells us that the inflation rate is given by:

   % Change in P = % Change in M + % Change in V – % Change in Y.

   Substituting the numbers given in the problem, we thus find:

   % Change in P = 14% + 0% – 5%

   = 9%.

   Thus, the real interest rate is 2 percent: the nominal interest rate of 11 percent minus the inflation rate of 9 percent.

2. a. Legislators wish to ensure that the real value of Social Security and other benefits stays constant over time. This is achieved by indexing benefits to the cost of living as measured by the consumer price index. With indexing, nominal benefits change at the same rate as prices.

   b. Assuming the inflation rate is measured correctly (see Chapter 2 for more on this issue), senior citizens are unaffected by the lower rate of inflation. Although they get less money from the government, the goods they purchase are cheaper; their purchasing power is exactly the same as it was with the higher inflation rate.

3. The money demand function is given as

   $$\left(\frac{M}{P}\right)^d = kY.$$

   a. To find the average inflation rate the money demand function can be expressed in terms of growth rates:

   % growth M^d – % growth P = % growth Y.

   The parameter k is a constant, so it can be ignored. The percentage change in nominal money demand M^d is the same as the growth in the money supply because nominal money demand has to equal nominal money supply. If nominal money demand grows 12 percent and real income (Y) grows 4 percent then the growth of the price level is 8 percent.

   b. From the answer to part (a), it follows that an increase in real income growth will result in a lower average inflation rate. For example, if real income grows at 6 percent and money supply growth remains at 12 percent, then inflation falls to 6 percent. In this case, a larger money supply is required to support a higher level of GDP, resulting in lower inflation.

   c. The parameter k defines how much money people want to hold for every dollar of income. The parameter k is inversely related to the velocity of money. All else the same, if people are holding fewer dollars, then each dollar must be used more times to purchase the same quantity of goods and services.

   d. If velocity growth is positive, then all else the same inflation will be higher. From the quantity equation we know that:

   % growth M + % growth V = % growth P + % growth Y.

   Suppose that the money supply grows by 12 percent and real income grows by 4 percent. When velocity growth is zero, inflation is 8 percent. Suppose now that velocity grows 2 percent: this will cause prices to grow by 10 percent. Inflation increases because the same quantity of money is being used more often to chase the same amount of goods. In this case, the money supply should grow more slowly to compensate for the positive growth in velocity.

4. A paper weapon might have been effective for all the reasons that hyperinflation is bad. For example, a large increase in the money supply increases shoeleather and menu costs; it makes relative prices more variable; it alters tax liabilities in arbitrary ways; it increases variability in relative prices; it makes the unit of account less useful; and finally, it increases uncertainty and causes arbitrary redistributions of wealth. If the hyperinflation is sufficiently extreme, it can undermine the public's confidence in the economy and economic policy.

   Note that if foreign airplanes dropped the money, then the government would not receive seigniorage revenue from the resulting inflation, so this benefit usually associated with inflation is lost.

5. The money demand function is given as

$$\left(\frac{M}{P}\right)^d = L(i,Y) = \frac{Y}{5i}.$$

   a. If output Y grows at rate g, then real money balances $(M/P)^d$ must also grow at rate g, given that the nominal interest rate i is a constant.
   b. To find the velocity of money, start with the quantity equation $MV = PY$ and rewrite the equation as $V = (PY)/M = (P/M)Y$. Now, note that P/M is the inverse of the real money supply, which is equal to real money demand. Therefore, the velocity of money is $V = (5i/Y) \times Y$, or $V = 5i$.
   c. If the nominal interest rate is constant, then the velocity of money must be constant.
   d. A one-time increase in the nominal interest rate will cause a one-time increase in the velocity of money. There will be no further changes in the velocity of money.

6. a. When the company decides to issue a new catalogue quarterly instead of annually, this is an example of menu costs. Productive resources will be taken from other activities in order to update the catalogue more frequently, so the price of the goods keeps up with the costs incurred by the company and the real value of their profit is maintained.
   b. Unexpected inflation is reducing the real value of the annuity. When there is unexpected inflation, creditors lose and debtors win. In this case, grandma is the creditor since she is owed the $10,000 per year from the insurance company. The insurance company is the debtor and it wins because it is paying grandma each year with dollars that are less valuable, reducing the real value of the amount it has to pay.
   c. Spending money quickly before it loses value is an example of shoe leather costs. Maria is diverting time and energy from other activities so that she can convert her money into goods and services before its value has eroded from the hyperinflation. She has no incentive to save her income.
   d. Warren is being taxed on his nominal gain and not his real gain. Warren earned a 5 percent nominal return (the $50,000) and had to pay 20 percent of this amount in taxes. His real return was actually –5 percent (the 5 percent nominal return minus the 10 percent inflation), so if the tax rate had been defined as a percentage of real earnings, then he would not owe any tax.
   e. You are only luckier than your father if the rate of inflation has not been greater than 133 percent across this time period. If he earned $3 and you earn $7, then you are paid 133 percent more in nominal terms (4/3 times 100). To figure out whether you are better off than your father, you would need to compare the two real wages.

7. One way to understand Coolidge's statement is to think of a government that is a net debtor in nominal terms to the private sector. Let B denote the government's outstanding debt measured in U.S. dollars. The debt in real terms equals B/P, where P is the price level. By increasing inflation, the government raises the price level and reduces in real terms the value of its outstanding debt. In this sense we can say that the government repudiates the debt. This only matters, however, when inflation is unexpected. If inflation is expected, people demand a higher nominal interest rate. Repudiation still

occurs (i.e., the real value of the debt still falls when the price level rises), but it is not at the expense of the holders of the debt, since they are compensated with a higher nominal interest rate.

8. Deflation is defined as a fall in the general price level, which is the same as a rise in the value of money. Under a gold standard, a rise in the value of money is a rise in the value of gold because money and gold are in a fixed ratio. Therefore, after a period of deflation, an ounce of gold buys more goods and services. This creates an incentive to look for new gold deposits and, thus, more gold is found after a period of deflation.

More Problems and Applications to Chapter 5

1. With constant money growth at rate μ, the question tells us that the Cagan model implies that $p_t = m_t + \gamma\mu$. This question draws out the implications of this equation.

   a. One way to interpret this result is to rearrange to find:

   $$m_t - p_t = -\gamma\mu.$$

   That is, real balances depend on the money growth rate. As the growth rate of money rises, real balances fall. This makes sense in terms of the model in this chapter, since faster money growth implies faster inflation, which makes it less desirable to hold money balances.

   b. With unchanged growth in the money supply, the increase in the level of the money supply m_t increases the price level p_t one-for-one.

   c. With unchanged current money supply m_t, a change in the growth rate of money μ changes the price level in the same direction.

   d. When the central bank reduces the rate of money growth μ, the price level will immediately fall. To offset this decline in the price level, the central bank can increase the current level of the money supply m_t, as we found in part (b). These answers assume that at each point in time, private agents expect the growth rate of money to remain unchanged, so that the change in policy takes them by surprise—but once it happens, it is completely credible. A practical problem is that the private sector might not find it credible that an *increase* in the current money supply signals a *decrease* in future money growth rates.

   e. If money demand does not depend on the expected rate of inflation, then the price level changes only when the money supply itself changes. That is, changes in the growth rate of money μ do not affect the price level. In part (d), the central bank can keep the current price level p_t constant simply by keeping the current money supply m_t constant.

CHAPTER **6**   The Open Economy

Questions for Review

1. By rewriting the national income accounts identity, we show in the text that

$$S - I = NX.$$

This form of the national income accounts identity shows the relationship between the international flow of funds for capital accumulation, $S - I$, and the international flow of goods and services, NX.

   Net capital outflow refers to the $(S - I)$ part of this identity: it is the excess of domestic saving over domestic investment. In an open economy, domestic saving need not equal domestic investment, because investors can borrow and lend in world financial markets. The trade balance refers to the (NX) part of the identity: it is the difference between what we export and what we import.

   Thus, the national accounts identity shows that the international flow of funds to finance capital accumulation and the international flow of goods and services are two sides of the same coin.

2. The *nominal exchange rate* is the relative price of the *currency* of two countries. The *real exchange rate*, sometimes called the *terms of trade*, is the relative price of the *goods* of two countries. It tells us the rate at which we can trade the goods of one country for the goods of another.

3. A cut in defense spending increases government saving and, hence, increases national saving. Investment depends on the world rate and is unaffected. Hence, the increase in saving causes the $(S - I)$ schedule to shift to the right, as in Figure 6-1. The trade balance rises, and the real exchange rate falls.

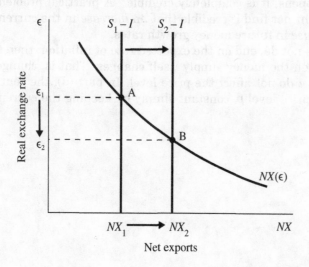

Figure 6-1

4. If a small open economy bans the import of Japanese DVD players, then for any given real exchange rate, imports are lower, so that net exports are higher. Hence, the net export schedule shifts out, as in Figure 6-2.

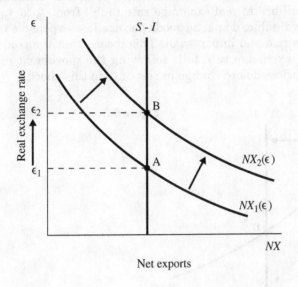

Figure 6-2

Net exports

The protectionist policy of banning DVD players does not affect saving, investment, or the world interest rate, so the $S - I$ schedule does not change. Because protectionist policies do not alter either saving or investment in the model of this chapter, they cannot alter the trade balance. Instead, a protectionist policy drives the real exchange rate higher.

5. We can relate the real and nominal exchange rates by the expression

Nominal		Real		Ratio of
Exchange	=	Exchange	×	Price
Rate		Rate		Levels
e	=	ϵ	×	(P^*/P).

Let P^* be the Mexican price level and P be the Japanese price level. The nominal exchange rate e is the number of Mexican pesos per Japanese yen (this is as if we take Japan to be the "domestic" country). We can express this in terms of percentage changes over time as

$$\% \text{ Change in } e = \% \text{ Change in } \epsilon + (\pi^* - \pi),$$

where π^* is the Mexican inflation rate and π is the Japanese inflation rate. If Mexican inflation is higher than Japanese inflation, then this equation tells us that a yen buys an increasing amount of pesos over time: the yen rises relative to the peso. Alternatively, viewed from the Mexican perspective, the exchange rate in terms of yen per peso falls.

Problems and Applications

1. a.   An increase in saving shifts the $(S - I)$ schedule to the right, increasing the supply of dollars available to be invested abroad, as in Figure 6-3. The increased supply of dollars causes the equilibrium real exchange rate to fall from ϵ_1 to ϵ_2. Because the dollar becomes less valuable, domestic goods become less expensive relative to foreign goods, so exports rise and imports fall. This means that the trade balance increases. The nominal exchange rate falls following the movement of the real exchange rate, because prices do not change in response to this shock.

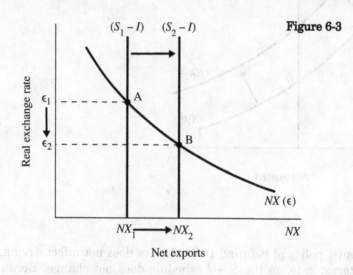

Figure 6-3

b.   The increase in investment will shift the $S - I$ schedule to the left, from $S - I_1$ to $S - I_2$, as in Figure 6-4. Since there are now fewer dollars available to invest abroad, the real exchange rate will increase. The increase in the exchange rate value of the dollar will cause net exports to fall as imports rise and exports fall. The nominal exchange rate will increase along with the real exchange rate because there has been no change in the price level.

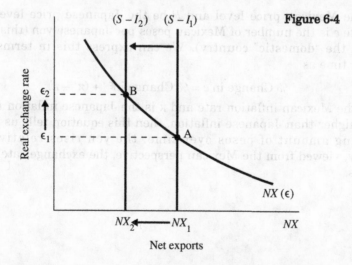

Figure 6-4

c.   The introduction of a stylish line of Toyotas that makes some consumers prefer foreign cars over domestic cars has no effect on saving or investment, but it shifts the $NX(\epsilon)$ schedule inward, as in Figure 6-5. The trade balance does not change, but the real exchange rate falls from ϵ_1 to ϵ_2. Because prices are not affected, the nominal exchange rate follows the real exchange rate.

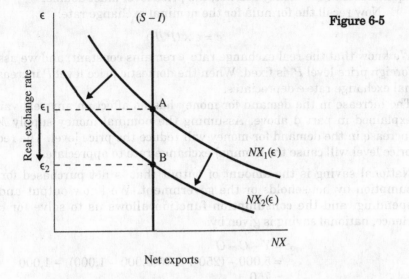

Figure 6-5

d. In the model we considered in this chapter, the doubling of the money supply has no effect on any real variables. The amounts of capital and labor determine output $\overline{Y}$. The world interest rate r^* determines investment $I(r^*)$. The difference between domestic saving and domestic investment $(S - I)$ determines net exports. Finally, the intersection of the $NX(\epsilon)$ schedule and the $(S - I)$ schedule determines the real exchange rate, as in Figure 6-6.

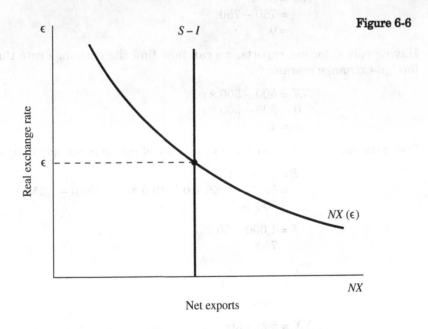

Figure 6-6

The doubling of the money supply does affect the nominal exchange rate through its effect on the domestic price level. The price level adjusts to equilibrate the demand and supply of real balances, so that

$$M/P = (M/P)^d.$$

Real money demand is determined by the level of output (or income) and the real interest rate so it does not change when the money supply doubles. To restore equilibrium in the money market, the price level must double.

Now recall the formula for the nominal exchange rate:

$$e = \epsilon \times (P^*/P).$$

We know that the real exchange rate ϵ remains constant, and we assume that the foreign price level P^* is fixed. When the domestic price level P increases, the nominal exchange rate e depreciates.

e. The increase in the demand for money has no affect on any real vaiables, as was explained in part d above. Assuming the nominal money supply M is fixed, an increase in the demand for money will reduce the price level. The reduction in the price level will cause the nominal exchange rate to appreciate.

2. a. National saving is the amount of output that is not purchased for current consumption by households or the government. We know output and government spending, and the consumption function allows us to solve for consumption. Hence, national saving is given by:

$$
\begin{aligned}
S &= Y - C - G \\
&= 5{,}000 - (250 + 0.75(5{,}000 - 1{,}000)) - 1{,}000 \\
&= 750.
\end{aligned}
$$

Investment depends negatively on the interest rate, which equals the world rate r^* of 5. Thus,

$$
\begin{aligned}
I &= 1{,}000 - 50 \times 5 \\
&= 750.
\end{aligned}
$$

Net exports equals the difference between saving and investment. Thus,

$$
\begin{aligned}
NX &= S - I \\
&= 750 - 750 \\
&= 0.
\end{aligned}
$$

Having solved for net exports, we can now find the exchange rate that clears the foreign-exchange market:

$$
\begin{aligned}
NX &= 500 - 500 \times \varepsilon \\
0 &= 500 - 500 \times \varepsilon \\
\varepsilon &= 1.
\end{aligned}
$$

b. Doing the same analysis with the new value of government spending we find:

$$
\begin{aligned}
S &= Y - C - G \\
&= 5{,}000 - (250 + 0.75(5{,}000 - 1{,}000)) - 1{,}250 \\
&= 500
\end{aligned}
$$

$$
\begin{aligned}
I &= 1{,}000 - 50 \times 5 \\
&= 750
\end{aligned}
$$

$$
\begin{aligned}
NX &= S - I \\
&= 500 - 750 \\
&= -250
\end{aligned}
$$

$$NX = 500 - 500 \times \varepsilon$$

$$-250 = 500 - 500 \times \varepsilon$$

$$\varepsilon = 1.5.$$

The increase in government spending reduces national saving, but with an unchanged world real interest rate, investment remains the same. Therefore, domestic investment now exceeds domestic saving, so some of this investment must be financed by borrowing from abroad. This capital inflow is accomplished by reducing net exports, which requires that the currency appreciate.

c. Repeating the same steps with the new interest rate,

$$S = Y - C - G$$
$$= 5{,}000 - (250 + 0.75(5{,}000 - 1{,}000)) - 1{,}000$$
$$= 750$$

$$I = 1{,}000 - 50 \times 10$$
$$= 500$$

$$NX = S - I$$
$$= 750 - 500$$
$$= 250$$

$$NX = 500 - 500 \times \varepsilon$$
$$250 = 500 - 500 \times \varepsilon$$
$$\varepsilon = 0.5.$$

Saving is unchanged from part (a), but the higher world interest rate lowers investment. This capital outflow is accomplished by running a trade surplus, which requires that the currency depreciate.

3. a. When Leverett's exports become less popular, its domestic saving $Y - C - G$ does not change. This is because we assume that Y is determined by the amount of capital and labor, consumption depends only on disposable income, and government spending is a fixed exogenous variable. Investment also does not change, since investment depends on the interest rate, and Leverett is a small open economy that takes the world interest rate as given. Because neither saving nor investment changes, net exports, which equal $S - I$, do not change either. This is shown in Figure 6-7 as the unmoving $S - I$ curve.

The decreased popularity of Leverett's exports leads to a shift inward of the net exports curve, as shown in Figure 6-7. At the new equilibrium, net exports are unchanged but the currency has depreciated.

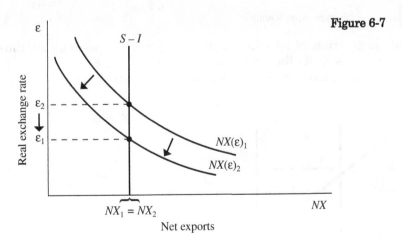

Figure 6-7

Even though Leverett's exports are less popular, its trade balance has remained the same. The reason for this is that the depreciated currency provides a stimulus to net exports, which overcomes the unpopularity of its exports by making them cheaper.

b.   Leverett's currency now buys less foreign currency, so traveling abroad is more expensive. This is an example of the fact that imports (including foreign travel) have become more expensive—as required to keep net exports unchanged in the face of decreased demand for exports.

c.   If the government reduces taxes, then disposable income and consumption rise. Hence, saving falls so that net exports also fall. In Figure 6-7, the $S - I$ curve shifts to the left, lowering net exports until the exchange rate is again equal to its initial value. This fall in net exports puts upward pressure on the exchange rate that offsets the decreased world demand. Investment and the interest rate would be unaffected by this policy since Leverett takes the world interest rate as given.

4.   Governor Bernanke's statement is consistent with the models in the chapter. Suppose we consider the United States as a small open economy, for example. The increase in the global supply of saving pushes the global interest rate down, which encourages U.S. investment. If we assume that this is primarily non-U.S. saving, then for the United States, the saving curve doesn't shift but we get a movement along the investment curve from point A to point B in Figure 6-8. The interest rate falls, and the trade deficit rises ($S - I$ falls).

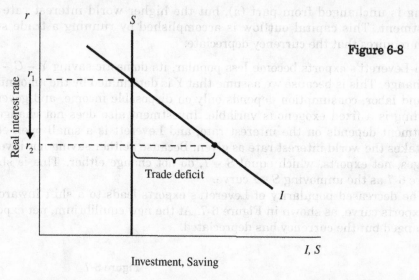

Figure 6-8

5.   The increase in government spending decreases government saving and, thus, decreases national saving; this shifts the saving schedule to the left, as in Figure 6-9. Given the world interest rate r^*, the decrease in domestic saving causes the trade balance to fall.

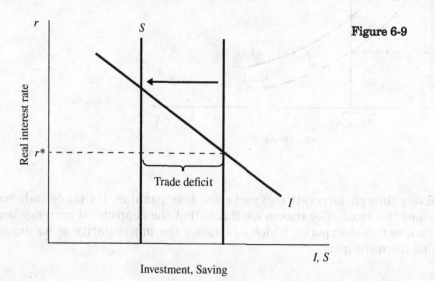

Figure 6-9

Figure 6-10 shows the impact of this increase in government purchases on the real exchange rate. The decrease in national saving causes the $(S - I)$ schedule to shift to the left, lowering the supply of dollars to be invested abroad. The lower supply of dollars causes the equilibrium real exchange rate to rise. As a result, domestic goods become more expensive relative to foreign goods, which causes exports to fall and imports to rise. In other words, as we determined in Figure 6-9, the trade balance falls.

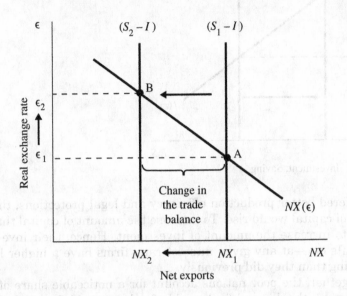

Figure 6-10

The answer to this question does depend on whether this is a local war or a world war. A world war causes many governments to increase expenditures; this increases the world interest rate r^*. The effect on a country's external accounts depends on the size of the change in the world interest rate relative to the size of the decrease in saving. For example, an increase in the world interest rate could cause a country to have a smaller trade deficit, as in Figure 6-11, or even a trade surplus, as in Figure 6-12.

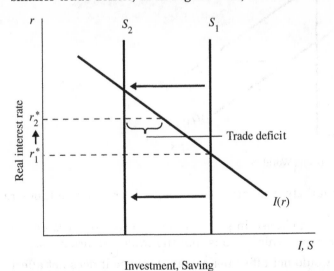

Figure 6-11

Figure 6-12

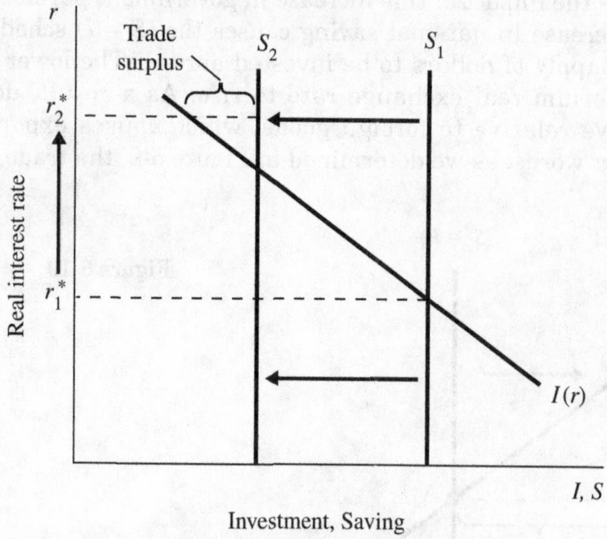

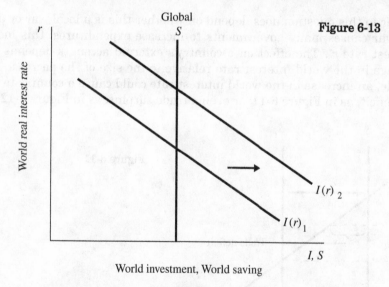

6. a.   If poor nations offered better production efficiency and legal protections, then the marginal product of capital would rise. To increase the amount of capital that they have, firms need to increase the amount of investment. Hence, their investment demand curve shifts out—at any given interest rate, firms have a higher level of investment spending than they did previously.

    b.   Assuming that together, the poor nations account for a noticeable share of world demand for investment, the demand for loanable funds in world financial markets rises. For the world overall, the picture looks like Figure 6-13, which follows.

Figure 6-13

    c.   In global financial markets, the increase in demand for loanable funds raises the interest rate.

    d.   For rich countries, the increase in global interest rates reduces desired investment. Hence, $S - I(r)$ rises, which means that the trade balance rises.

7. The tariff on luxury cars would not affect net exports because it does not affect national saving (because it would not affect Y, C, or G) or investment. It would, however, shift the NX curve by decreasing U.S. demand for Japanese auto imports. This shift of the curve, shown in Figure 6-14, would raise the exchange rate. Although net exports would not change, the volume of both imports and exports would fall by the same amount.

Figure 6-14

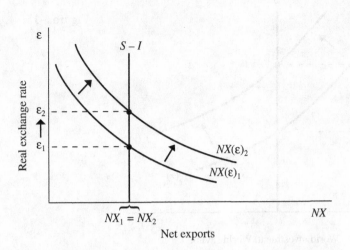

There are also important compositional effects of this policy. On the production side, the higher exchange rate increases imports and puts pressure on the sales of American companies with the exception of American luxury car production, which is shielded by the tariff. Also American exporters will be hurt by the higher exchange rate, which makes their imported goods more expensive to foreign countries. Consumers of Japanese luxury cars will be hurt by the tariffs while all other consumers will benefit from the appreciated dollar, which allows them to purchase goods more cheaply. In sum, the policy would shift demand to American luxury car producers at the expense of the rest of American production and also shift consumption from Japanese luxury cars to all other imports.

8. The real exchange rate measures the rate at which the goods of one country can be traded for the goods of the other country. In this case, the real exchange rate measures the number of bottles of vodka that must be exchanged for one TV. If Russia is experiencing no technological progress in vodka production, then the number of bottles produced is fixed. Since China is experiencing positive technological progress in TV production, the number of TVs produced will be increasing. Given that TVs are relatively more abundant and vodka is relatively more scarce, we would expect the real exchange rate to decrease—that is, it takes fewer bottles of vodka to buy one TV. The nominal exchange rate (e), measured as rubles per yuan, is determined by the following equation:

$$e = \varepsilon \times \left(\frac{P*}{P} \right)$$

where ε. measures the real exchange rate, $P*$ measures the price level in Russia, and P measures the price level in China. Given China has stable money growth and Russia has rapid money growth, Russia's price level will be increasing at a faster rate than the price level in China. The effect on the nominal exchange rate is ambiguous. The decline in the real exchange rate will push the nominal exchange rate down, but the rapidly rising price level in Russia relative to China will push the nominal exchange rate up.

9. a. If the countries that institute an investment tax credit are large enough to shift the world investment demand schedule, then the tax credits shift the world investment demand schedule upward, as in Figure 6-15.

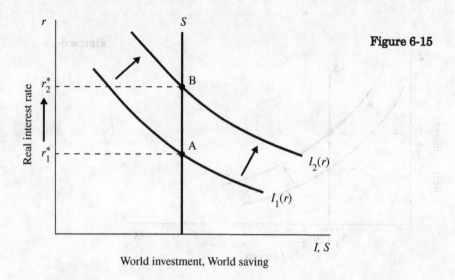

Figure 6-15

World investment, World saving

b. The world interest rate increases from r_1^* to r_2^* because of the increase in world investment demand; this is shown in Figure 6-15. (Remember that the world is a closed economy.)

c. The increase in the world interest rate increases the required rate of return on investments in Oceana. Because the investment schedule slopes downward, we know that a higher world interest rate means lower investment, as in Figure 6-16.

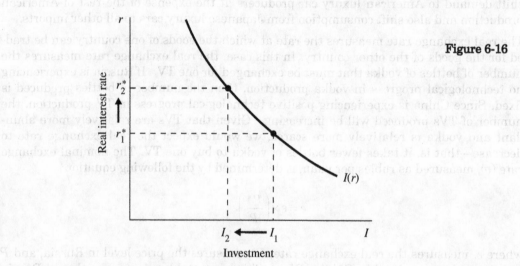

Figure 6-16

Investment

d. Given that our saving has not changed, the higher world interest rate means that our trade balance increases, as in Figure 6-17.

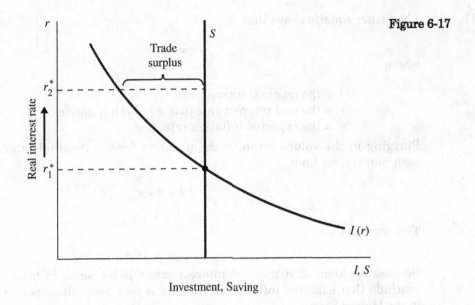

Figure 6-17

e. The increase in the world interest rate reduces domestic investment, which increases the supply of dollars that are available to invest abroad. The domestic currency becomes less valuable, and domestic goods become less expensive relative to foreign goods. The real exchange rate falls, as is shown in Figure 6-18.

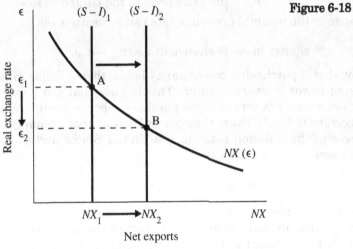

Figure 6-18

10. The easiest way to tell if your friend is right or wrong is to consider an example. Suppose that ten years ago, an American hot dog cost $1, while a Mexican taco cost 10 pesos. Since $1 bought 10 pesos ten years ago, it cost the same amount of money to buy a hot dog as to buy a taco. Since total U.S. inflation has been 25 percent, the American hot dog now costs $1.25. Total Mexican inflation has been 100 percent, so the Mexican taco now costs 20 pesos. This year, $1 buys 15 pesos, so that the taco costs 20 pesos [15 pesos/dollar] = $1.33. This means that it is now more expensive to purchase a Mexican taco than a U.S. hot dog.

Thus, your friend is simply wrong to conclude that it is cheaper to travel in Mexico. Even though the dollar buys more pesos than it used to, the relatively rapid inflation in Mexico means that pesos buy fewer goods than they used to—it is more expensive now for an American to travel there.

11. a.   The Fisher equation says that

$$i = r + \pi^e$$

where

i = the nominal interest rate
r = the real interest rate (same in both countries)
π^e = the expected inflation rate.

Plugging in the values given in the question for the nominal interest rates for each country, we find:

$$12 = r + \pi^e_{Can}$$
$$8 = r + \pi^e_{US}$$

This implies that

$$\pi^e_{Can} - \pi^e_{US} = 4.$$

Because we know that the real interest rate r is the same in both countries, we conclude that expected inflation in Canada is four percentage points higher than in the United States.

  b.   As in the text, we can express the nominal exchange rate as

$$e = \varepsilon \times (P_{Can}/P_{US}),$$

where

ε = the real exchange rate
P_{Can} = the price level in Canada
P_{US} = the price level in the United States.

The change in the nominal exchange rate can be written as:

% change in e = % change in $\varepsilon + (\pi_{Can} - \pi_{US})$.

We know that if purchasing-power parity holds, then a dollar must have the same purchasing power in every country. This implies that the percent change in the real exchange rate ε is zero because purchasing-power parity implies that the real exchange rate is fixed. Thus, changes in the nominal exchange rate result from differences in the inflation rates in the United States and Canada. In equation form this says

% change in $e = (\pi_{Can} - \pi_{US})$.

Because people know that purchasing-power parity holds, they expect this relationship to hold. In other words, the expected change in the nominal exchange rate equals the expected inflation rate in Canada minus the expected inflation rate in the United States. That is,

Expected % change in $e = \pi^e_{Can} - \pi^e_{US}$

In part (a), we found that the difference in expected inflation rates is 4 percent. Therefore, the expected change in the nominal exchange rate e is 4 percent.

  c.   The problem with your friend's scheme is that it does not take into account the change in the nominal exchange rate e between the U.S. and Canadian dollars. Given that the real interest rate is fixed and identical in the United States and Canada, and given purchasing-power parity, we know that the difference in nominal interest rates accounts for the expected change in the nominal exchange rate between U.S. and Canadian dollars. In this example, the Canadian nominal interest rate is 12 percent, while the U.S. nominal interest rate is 8 percent. We conclude from this that the expected change in the nominal exchange rate is 4 percent. Therefore,

e this year = 1 C$/US$.
e next year = 1.04 C$/US$.

Assume that your friend borrows 1 U.S. dollar from an American bank at 8 percent, exchanges it for 1 Canadian dollar, and puts it in a Canadian Bank. At the end of the year your friend will have $1.12 in Canadian dollars. But to repay the American bank, the Canadian dollars must be converted back into U.S. dollars. The $1.12 (Canadian) becomes $1.08 (American), which is the amount owed to the U.S. bank. So in the end, your friend breaks even. In fact, after paying for transaction costs, your friend loses money.

More Problems and Applications to Chapter 6

1. a.   As shown in Figure 6-19, an increase in government purchases reduces national saving. This reduces the supply of loans and raises the equilibrium interest rate. This causes both domestic investment and net capital outflow to fall. The fall in net capital outflow reduces the supply of dollars to be exchanged into foreign currency, so the exchange rate appreciates and the trade balance falls.

Figure 6-19

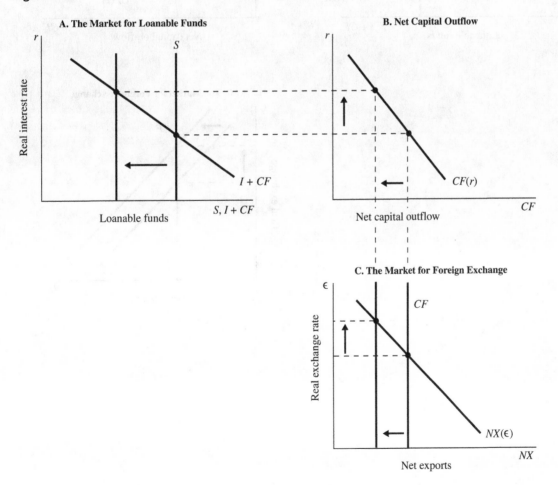

b. As shown in Figure 6-20, the increase in demand for exports shifts the net exports schedule outward. Since nothing has changed in the market for loanable funds, the interest rate remains the same, which in turn implies that net capital outflow remains the same. The shift in the net exports schedule causes the exchange rate to appreciate. The rise in the exchange rate makes U.S. goods more expensive relative to foreign goods, which depresses exports and stimulates imports. In the end, the increase in demand for American goods does not affect the trade balance.

Figure 6-20

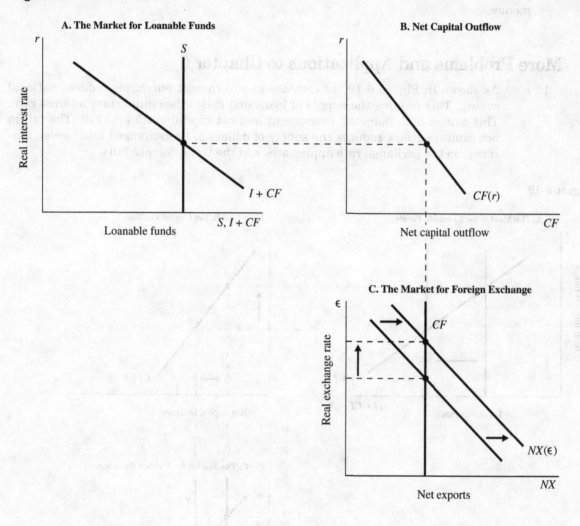

c.   As shown in Figure 6-21, the U.S. investment demand schedule shifts inward. The demand for loans falls, so the equilibrium interest rate falls. The lower interest rate increases net capital outflow. Despite the fall in the interest rate, domestic investment falls; we know this because $I + CF$ does not change, and CF rises. The rise in net capital outflow increases the supply of dollars in the market for foreign exchange. The exchange rate depreciates, and net exports rise.

Figure 6-21

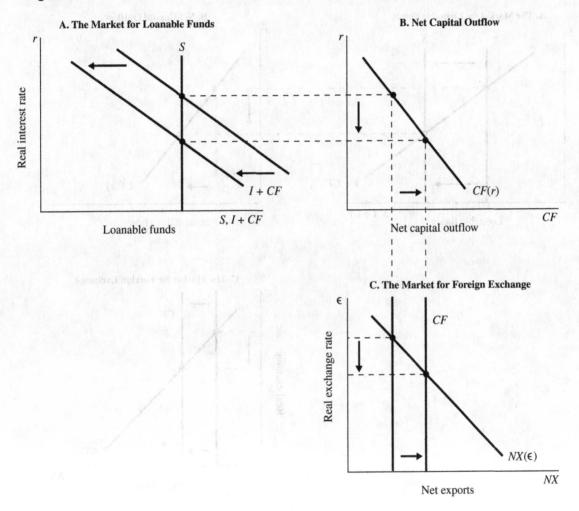

A. The Market for Loanable Funds

B. Net Capital Outflow

C. The Market for Foreign Exchange

d.   As shown in Figure 6-22, the increase in saving increases the supply of loans and lowers the equilibrium interest rate. This causes both domestic investment and net capital outflow to rise. The increase in net capital outflow increases the supply of dollars to be exchanged into foreign currency, so the exchange rate depreciates and the trade balance rises.

Figure 6-22

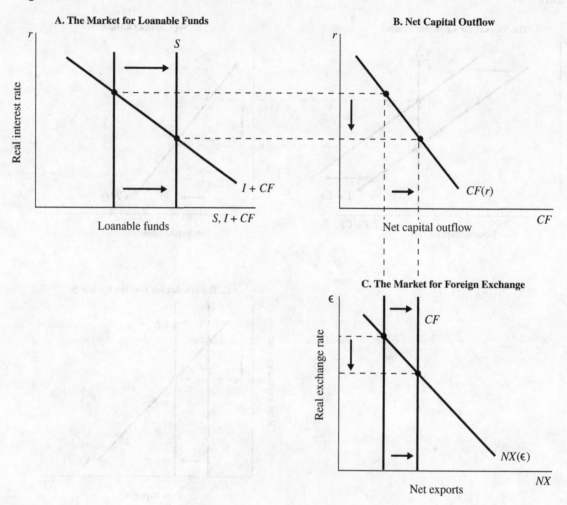

e. The reduction in the willingness of Americans to travel abroad reduces imports, since foreign travel counts as an import. As shown in Figure 6-23, this shifts the net exports schedule outward. Since nothing has changed in the market for loanable funds, the interest rate remains the same, which in turn implies that net capital outflow remains the same. The shift in the net exports schedule causes the exchange rate to appreciate. The rise in the exchange rate makes U.S. goods more expensive relative to foreign goods, which depresses exports and stimulates imports. In the end, the fall in Americans' desire to travel abroad does not affect the trade balance.

Figure 6-23

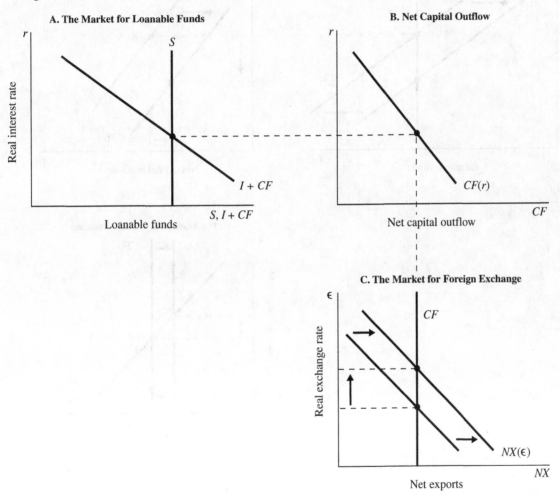

f. As shown in Figure 6-24, the net capital outflow schedule shifts in. This reduces demand for loans, so the equilibrium interest rate falls and investment rises. Net capital outflow falls, despite the fall in the interest rate; we know this because $I + CF$ is unchanged and investment rises. The fall in net foreign investment reduces the supply of dollars to be exchanged into foreign currency, so the exchange rate appreciates and the trade balance falls.

Figure 6-24

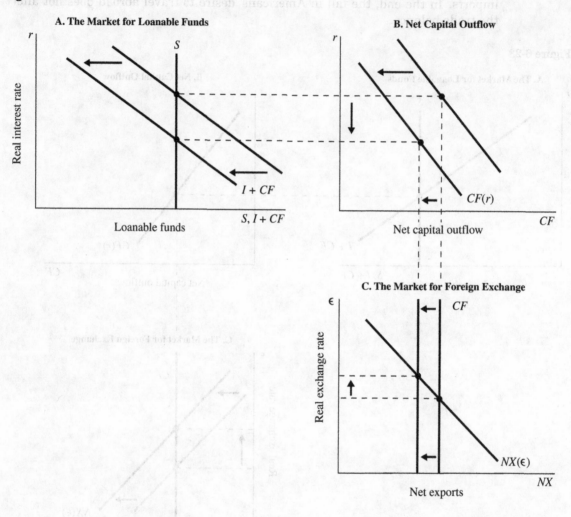

A. The Market for Loanable Funds

B. Net Capital Outflow

C. The Market for Foreign Exchange

2. Gingrich's statement has no immediate effect on any of the "fundamentals" in the economy: consumption, government purchases, taxes, and output are all unchanged. International investors, however, will be more reluctant to invest in the American economy, particularly to purchase U.S. government debt, because of the default risk. As both Americans and foreigners move their money out of the United States, the *CF* curve shifts outward (there is more capital outflow), as shown in Figure 6-25(B). This raises the interest rate in order to keep *I* + *CF* equal to the unchanged *S*, shown in Figure 6-25(A). The increase in *CF* raises the supply in the market for foreign exchange, which lowers the equilibrium exchange rate as shown in Figure 6-25(C).

Figure 6-25

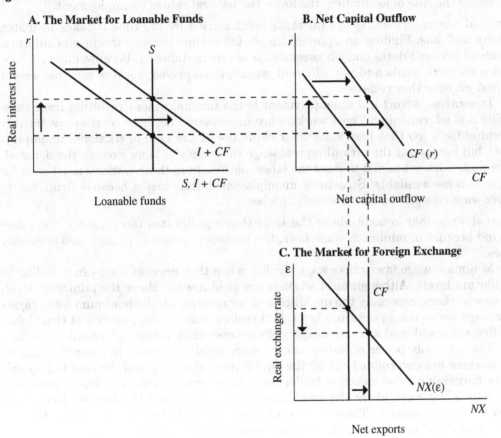

Questions for Review

1. The rates of job separation and job finding determine the natural rate of unemployment. The rate of job separation is the fraction of people who lose their job each month. The higher the rate of job separation, the higher the natural rate of unemployment. The rate of job finding is the fraction of unemployed people who find a job each month. The higher the rate of job finding, the lower the natural rate of unemployment.

2. Frictional unemployment is the unemployment caused by the time it takes to match workers and jobs. Finding an appropriate job takes time because the flow of information about job candidates and job vacancies is not instantaneous. Because different jobs require different skills and pay different wages, unemployed workers may not accept the first job offer they receive.

   In contrast, structural unemployment is the unemployment resulting from wage rigidity and job rationing. These workers are unemployed not because they are actively searching for a job that best suits their skills (as in the case of frictional unemployment), but because at the prevailing real wage the supply of labor exceeds the demand. If the wage does not adjust to clear the labor market, then these workers must wait for jobs to become available. Structural unemployment thus arises because firms fail to reduce wages despite an excess supply of labor.

3. The real wage may remain above the level that equilibrates labor supply and labor demand because of minimum wage laws, the monopoly power of unions, and efficiency wages.

   Minimum-wage laws cause wage rigidity when they prevent wages from falling to equilibrium levels. Although most workers are paid a wage above the minimum level, for some workers, especially the unskilled and inexperienced, the minimum wage raises their wage above the equilibrium level. It therefore reduces the quantity of their labor that firms demand, and an excess supply of workers—that is, unemployment—results.

   The monopoly power of unions causes wage rigidity because the wages of unionized workers are determined not by the equilibrium of supply and demand but by collective bargaining between union leaders and firm management. The wage agreement often raises the wage above the equilibrium level and allows the firm to decide how many workers to employ. These high wages cause firms to hire fewer workers than at the market-clearing wage, so structural unemployment increases.

   Efficiency-wage theories suggest that high wages make workers more productive. The influence of wages on worker efficiency may explain why firms do not cut wages despite an excess supply of labor. Even though a wage reduction decreases the firm's wage bill, it may also lower worker productivity and therefore the firm's profits.

4. Depending on how one looks at the data, most unemployment can appear to be *either* short term or long term. Most spells of unemployment are short; that is, most of those who became unemployed find jobs quickly. On the other hand, most weeks of unemployment are attributable to the small number of long-term unemployed. By definition, the long-term unemployed do not find jobs quickly, so they appear on unemployment rolls for many weeks or months.

5. Europeans work fewer hours than Americans. One explanation is that the higher income tax rates in Europe reduce the incentive to work. A second explanation is a larger underground economy in Europe as a result of more people attempting to evade the high tax rates. A third explanation is the greater importance of unions in Europe

and their ability to bargain for reduced work hours. A final explanation is based on preferences, whereby Europeans value leisure more than Americans do, and therefore elect to work fewer hours.

Problems and Applications

1. a. In the example that follows, we assume that during the school year you look for a part-time job, and that on average it takes 2 weeks to find one. We also assume that the typical job lasts 1 semester, or 12 weeks.

   b. If it takes 2 weeks to find a job, then the rate of job finding in weeks is:

   $$f = (1 \text{ job/2 weeks}) = 0.5 \text{ jobs/week.}$$

   If the job lasts for 12 weeks, then the rate of job separation in weeks is:

   $$s = (1 \text{ job/12 weeks}) = 0.083 \text{ jobs/week.}$$

   c. From the text, we know that the formula for the natural rate of unemployment is

   $$(U/L) = (s/(s+f)),$$

   where U is the number of people unemployed and L is the number of people in the labor force.

   Plugging in the values for f and s that were calculated in part (b), we find:

   $$(U/L) = (0.083/(0.083 + 0.5)) = 0.14.$$

   Thus, if on average it takes 2 weeks to find a job that lasts 12 weeks, the natural rate of unemployment for this population of college students seeking part-time employment is 14 percent.

2. To show that the unemployment rate evolves over time to the steady-state rate, let's begin by defining how the number of people unemployed changes over time. The change in the number of unemployed equals the number of people losing jobs (sE) minus the number finding jobs (fU). In equation form, we can express this as:

   $$U_{t+1} - U_t = \Delta U_{t+1} = sE_t - fU_t.$$

   Recall from the text that $L = E_t + U_t$, or $E_t = L - U_t$, where L is the total labor force (we will assume that L is constant). Substituting for E_t in the above equation, we find:

   $$\Delta U_{t+1} = s(L - U_t) - fU_t.$$

   Dividing by L, we get an expression for the change in the unemployment rate from t to $t + 1$:

   $$\Delta U_{t+1}/L = (U_{t+1}/L) - (U_t/L) = \Delta[U/L]_{t+1} = s(1 - U_t/L) - fU_t/L.$$

   Rearranging terms on the right-hand side of the equation above, we end up with line 1 below. Now take line 1 below, multiply the right-hand side by $(s + f)/(s + f)$ and rearrange terms to end up with line 2 below:

   $$\Delta[U/L]_{t+1} = s - (s + f)U_t/L$$
   $$= (s + f)[s/(s + f) - U_t/L].$$

   The first point to note about this equation is that in steady state, when the unemployment rate equals its natural rate, the left-hand side of this expression equals zero. This tells us that, as we found in the text, the natural rate of unemployment $(U/L)^n$ equals $s/(s + f)$. We can now rewrite the above expression, substituting $(U/L)^n$ for $s/(s + f)$, to get an equation that is easier to interpret:

   $$\Delta[U/L]_{t+1} = (s + f)[(U/L)^n - U_t/L].$$

This expression shows the following:

- If $U_t/L > (U/L)^n$ (that is, the unemployment rate is above its natural rate), then $\Delta[U/L]_{t+1}$ is negative: the unemployment rate falls.
- If $U_t/L < (U/L)^n$ (that is, the unemployment rate is below its natural rate), then $\Delta[U/L]_{t+1}$ is positive: the unemployment rate rises.

This process continues until the unemployment rate U/L reaches the steady-state rate $(U/L)^n$.

3. Call the number of residents of the dorm who are involved I, the number who are uninvolved U, and the total number of students $T = I + U$. In steady state the total number of involved students is constant. For this to happen we need the number of newly uninvolved students, $(0.10)I$, to be equal to the number of students who just became involved, $(0.05)U$. Following a few substitutions:

$$(0.05)U = (0.10)I$$
$$= (0.10)(T - U),$$

so

$$\frac{U}{T} = \frac{0.10}{0.10 + 0.05}$$
$$= \frac{2}{3}.$$

We find that two-thirds of the students are uninvolved.

4. Consider the formula for the natural rate of unemployment,

$$\frac{U}{L} = \frac{s}{s+f}.$$

If the new law lowers the chance of separation s, but has no effect on the rate of job finding f, then the natural rate of unemployment falls.

For several reasons, however, the new law might tend to reduce f. First, raising the cost of firing might make firms more careful about hiring workers, since firms have a harder time firing workers who turn out to be a poor match. Second, if searchers think that the new legislation will lead them to spend a longer period of time on a particular job, then they might weigh more carefully whether or not to take that job. If the reduction in f is large enough, then the new policy may even increase the natural rate of unemployment.

5. a. The demand for labor is determined by the amount of labor that a profit-maximizing firm wants to hire at a given real wage. The profit-maximizing condition is that the firm hire labor until the marginal product of labor equals the real wage,

$$MPL = \frac{W}{P}.$$

The marginal product of labor is found by differentiating the production function with respect to labor (see Chapter 3 for more discussion),

$$MPL = \frac{dY}{dL}$$
$$= \frac{d(K^{1/3}L^{2/3})}{dL}$$
$$= \frac{2}{3}K^{1/3}L^{-1/3}.$$

In order to solve for labor demand, we set the *MPL* equal to the real wage and solve for *L*:

$$\frac{2}{3} K^{1/3} L^{-1/3} = \frac{W}{P}$$

$$L = \frac{8}{27} K\left(\frac{W}{P}\right)^{-3}.$$

Notice that this expression has the intuitively desirable feature that increases in the real wage reduce the demand for labor.

b. We asume that the 1,000 units of capital and the 1,000 units of labor are supplied inelastically (i.e., they will work at any price). In this case we know that all 1,000 units of each will be used in equilibrium, so we can substitute them into the above labor demand function and solve for $\frac{W}{P}$.

$$1,000 = \frac{8}{27} 1,000\left(\frac{W}{P}\right)^{-3}$$

$$\frac{W}{P} = \frac{2}{3}.$$

In equilibrium, employment will be 1,000, and multiplying this by 2/3 we find that the workers earn 667 units of output. The total output is given by the production function:

$$Y = K^{1/3} L^{2/3}$$

$$= 1,000^{1/3} 1,000^{2/3}$$

$$= 1,000.$$

Notice that workers get two-thirds of output, which is consistent with what we know about the Cobb–Douglas production function from Chapter 3.

c. The congressionally mandated wage of 1 unit of output is above the equilibrium wage of 2/3 units of output.

d. Firms will use their labor demand function to decide how many workers to hire at the given real wage of 1 and capital stock of 1,000:

$$L = \frac{8}{27} 1,000(1)^{-3}$$

$$= 296,$$

so 296 workers will be hired for a total compensation of 296 units of output. To find the new level of output, plug the new value for labor and the value for capital into the production function and you will find $Y = 444$.

e. The policy redistributes output from the 704 workers who become involuntarily unemployed to the 296 workers who get paid more than before. The lucky workers benefit less than the losers lose as the total compensation to the working class falls from 667 to 296 units of output.

f. This problem does focus the analysis of minimum-wage laws on the two effects of these laws: they raise the wage for some workers while downward-sloping labor demand reduces the total number of jobs. Note, however, that if labor demand is less elastic than in this example, then the loss of employment may be smaller, and the change in worker income might be positive.

6. a. The labor demand curve is given by the marginal product of labor schedule faced by firms. If a country experiences a reduction in productivity, then the labor demand curve shifts to the left as in Figure 7-1. If labor becomes less productive, then at any given real wage, firms demand less labor.

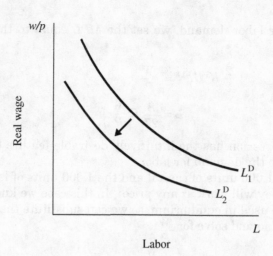

Figure 7-1

b.   If the labor market is always in equilibrium, then, assuming a fixed labor supply, an adverse productivity shock causes a decrease in the real wage but has no effect on employment or unemployment, as in Figure 7-2.

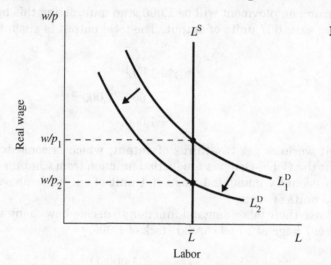

Figure 7-2

c.   If unions constrain real wages to remain unaltered, then as illustrated in Figure 7-3, employment falls to L_1 and unemployment equals $\overline{L} - L_1$.

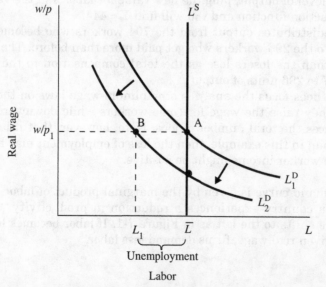

Figure 7-3

This example shows that the effect of a productivity shock on an economy depends on the role of unions and the response of collective bargaining to such a change.

7. Real wages have risen over time in both the United States and Europe, increasing the reward for working (the substitution effect) but also making people richer, so they want to "buy" more leisure (the income effect). If the income effect dominates, then people want to work less as real wages go up. This could explain the European experience, in which hours worked per employed person have fallen over time. If the income and substitution effects approximately cancel, then this could explain the U.S. experience, in which hours worked per person have stayed about constant. Economists do not have good theories for why tastes might differ, so they disagree on whether it is reasonable to think that Europeans have a larger income effect than do Americans.

8. The vacant office space problem is similar to the unemployment problem; we can apply the same concepts we used in analyzing unemployed labor to analyze why vacant office space exists. There is a rate of office separation: firms that occupy offices leave, either to move to different offices or because they go out of business. There is a rate of office finding: firms that need office space (either to start up or expand) find empty offices. It takes time to match firms with available space. Different types of firms require spaces with different attributes depending on what their specific needs are. Also, because demand for different goods fluctuates, there are "sectoral shifts"—changes in the composition of demand among industries and regions—that affect the profitability and office needs of different firms.

CHAPTER **8**   Economic Growth I: Capital Accumulation and Population Growth

Questions for Review

1. In the Solow growth model, a high saving rate leads to a large steady-state capital stock and a high level of steady-state output. A low saving rate leads to a small steady-state capital stock and a low level of steady-state output. Higher saving leads to faster economic growth only in the short run. An increase in the saving rate raises growth until the economy reaches the new steady state. That is, if the economy maintains a high saving rate, it will also maintain a large capital stock and a high level of output, but it will *not* maintain a high rate of growth forever. In the steady state, the growth rate of output (or income) is independent of the saving rate.

2. It is reasonable to assume that the objective of an economic policymaker is to maximize the economic well-being of the individual members of society. Since economic well-being depends on the amount of consumption, the policymaker should choose the steady state with the highest level of consumption. The Golden Rule level of capital represents the level that maximizes consumption in the steady state.

   Suppose, for example, that there is no population growth or technological change. If the steady-state capital stock increases by one unit, then output increases by the marginal product of capital MPK; depreciation, however, increases by an amount δ, so that the net amount of extra output available for consumption is $MPK - \delta$. The Golden Rule capital stock is the level at which $MPK = \delta$, so that the marginal product of capital equals the depreciation rate.

3. When the economy begins above the Golden Rule level of capital, reaching the Golden Rule level leads to higher consumption at all points in time. Therefore, the policymaker would always want to choose the Golden Rule level, because consumption is increased for all periods of time. On the other hand, when the economy begins below the Golden Rule level of capital, reaching the Golden Rule level means reducing consumption today to increase consumption in the future. In this case, the policymaker's decision is not as clear. If the policymaker cares more about current generations than about future generations, he or she may decide *not* to pursue policies to reach the Golden Rule steady state. If the policymaker cares equally about all generations, then he or she chooses to reach the Golden Rule. Even though the current generation will have to consume less, an infinite number of future generations will benefit from increased consumption by moving to the Golden Rule.

4. The higher the population growth rate is, the lower the steady-state level of capital per worker, and therefore there is a lower level of steady-state income per worker. For example, Figure 8-1 shows the steady state for two levels of population growth, a low level n_1 and a higher level n_2. The higher population growth n_2 means that the line representing population growth and depreciation is higher, so the steady-state level of capital per worker is lower.

Figure 8-1

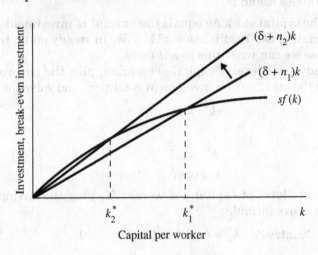

In a model with no technological change, the steady-state growth rate of total income is n: the higher the population growth rate n is, the higher the growth rate of total income. Income per worker, however, grows at rate zero in steady state and, thus, is not affected by population growth.

Problems and Applications

1. a.   A production function has constant returns to scale if increasing all factors of production by an equal percentage causes output to increase by the same percentage. Mathematically, a production function has constant returns to scale if $zY = F(zK, zL)$ for any positive number z. That is, if we multiply both the amount of capital and the amount of labor by some amount z, then the amount of output is multiplied by z. For example, if we double the amounts of capital and labor we use (setting $z = 2$), then output also doubles.

   To see if the production function $Y = F(K, L) = K^{1/2}L^{1/2}$ has constant returns to scale, we write:

$$F(zK, zL) = (zK)^{1/2}(zL)^{1/2} = zK^{1/2}L^{1/2} = zY.$$

Therefore, the production function $Y = K^{1/2}L^{1/2}$ has constant returns to scale.

   b.   To find the per-worker production function, divide the production function $Y = K^{1/2}L^{1/2}$ by L:

$$\frac{Y}{L} = \frac{K^{1/2}L^{1/2}}{L}.$$

If we define $y = Y/L$, we can rewrite the above expression as:

$$y = K^{1/2}/L^{1/2}.$$

Defining $k = K/L$, we can rewrite the above expression as:

$$y = k^{1/2}.$$

c.   We know the following facts about countries A and B:

δ = depreciation rate = 0.05,

s_a = saving rate of country A = 0.1,

s_b = saving rate of country B = 0.2, and

$y = k^{1/2}$ is the per-worker production function derived
in part (b) for countries A and B.

The growth of the capital stock Δk equals the amount of investment $sf(k)$, less the amount of depreciation δk. That is, $\Delta k = sf(k) - \delta k$. In steady state, the capital stock does not grow, so we can write this as $sf(k) = \delta k$.

To find the steady-state level of capital per worker, plug the per-worker production function into the steady-state investment condition, and solve for k^*:

$$sk^{1/2} = \delta k.$$

Rewriting this:

$$k^{1/2} = s/\delta$$
$$k = (s/\delta)^2.$$

To find the steady-state level of capital per worker k^*, plug the saving rate for each country into the above formula:

Country A: $k_a^* = (s_a/\delta)^2 = (0.1/0.05)^2 = 4.$

Country B: $k_b^* = (s_b/\delta)^2 = (0.2/0.05)^2 = 16.$

Now that we have found k^* for each country, we can calculate the steady-state levels of income per worker for countries A and B because we know that $y = k^{1/2}$:

$$y_a^* = (4)^{1/2} = 2.$$
$$y_b^* = (16)^{1/2} = 4.$$

We know that out of each dollar of income, workers save a fraction s and consume a fraction $(1 - s)$. That is, the consumption function is $c = (1 - s)y$. Since we know the steady-state levels of income in the two countries, we find

Country A: $c_a^* = (1 - s_a)y_a^* = (1 - 0.1)(2)$
$$= 1.8.$$

Country B: $c_b^* = (1 - s_b)y_b^* = (1 - 0.2)(4)$
$$= 3.2.$$

d.   Using the following facts and equations, we calculate income per worker y, consumption per worker c, and capital per worker k:

$s_a = 0.1.$

$s_b = 0.2.$

$\delta = 0.05.$

$k_0 = 2$ for both countries.

$y = k^{1/2}.$

$c = (1 - s)y.$

Country A

Year	k	$y = k^{1/2}$	$c = (1 - s_a)y$	$i = s_a y$	δk	$\Delta k = i - \delta k$
1	2	1.414	1.273	0.141	0.100	0.041
2	2.041	1.429	1.286	0.143	0.102	0.041
3	2.082	1.443	1.299	0.144	0.104	0.040
4	2.122	1.457	1.311	0.146	0.106	0.040
5	2.162	1.470	1.323	0.147	0.108	0.039

Country B

Year	k	$y = k^{1/2}$	$c = (1 - s_a)y$	$i = s_a y$	δk	$\Delta k = i - \delta k$
1	2	1.414	1.131	0.283	0.100	0.183
2	2.183	1.477	1.182	0.295	0.109	0.186
3	2.369	1.539	1.231	0.308	0.118	0.190
4	2.559	1.600	1.280	0.320	0.128	0.192
5	2.751	1.659	1.327	0.332	0.138	0.194

Note that it will take five years before consumption in country B is higher than consumption in country A.

2. a. The production function in the Solow growth model is $Y = F(K, L)$, or expressed terms of output per worker, $y = f(k)$. If a war reduces the labor force through casualties, then L falls but $k = K/L$ rises. The production function tells us that total output falls because there are fewer workers. Output per worker increases, however, since each worker has more capital.

   b. The reduction in the labor force means that the capital stock per worker is higher after the war. Therefore, if the economy were in a steady state prior to the war, then after the war the economy has a capital stock that is higher than the steady-state level. This is shown in Figure 8-2 as an increase in capital per worker from k^* to k_1. As the economy returns to the steady state, the capital stock per worker falls from k_1 back to k^*, so output per worker also falls.

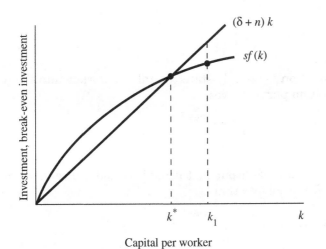

Figure 8-2

Hence, in the transition to the new steady state, the growth of output per worker is slower than normal. In the steady state, we know that the growth rate of output per worker is equal to zero, given there is no technological change in this model. Therefore, in this case, the growth rate of output per worker must be less than zero until the new steady state is reached.

3. a. We follow Section 8-1, "Approaching the Steady State: A Numerical Example." The production function is $Y = K^{0.3}L^{0.7}$. To derive the per-worker production function $f(k)$, divide both sides of the production function by the labor force L:

$$\frac{Y}{L} = \frac{K^{0.3}L^{0.7}}{L}.$$

Rearrange to obtain:

$$\frac{Y}{L} = \left(\frac{K}{L}\right)^{0.3}.$$

Because $y = Y/L$ and $k = K/L$, this becomes:

$$y = k^{0.3}.$$

b. Recall that

$$\Delta k = sf(k) - \delta k.$$

The steady-state value of capital per worker k^* is defined as the value of k at which capital per worker is constant, so $\Delta k = 0$. It follows that in steady state

$$0 = sf(k) - \delta k,$$

or, equivalently,

$$\frac{k^*}{f(k^*)} = \frac{s}{\delta}.$$

For the production function in this problem, it follows that:

$$\frac{k^*}{(k^*)^{0.3}} = \frac{s}{\delta}.$$

Rearranging:

$$(k^*)^{0.7} = \frac{s}{\delta},$$

or

$$k^* = \left(\frac{s}{\delta}\right)^{1/0.7}.$$

Substituting this equation for steady-state capital per worker into the per-worker production function from part (a) gives:

$$y^* = \left(\frac{s}{\delta}\right)^{0.3/0.7}.$$

Consumption is the amount of output that is not invested. Since investment in the steady state equals δk^*, it follows that

$$c^* = f(k^*) - \delta k^* = \left(\frac{s}{\delta}\right)^{0.3/0.7} - \delta\left(\frac{s}{\delta}\right)^{1/0.7}.$$

(*Note:* An alternative approach to the problem is to note that consumption also equals the amount of output that is not saved:

$$c^* = (1-s)f(k^*) = (1-s)(k^*)^{0.3} = (1-s)\left(\frac{s}{\delta}\right)^{0.3/0.7}$$

Some algebraic manipulation shows that this equation is equal to the equation above.)

c. The table below shows k^*, y^*, and c^* for the saving rate in the left column, using the equations from part (b). We assume a depreciation rate of 10 percent (i.e., 0.1). (The last column shows the marginal product of capital, derived in part (d) below).

	k^*	y^*	c^*	$MPK\text{-}\delta k^*$
0	0.00	0.00	0.00	
0.1	1.00	1.00	0.90	0.2000
0.2	2.69	1.35	1.08	0.0500
0.3	4.80	1.60	1.12	0.0000
0.4	7.25	1.81	1.09	–0.0250
0.5	9.97	1.99	1.00	–0.0400
0.6	12.93	2.16	0.86	–0.0500
0.7	16.12	2.30	0.69	–0.0571
0.8	19.50	2.44	0.49	–0.0625
0.9	23.08	2.56	0.26	–0.0667
1	26.83	2.68	0.00	–0.0700

Note that a saving rate of 100 percent ($s = 1.0$) maximizes output per worker. In that case, of course, nothing is ever consumed, so $c^* = 0$. Consumption per worker is maximized at a rate of saving of 0.3 percent—that is, where s equals capital's share in output. This is the Golden Rule level of s.

d. The marginal product of capital (*MPK*) is the change in output per worker (y) for a given change in capital per worker (k). To find the marginal product of capital, differentiate the per-worker production function with respect to capital per worker (k):

$$MPK = 0.3k^{-0.7} = \frac{0.3}{k^{0.7}}.$$

To find the marginal product of capital net of depreciation, use the equation above to calculate the marginal product of capital and then subtract depreciation, which is 10 percent of the value of the steady-state level of capital per worker. These values appear in the table above. Note that when consumption per worker is maximized, the value of the marginal product of capital net of depreciation is zero.

4. Suppose the economy begins with an initial steady-state capital stock below the Golden Rule level. The immediate effect of devoting a larger share of national output to investment is that the economy devotes a smaller share to consumption; that is, "living standards" as measured by consumption fall. The higher investment rate means that the capital stock increases more quickly, so the growth rates of output and output per worker rise. The productivity of workers is the average amount produced by each worker—that is, output per worker. So productivity growth rises. Hence, the immediate effect is that living standards fall but productivity growth rises.

In the new steady state, output grows at rate n, while output per worker grows at rate zero. This means that in the steady state, productivity growth is independent of the rate of investment. Since we begin with an initial steady-state capital stock below the Golden Rule level, the higher investment rate means that the new steady state has a higher level of consumption, so living standards are higher.

Thus, an increase in the investment rate increases the productivity growth rate in the short run but has no effect in the long run. Living standards, on the other hand, fall immediately and only rise over time. That is, the quotation emphasizes growth, but not the sacrifice required to achieve it.

5. a.   An increase in the saving rate will shift the saving curve upwards, as illustrated in Figure 8-3, which follows. Since actual investment is now greater than break-even investment, the level of capital per worker will increase and the steady-state level of capital per worker will be higher. The increase in capital per worker will increase output per worker.

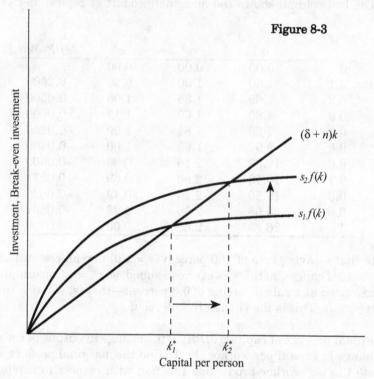

Figure 8-3

b.   An increase in the depreciation rate will shift the break-even investment line upwards to $(\delta_2 + n)$ as illustrated in Figure 8-4, which follows. Since actual investment is now less than break-even investment, the level of capital per worker will decrease and the steady-state level of capital per worker will be lower. The decrease in capital per worker will decrease output per worker.

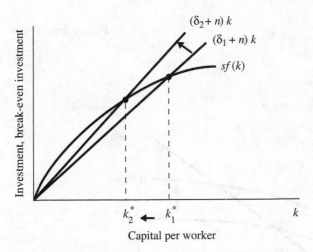

Figure 8-4

c. A reduction in the rate of population growth will shift the break-even investment line down and to the right to $(\delta + n_2)$ as illustrated in Figure 8-5, which follows. Since actual investment is now greater than break-even investment, the level of capital per worker will increase and the steady-state level of capital per worker will be higher. The increase in capital per worker will increase output per worker.

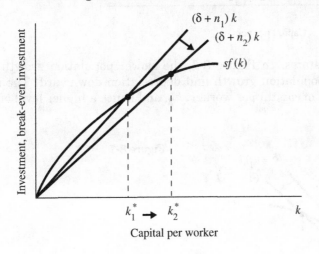

Figure 8-5

d. The technological improvement increases output $f(k)$, and as a result the saving curve shifts upwards. Since actual investment is now greater than break-even investment, the level of capital per worker will increase and the steady-state level of capital per worker will be higher. The increase in capital per worker will increase output per worker.

Figure 8-6

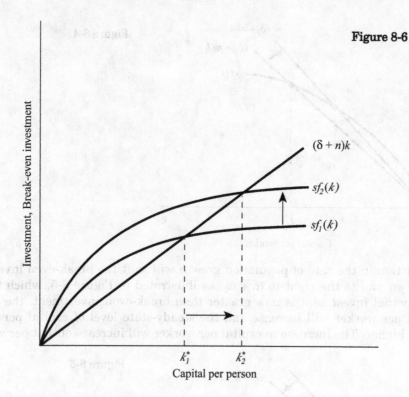

6. First, consider steady states. In Figure 8-7, the slower population growth rate shifts the line representing population growth and depreciation downward. The new steady state has a higher level of capital per worker, k_2^*, and hence a higher level of output per worker.

Figure 8-7

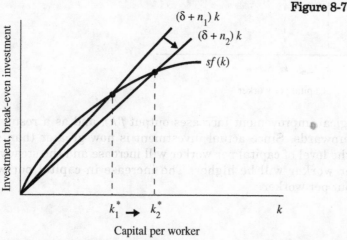

What about steady-state growth rates? In steady state, total output grows at rate n, whereas output per-worker grows at rate 0. Hence, slower population growth will lower *total* output growth, but *per-worker* output growth will be the same.

Now consider the transition. We know that the steady-state level of output per worker is higher with low population growth. Hence, during the transition to the new steady state, output per worker must grow at a rate faster than 0 for a while. In the decades after the fall in population growth, growth in total output will transition to its new lower level while growth in output per worker will jump up but then transition back to zero.

7. If there are decreasing returns to labor and capital, then increasing both capital and labor by the same proportion increases output by less than this proportion. For exam-

ple, if we double the amounts of capital and labor, then output less than doubles. This may happen if there is a fixed factor such as land in the production function, and it becomes scarce as the economy grows larger. Then population growth will increase total output but decrease output per worker, since each worker has less of the fixed factor to work with.

If there are increasing returns to scale, then doubling inputs of capital and labor more than doubles output. This may happen if specialization of labor becomes greater as population grows. Then population growth increases total output and also increases output per worker, since the economy is able to take advantage of the scale economy more quickly.

8. a.   To find output per worker y we divide total output by the number of workers:

$$\frac{Y}{L} = \frac{K^\alpha \left[(1-u)L\right]^{1-\alpha}}{L}$$

$$y = \left(\frac{K}{L}\right)^\alpha (1-u)^{1-\alpha}$$

$$y = k^\alpha (1-u)^{1-\alpha},$$

where the final step uses the definition $k = \frac{K}{L}$. Notice that unemployment reduces the amount of output per worker for any given capital–labor ratio because some of the workers are not producing anything.

The steady state is the level of capital per worker at which the increase in capital per worker from investment equals its decrease from depreciation and population growth.

$$sy = (\delta + n)k$$

$$sk^\alpha (1-u)^{1-\alpha} = (\delta + n)k$$

$$k^* = (1-u)\left(\frac{s}{\delta+n}\right)^{\frac{1}{1-\alpha}}$$

Finally, to get steady-state output per worker, plug the steady-state level of capital per worker into the production function:

$$y^* = \left((1-u^*)\left(\frac{s}{\delta+n}\right)^{\frac{1}{1-\alpha}}\right)^\alpha (1-u^*)^{1-\alpha}$$

$$= (1-u^*)\left(\frac{s}{\delta+n}\right)^{\frac{\alpha}{1-\alpha}}$$

Unemployment lowers steady-state output for two reasons: for a given k, unemployment lowers y, and unemployment also lowers the steady-state value k^*.

   b.   The steady state can be graphically illustrated using the equations that describe the steady state from part a above. Unemployment lowers the marginal product of capital per worker and, hence, acts like a negative technological shock that reduces the amount of capital the economy can maintain in steady state. Figure 8–8 shows this graphically: an increase in unemployment lowers the $sf(k)$ line and the steady-state level of capital per worker.

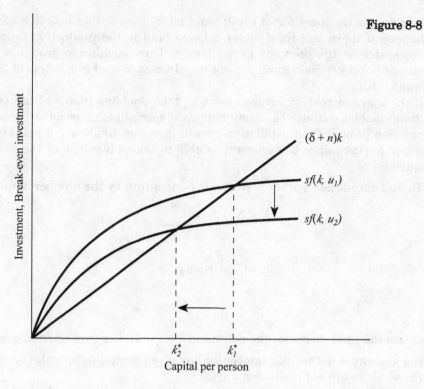

Figure 8-8

c. Figure 8-9 below shows the pattern of output over time. As soon as unemployment falls from u_1 to u_2, output jumps up from its initial steady-state value of $y^*(u_1)$. The economy has the same amount of capital (since it takes time to adjust the capital stock), but this capital is combined with more workers. At that moment the economy is out of steady state: it has less capital than it wants to match the increased number of workers in the economy. The economy begins its transition by accumulating more capital, raising output even further than the original jump. Eventually the capital stock and output converge to their new, higher steady-state levels.

Figure 8-9

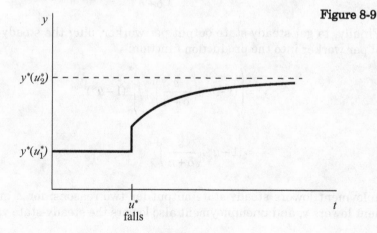

CHAPTER 9

Economic Growth II: Technology, Empirics, and Policy

Questions for Review

1. In the Solow model, we find that only technological progress can affect the steady-state rate of growth in income per worker. Growth in the capital stock (through high saving) has no effect on the steady-state growth rate of income per worker; neither does population growth. But technological progress can lead to sustained growth.

2. In the steady state, output per person in the Solow model grows at the rate of technological progress g. Capital per person also grows at rate g. Note that this implies that output and capital per *effective* worker are constant in steady state. In the U.S. data, output and capital per worker have both grown at about 2 percent per year for the past half-century.

3. To decide whether an economy has more or less capital than the Golden Rule, we need to compare the marginal product of capital net of depreciation ($MPK - \delta$) with the growth rate of total output ($n + g$). The growth rate of GDP is readily available. Estimating the net marginal product of capital requires a little more work but, as shown in the text, can be backed out of available data on the capital stock relative to GDP, the total amount of depreciation relative to GDP, and capital's share in GDP.

4. Economic policy can influence the saving rate by either increasing public saving or providing incentives to stimulate private saving. Public saving is the difference between government revenue and government spending. If spending exceeds revenue, the government runs a budget deficit, which is negative saving. Policies that decrease the deficit (such as reductions in government purchases or increases in taxes) increase public saving, whereas policies that increase the deficit decrease saving. A variety of government policies affect private saving. The decision by a household to save may depend on the rate of return; the greater the return to saving, the more attractive saving becomes. Tax incentives such as tax-exempt retirement accounts for individuals and investment tax credits for corporations increase the rate of return and encourage private saving.

5. The rate of growth of output per person slowed worldwide after 1972. This slowdown appears to reflect a slowdown in productivity growth—the rate at which the production function is improving over time. Various explanations have been proposed, but the slowdown remains a mystery. In the second half of the 1990s, productivity grew more quickly again in the United States and, it appears, a few other countries. Many commentators attribute the productivity revival to the effects of information technology.

6. Endogenous growth theories attempt to explain the rate of technological progress by explaining the decisions that determine the creation of knowledge through research and development. By contrast, the Solow model simply took this rate as exogenous. In the Solow model, the saving rate affects growth temporarily, but diminishing returns to capital eventually force the economy to approach a steady state in which growth depends only on exogenous technological progress. By contrast, many endogenous growth models in essence assume that there are constant (rather than diminishing) returns to capital, interpreted to include knowledge. Hence, changes in the saving rate can lead to persistent growth.

Problems and Applications

1. a.   In the Solow model with technological progress, y is defined as output per effective worker and k is defined as capital per effective worker. The number of effective workers is defined as $L \times E$ (or LE), where L is the number of workers and E measures the efficiency of each worker. To find output per effective worker y, divide total output by the number of effective workers:

$$\frac{Y}{LE} = \frac{K^{\frac{1}{2}}(LE)^{\frac{1}{2}}}{LE}$$

$$\frac{Y}{LE} = \frac{K^{\frac{1}{2}}L^{\frac{1}{2}}E^{\frac{1}{2}}}{LE}$$

$$\frac{Y}{LE} = \frac{K^{\frac{1}{2}}}{L^{\frac{1}{2}}E^{\frac{1}{2}}}$$

$$\frac{Y}{LE} = \left(\frac{K}{LE}\right)^{\frac{1}{2}}$$

$$y = k^{\frac{1}{2}}.$$

   b.   To solve for the steady-state value of y as a function of s, n, g, and δ, we begin with the equation for the change in the capital stock in the steady state:

$$\Delta k = sf(k) - (\delta + n + g)k = 0.$$

The production function $y = \sqrt{k}$ can also be rewritten as $y^2 = k$. Plugging this production function into the equation for the change in the capital stock, we find that in the steady state:

$$sy - (\delta + n + g)y^2 = 0.$$

Solving this, we find the steady-state value of y:

$$y^* = s/(\delta + n + g).$$

   c.   The question provides us with the following information about each country:

   Atlantis: $s = 0.28$ Xanadu: $s = 0.10$
   $n = 0.01$ $n = 0.04$
   $g = 0.02$ $g = 0.02$
   $\delta = 0.04$ $\delta = 0.04$

Using the equation for y^* that we derived in part (a), we can calculate the steady-state values of y for each country.

   Developed country: $y^* = 0.28/(0.04 + 0.01 + 0.02) = 4.$
   Less-developed country: $y^* = 0.10/(0.04 + 0.04 + 0.02) = 1.$

2. To solve this problem, it is useful to establish what we know about the U.S. economy:

A Cobb–Douglas production function has the form $y = k^\alpha$, where α is capital's share of income. The question tells us that $\alpha = 0.3$, so we know that the production function is $y = k^{0.3}$.

In the steady state, we know that the growth rate of output equals 3 percent, so we know that $(n + g) = 0.03$.

The depreciation rate $\delta = 0.04$.

The capital–output ratio $K/Y = 2.5$. Because $k/y = [K/(L \times E)]/[Y/(L \times E)] = K/Y$, we also know that $k/y = 2.5$. (That is, the capital–output ratio is the same in terms of effective workers as it is in levels.)

a. Begin with the steady-state condition, $sy = (\delta + n + g)k$. Rewriting this equation leads to a formula for saving in the steady state:

$$s = (\delta + n + g)(k/y).$$

Plugging in the values established above:

$$s = (0.04 + 0.03)(2.5) = 0.175.$$

The initial saving rate is 17.5 percent.

b. We know from Chapter 3 that with a Cobb–Douglas production function, capital's share of income $\alpha = MPK(K/Y)$. Rewriting, we have:

$$MPK = \alpha/(K/Y).$$

Plugging in the values established above, we find:

$$MPK = 0.3/2.5 = 0.12.$$

c. We know that at the Golden Rule steady state:

$$MPK = (n + g + \delta).$$

Plugging in the values established above:

$$MPK = (0.03 + 0.04) = 0.07.$$

At the Golden Rule steady state, the marginal product of capital is 7 percent, whereas it is 12 percent in the initial steady state. Hence, from the initial steady state we need to increase k to achieve the Golden Rule steady state.

d. We know from Chapter 3 that for a Cobb–Douglas production function, $MPK = \alpha (Y/K)$. Solving this for the capital–output ratio, we find:

$$K/Y = \alpha/MPK.$$

We can solve for the Golden Rule capital–output ratio using this equation. If we plug in the value 0.07 for the Golden Rule steady-state marginal product of capital, and the value 0.3 for α, we find:

$$K/Y = 0.3/0.07 = 4.29.$$

In the Golden Rule steady state, the capital–output ratio equals 4.29, compared to the current capital–output ratio of 2.5.

e. We know from part (a) that in the steady state

$$s = (\delta + n + g)(k/y),$$

where k/y is the steady-state capital–output ratio. In the introduction to this answer, we showed that $k/y = K/Y$, and in part (d) we found that the Golden Rule $K/Y = 4.29$. Plugging in this value and those established above:

$$s = (0.04 + 0.03)(4.29) = 0.30.$$

To reach the Golden Rule steady state, the saving rate must rise from 17.5 to 30 percent. This result implies that if we set the saving rate equal to the share going to capital (30%), we will achieve the Golden Rule steady state.

3. a. In the steady state, we know that $sy = (\delta + n + g)k$. This implies that

$$k/y = s/(\delta + n + g).$$

Since s, δ, n, and g are constant, this means that the ratio k/y is also constant. Since $k/y = [K/(L \times E)]/[Y/(L \times E)] = K/Y$, we can conclude that in the steady state, the capital–output ratio is constant.

b. We know that capital's share of income $= MPK \times (K/Y)$. In the steady state, we know from part (a) that the capital–output ratio K/Y is constant. We also know from the hint that the MPK is a function of k, which is constant in the steady state; therefore the MPK itself must be constant. Thus, capital's share of income is constant. Labor's share of income is 1 – [capital's share]. Hence, if capital's share is constant, we see that labor's share of income is also constant.

c. We know that in the steady state, total income grows at $n + g$—the rate of population growth plus the rate of technological change. In part (b) we showed that labor's and capital's share of income is constant. If the shares are constant, and total income grows at the rate $n + g$, then labor income and capital income must also grow at the rate $n + g$.

d. Define the real rental price of capital R as:

$$R = \text{Total Capital Income/Capital Stock}$$
$$= (MPK \times K)/K$$
$$= MPK.$$

We know that in the steady state, the MPK is constant because capital per effective worker k is constant. Therefore, we can conclude that the real rental price of capital is constant in the steady state.

To show that the real wage w grows at the rate of technological progress g, define:

$$TLI = \text{Total Labor Income.}$$
$$L = \text{Labor Force.}$$

Using the hint that the real wage equals total labor income divided by the labor force:

$$w = TLI/L.$$

Equivalently,

$$wL = TLI.$$

In terms of percentage changes, we can write this as

$$\Delta w/w + \Delta L/L = \Delta TLI/TLI.$$

This equation says that the growth rate of the real wage plus the growth rate of the labor force equals the growth rate of total labor income. We know that the labor force grows at rate n, and from part (c) we know that total labor income grows at rate $n + g$. We therefore conclude that the real wage grows at rate g.

4. a. The per worker production function is

$$F(K,L)/L = AK^{\alpha} L^{1-\alpha}/L = A(K/L)^{\alpha} = Ak^{\alpha}.$$

b. In the steady state, $\Delta k = sf(k) - (\delta + n + g)k = 0$. Hence, $sAk^{\alpha} = (\delta + n + g)k$, or, after rearranging:

$$k^* = \left[\frac{sA}{\delta + n + g}\right]^{\left(\frac{1}{1-\alpha}\right)}$$

Plugging into the per-worker production function from part (a) gives:

$$y^* = A^{\left(\frac{1}{1-\alpha}\right)}\left[\frac{s}{\delta + n + g}\right]^{\left(\frac{\alpha}{1-\alpha}\right)}$$

Thus, the ratio of steady-state income per worker in Richland to Poorland is:

$$\left(y^*_{Richland} \, / \, y^*_{Poorland}\right) = \left[\frac{\dfrac{s_{Richland}}{\delta + n_{Richland} + g}}{\dfrac{s_{Poorland}}{\delta + n_{Poorland} + g}}\right]^{\frac{\alpha}{1-\alpha}}$$

$$= \left[\frac{\dfrac{0.32}{0.05 + 0.01 + 0.02}}{\dfrac{0.10}{0.05 + 0.03 + 0.02}}\right]^{\frac{\alpha}{1-\alpha}}$$

$$= [4]^{\left(\frac{\alpha}{1-\alpha}\right)}$$

c. If α equals 1/3, then Richland should be $4^{1/2}$, or two times, richer than Poorland.

d. If $4^{\left(\frac{\alpha}{1-\alpha}\right)} = 16$, then it must be the case that $\left(\dfrac{\alpha}{1-\alpha}\right) = 2$, which in turn requires that α equals 2/3. Hence, If the Cobb-Douglas production function puts 2/3 of the weight on capital and only 1/3 on labor, then we can explain a 16-fold difference in levels of income per worker. One way to justify this might be to think about capital more broadly to include human capital—which must also be accumulated through investment, much in the way one accumulates physical capital.

5. How do differences in education across countries affect the Solow model? Education is one factor affecting the *efficiency of labor*, which we denoted by E. (Other factors affecting the efficiency of labor include levels of health, skill, and knowledge.) Since country 1 has a more highly educated labor force than country 2, each worker in country 1 is more efficient. That is, $E_1 > E_2$. We will assume that both countries are in steady state.

a. In the Solow growth model, the rate of growth of total income is equal to $n + g$, which is independent of the work force's *level* of education. The two countries will, thus, have the same rate of growth of total income because they have the same rate of population growth and the same rate of technological progress.

b. Because both countries have the same saving rate, the same population growth rate, and the same rate of technological progress, we know that the two countries will converge to the same steady-state level of capital per effective worker k^*. This is shown in Figure 9-1.

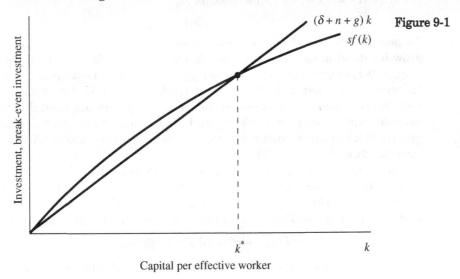

Figure 9-1

Hence, output per effective worker in the steady state, which is $y^* = f(k^*)$, is the same in both countries. But $y^* = Y/(L \times E)$ or $Y/L = y^* E$. We know that y^* will be the same in both countries, but that $E_1 > E_2$. Therefore, $y^*E_1 > y^*E_2$. This implies that $(Y/L)_1 > (Y/L)_2$. Thus, the level of income per worker will be higher in the country with the more educated labor force.

c. We know that the real rental price of capital R equals the marginal product of capital (MPK). But the MPK depends on the capital stock per efficiency unit of labor. In the steady state, both countries have $k_1^* = k_2^* = k^*$ because both countries have the same saving rate, the same population growth rate, and the same rate of technological progress. Therefore, it must be true that $R_1 = R_2 = MPK$. Thus, the real rental price of capital is identical in both countries.

d. Output is divided between capital income and labor income. Therefore, the wage per effective worker can be expressed as:

$$w = f(k) - MPK \cdot k.$$

As discussed in parts (b) and (c), both countries have the same steady-state capital stock k and the same MPK. Therefore, the wage per effective worker in the two countries is equal.

Workers, however, care about the wage per unit of labor, not the wage per effective worker. Also, we can observe the wage per unit of labor but not the wage per effective worker. The wage per unit of labor is related to the wage per effective worker by the equation

Wage per Unit of $L = wE$.

Thus, the wage per unit of labor is higher in the country with the more educated labor force.

6. a. In the two-sector endogenous growth model in the text, the production function for manufactured goods is

$$Y = F(K,(1-u)EL).$$

We assumed in this model that this function has constant returns to scale. As in Section 3-1, constant returns means that for any positive number z, $zY = F(zK, z(1-u)EL)$. Setting $z = 1/EL$, we obtain:

$$\frac{Y}{EL} = F\left(\frac{K}{EL},(1-u)\right).$$

Using our standard definitions of y as output per effective worker and k as capital per effective worker, we can write this as

$$y = F(k,(1-u)).$$

b. To begin, note that from the production function in research universities, the growth rate of labor efficiency, $\Delta E / E$, equals $g(u)$. We can now follow the logic of Section 9-1, substituting the function $g(u)$ for the constant growth rate g. In order to keep capital per effective worker (K/EL) constant, break-even investment includes three terms: δk is needed to replace depreciating capital, nk is needed to provide capital for new workers, and $g(u)$ is needed to provide capital for the greater stock of knowledge E created by research universities. That is, break-even investment is $(\delta + n + g(u))k$.

c. Again following the logic of Section 9-1, the growth of capital per effective worker is the difference between saving per effective worker and break-even investment per effective worker. We now substitute the per-effective-worker production function from part (a), and the function $g(u)$ for the constant growth rate g, to obtain:

$$\Delta k = sF(k,(1-u)) - (\delta + n + g(u))k.$$

In the steady state, $\Delta k = 0$, so we can rewrite the equation above as:

$$sF(k,(1-u)) = (\delta + n + g(u))k$$

As in our analysis of the Solow model, for a given value of u we can plot the left- and right-hand sides of this equation:

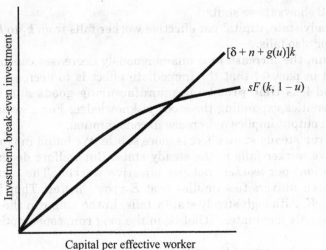

Figure 9-2

The steady state is given by the intersection of the two curves.

d. The steady state has constant capital per effective worker k as given by Figure 9-2 above. We also assume that in the steady state, there is a constant share of time spent in research universities, so u is constant. (After all, if u were not constant, it wouldn't be a "steady" state!). Hence, output per effective worker y is also constant. Output per worker equals yE, and E grows at rate $g(u)$. Therefore, output per worker grows at rate $g(u)$. The saving rate does not affect this growth rate. However, the amount of time spent in research universities does affect this rate: as more time is spent in research universities, the steady-state growth rate rises.

e. An increase in u shifts both lines in our figure. Output per effective worker falls for any given level of capital per effective worker, since less of each worker's time is spent producing manufactured goods. This is the immediate effect of the change, since at the time u rises, the capital stock K and the efficiency of each worker E are constant. Since output per effective worker falls, the curve showing saving per effective worker shifts down.

At the same time, the increase in time spent in research universities increases the growth rate of labor efficiency $g(u)$. Hence, break-even investment [which we found above in part (b)] rises at any given level of k, so the line showing break-even investment also shifts up.

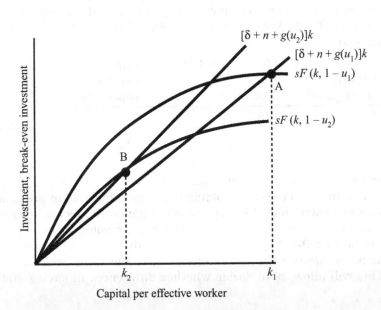

Figure 9-3

Figure 9-3 shows these shifts:

In the new steady state, capital per effective worker falls from k_1 to k_2. Output per effective worker also falls.

f.   In the short run, the increase in u unambiguously decreases consumption. After all, we argued in part (e) that the immediate effect is to decrease output, since workers spend less time producing manufacturing goods and more time in research universities expanding the stock of knowledge. For a given saving rate, the decrease in output implies a decrease in consumption.

The long-run steady-state effect is more subtle. We found in part (e) that output per effective worker falls in the steady state. But welfare depends on output (and consumption) per *worker*, not per effective worker. The increase in time spent in research universities implies that E grows faster. That is, output per worker equals yE. Although steady-state y falls, in the long run the faster growth rate of E necessarily dominates. That is, in the long run, consumption unambiguously rises.

Nevertheless, because of the initial decline in consumption, the increase in u is not unambiguously a good thing. That is, a policymaker who cares more about current generations than about future generations may decide not to pursue a policy of increasing u. (This is analogous to the question considered in Chapter 8 of whether a policymaker should try to reach the Golden Rule level of capital per effective worker if k is currently below the Golden Rule level.)

7.   There is no unique way to find the data to answer this question. For example, from the World Bank Web site, I followed links to "Data and Statistics." I then followed a link to "Quick Reference Tables" (http://www.worldbank.org/data/databytopic/GNPPC.pdf) to find a summary table of income per capita across countries. (Note that there are some subtle issues in converting currency values across countries that are beyond the scope of this book. The data in Table 9–1 use what are called "purchasing power parity.")

As an example, I chose to compare the United States (income per person of $31,900 in 1999) and Pakistan ($1,860), with a 17-fold difference in income per person. How can we decide what factors are most important? As the text notes, differences in income must come from differences in capital, labor, and/or technology. The Solow growth model gives us a framework for thinking about the importance of these factors.

One clear difference across countries is in educational attainment. One can think about differences in educational attainment as reflecting differences in broad "human capital" (analogous to physical capital) or as differences in the level of technology (e.g., if your work force is more educated, then you can implement better technologies). For our purposes, we will think of education as reflecting "technology," in that it allows more output per worker for any given level of physical capital per worker.

From the World Bank Web site (country tables) I found the following data (downloaded February 2002):

	Labor Force Growth (1994–2000)	Investment/GDP (1990) (percent)	Illiteracy (percent of population 15+)
United States	1.5	18	0
Pakistan	3.0	19	54

How can we decide which factor explains the most? It seems unlikely that the small difference in investment/GDP explains the large difference in per capital income, leaving labor-force growth and illiteracy (or, more generally, technology) as the likely culprits. But we can be more formal about this using the Solow model.

We follow Section 9-1, "Approaching the Steady State: A Numerical Example." For the moment, we assume the two countries have the same production technology: $Y=K^{0.5}L^{0.5}$. (This will allow us to decide whether differences in saving and population growth can explain the differences in income per capita; if not, then differences in technology will remain as the likely explanation.) As in the text, we can express this equation in terms of the per-worker production function $f(k)$:

$$y = k^{0.5}.$$

In steady-state, we know that

$$\Delta k = sf(k) - (n + \delta)k.$$

The steady-state value of capital per worker k^* is defined as the value of k at which capital per worker is constant, so $\Delta k = 0$. It follows that in steady state

$$0 = sf(k) - (n + \delta)k,$$

or, equivalently,

$$\frac{k^*}{f(k^*)} = \frac{s}{n + \delta}.$$

For the production function in this problem, it follows that:

$$\frac{k^*}{(k^*)^{0.5}} = \frac{s}{n + \delta},$$

Rearranging:

$$(k^*)^{0.5} = \frac{s}{n + \delta},$$

or

$$k^* = \left(\frac{s}{n + \delta}\right)^2.$$

Substituting this equation for steady-state capital per worker into the per-worker production function gives:

$$y^* = \left(\frac{s}{n + \delta}\right).$$

If we assume that the United States and Pakistan are in steady state and have the same rates of depreciation—say, 5 percent—then the ratio of income per capita in the two countries is:

$$\frac{y_{US}}{y_{Parkistan}} = \left[\frac{s_{US}}{s_{Pakistan}}\right]\left[\frac{n_{Pakistan} + 0.05}{n_{US} + 0.05}\right]$$

This equation tells us that if, say, the U.S. saving rate had been twice Pakistan's saving rate, then U.S. income per worker would be twice Pakistan's level (other things equal). Clearly, given that the U.S. has 17-times higher income per worker but very similar levels of investment relative to GDP, this variable is not a major factor in the comparison. Even population growth can only explain a factor of 1.2 (0.08/0.065) difference in levels of output per worker.

The remaining culprit is technology, and the high level of illiteracy in Pakistan is consistent with this conclusion.

More Problems and Applications to Chapter 9

1. a. The growth in total output (Y) depends on the growth rates of labor (L), capital (K), and total factor productivity (A), as summarized by the equation:

$$\Delta Y/Y = \alpha \Delta K/K + (1-\alpha)\Delta L/L + \Delta A/A,$$

where α is capital's share of output. We can look at the effect on output of a 5-percent increase in labor by setting $\Delta K/K = \Delta A/A = 0$. Since $\alpha = 2/3$, this gives us

$$\Delta Y/Y = (1/3)(5\%)$$
$$= 1.67\%.$$

A 5-percent increase in labor input increases output by 1.67 percent.

Labor productivity is Y/L. We can write the growth rate in labor productivity as

$$\frac{\Delta Y}{Y} = \frac{\Delta(Y/L)}{Y/L} - \frac{\Delta L}{L}.$$

Substituting for the growth in output and the growth in labor, we find

$$\Delta(Y/L)/(Y/L) = 1.67\% - 5.0\%$$
$$= -3.34\%.$$

Labor productivity falls by 3.34 percent.

To find the change in total factor productivity, we use the equation

$$\Delta A/A = \Delta Y/Y - \alpha \Delta K/K - (1-\alpha)\Delta L/L.$$

For this problem, we find

$$\Delta A/A = 1.67\% - 0 - (1/3)(5\%)$$
$$= 0.$$

Total factor productivity is the amount of output growth that remains after we have accounted for the determinants of growth that we can measure. In this case, there is no change in technology, so all of the output growth is attributable to measured input growth. That is, total factor productivity growth is zero, as expected.

   b. Between years 1 and 2, the capital stock grows by 1/6, labor input grows by 1/3, and output grows by 1/6. We know that the growth in total factor productivity is given by

$$\Delta A/A = \Delta Y/Y - \alpha \Delta K/K - (1-\alpha)\Delta L/L.$$

Substituting the numbers above, and setting $\alpha = 2/3$, we find

$$\Delta A/A = (1/6) - (2/3)(1/6) - (1/3)(1/3)$$
$$= 3/18 - 2/18 - 2/18$$
$$= -1/18$$
$$= -.056.$$

Total factor productivity falls by 1/18, or approximately 5.6 percent.

2. By definition, output Y equals labor productivity Y/L multiplied by the labor force L:

$$Y = (Y/L)L.$$

Using the mathematical trick in the hint, we can rewrite this as

$$\frac{\Delta Y}{Y} = \frac{\Delta(Y/L)}{Y/L} + \frac{\Delta L}{L}.$$

We can rearrange this as

$$\frac{\Delta(Y/L)}{Y/L} = \frac{\Delta Y}{Y} - \frac{\Delta L}{L}.$$

Substituting for $\Delta Y/Y$ from the text, we find

$$\frac{\Delta(Y/L)}{Y/L} = \frac{\Delta A}{A} + \frac{\alpha\Delta K}{K} + (1-\alpha)\frac{\Delta L}{L} - \frac{\Delta L}{L}$$

$$= \frac{\Delta A}{A} + \frac{\alpha\Delta K}{K} - \frac{\alpha\Delta L}{L}$$

$$= \frac{\Delta A}{A} + \alpha\left[\frac{\Delta K}{K} - \frac{\Delta L}{L}\right].$$

Using the same trick we used above, we can express the term in brackets as

$$\Delta K/K - \Delta L/L = \Delta(K/L)/(K/L).$$

Making this substitution in the equation for labor productivity growth, we conclude that

$$\frac{\Delta(Y/L)}{Y/L} = \frac{\Delta A}{A} + \frac{\alpha\Delta(K/L)}{K/L}.$$

3. We know the following:

$$\Delta Y/Y = n + g = 3.6\%$$
$$\Delta K/K = n + g = 3.6\%$$
$$\Delta L/L = n = 1.8\%$$
$$\text{Capital's share} = \alpha = 1/3$$
$$\text{Labor's share} = 1 - \alpha = 2/3.$$

Using these facts, we can easily find the contributions of each of the factors, and then find the contribution of total factor productivity growth, using the following equations:

Output Growth		Capital's Contribution		Labor's Contribution		Total Factor Productivity
$\dfrac{\Delta Y}{Y}$	=	$\dfrac{\alpha\Delta K}{K}$	+	$\dfrac{(1-\alpha)\Delta L}{L}$	+	$\dfrac{\Delta A}{A}$
3.6%	=	(1/3)(3.6%)	+	(2/3)(1.8%)	+	$\Delta A/A$

We can easily solve this for $\Delta A/A$, to find that

3.6%	=	1.2%	+	1.2%	+	1.2%.

We conclude that the contribution of capital is 1.2% per year, the contribution of labor is 1.2% per year, and the contribution of total factor productivity growth is 1.2% per year. These numbers match the ones in Table 9-3 in the text for the United States from 1948–2002.

Questions for Review

1. When GDP declines during a recession, growth in real consumption and investment spending both decline; unemployment rises sharply.

2. The price of a magazine is an example of a price that is sticky in the short run and flexible in the long run. Economists do not have a definitive answer as to why magazine prices are sticky in the short run. Perhaps customers would find it inconvenient if the price of a magazine they purchase changed every month.

3. Aggregate demand is the relation between the quantity of output demanded and the aggregate price level. To understand why the aggregate demand curve slopes downward, we need to develop a theory of aggregate demand. One simple theory of aggregate demand is based on the quantity theory of money. Write the quantity equation in terms of the supply and demand for real money balances as

$$M/P = (M/P)^d = kY,$$

where $k = 1/V$. This equation tells us that for any fixed money supply M, a negative relationship exists between the price level P and output Y, assuming that velocity V is fixed: the higher the price level, the lower the level of real balances and, therefore, the lower the quantity of goods and services demanded Y. In other words, the aggregate demand curve slopes downward, as in Figure 10-1.

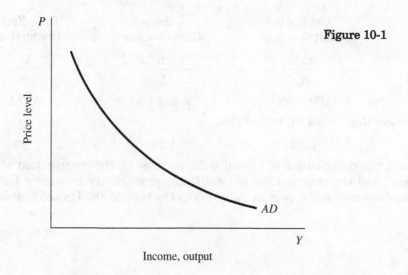

Figure 10-1

One way to understand this negative relationship between the price level and output is to note the link between money and transactions. If we assume that V is constant, then the money supply determines the dollar value of all transactions:

$$MV = PY.$$

An increase in the price level implies that each transaction requires more dollars. For the above identity to hold with constant velocity, the quantity of transactions and thus the quantity of goods and services purchased Y must fall.

4. If the Fed increases the money supply, then the aggregate demand curve shifts outward, as in Figure 10-2. In the short run, prices are sticky, so the economy moves along the short-run aggregate supply curve from point A to point B. Output rises above its natural rate level $\overline{Y}$: the economy is in a boom. The high demand, however, eventually causes wages and prices to increase. This gradual increase in prices moves the economy along the new aggregate demand curve AD_2 to point C. At the new long-run equilibrium, output is at its natural-rate level, but prices are higher than they were in the initial equilibrium at point A.

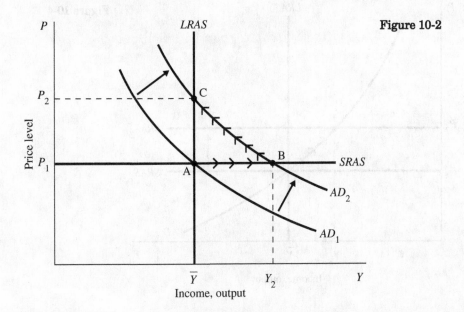

Figure 10-2

5. It is easier for the Fed to deal with demand shocks than with supply shocks because the Fed can reduce or even eliminate the impact of demand shocks on output by controlling the money supply. In the case of a supply shock, however, there is no way for the Fed to adjust aggregate demand to maintain both full employment and a stable price level.

   To understand why this is true, consider the policy options available to the Fed in each case. Suppose that a demand shock (such as the introduction of automatic teller machines, which reduces money demand by decreasing the parameter k and therefore increasing velocity V) shifts the aggregate demand curve outward, as in Figure 10-3. Output increases in the short run to Y_2. In the long run output returns to the natural-

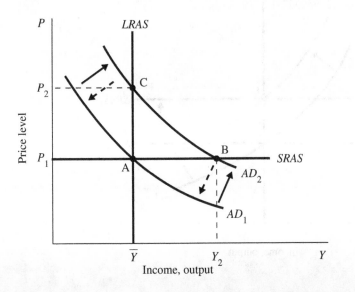

Figure 10-3

rate level, but at a higher price level P_2. The Fed can offset this increase in velocity, however, by reducing the money supply; this returns the aggregate demand curve to its initial position, AD_1. To the extent that the Fed can control the money supply, it can reduce or even eliminate the impact of demand shocks on output.

Now consider how an adverse supply shock (such as a crop failure or an increase in union aggressiveness) affects the economy. As shown in Figure 10-4, the short-run aggregate supply curve shifts up, and the economy moves from point A to point B.

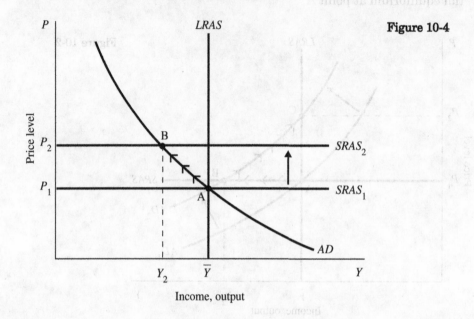

Figure 10-4

Output falls below the natural rate and prices rise. The Fed has two options. Its first option is to hold aggregate demand constant, in which case output falls below its natural rate. Eventually prices fall and restore full employment, but the cost is a painful

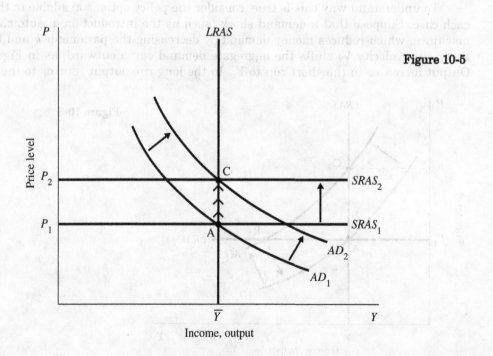

Figure 10-5

recession. Its second option is to increase aggregate demand by increasing the money supply, bringing the economy back toward the natural rate of output, as in Figure 10-5. This policy leads to a permanently higher price level at the new equilibrium, point C. Thus, in the case of a supply shock, there is no way to adjust aggregate demand to maintain both full employment and a stable price level.

Problems and Applications

1. a. Interest-bearing checking accounts make holding money more attractive. This increases the demand for money.

   b. The increase in money demand is equivalent to a decrease in the velocity of money. Recall the quantity equation

   $$M/P = kY,$$

   where $k = 1/V$. For this equation to hold, an increase in real money balances for a given amount of output means that k must increase; that is, velocity falls. Because interest on checking accounts encourages people to hold money, dollars circulate less frequently.

   c. If the Fed keeps the money supply the same, the decrease in velocity shifts the aggregate demand curve downward, as in Figure 10-6. In the short run when prices are sticky, the economy moves from the initial equilibrium, point A, to the short-run equilibrium, point B. The drop in aggregate demand reduces the output of the economy below the natural rate.

Figure 10-6

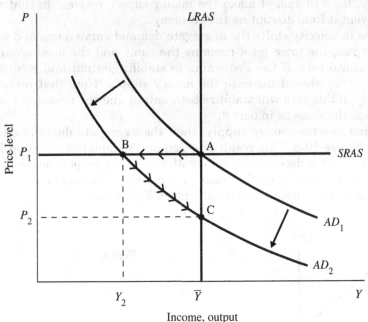

Over time, the low level of aggregate demand causes prices and wages to fall. As prices fall, output gradually rises until it reaches the natural-rate level of output at point C.

d.   The decrease in velocity causes the aggregate demand curve to shift downward. The Fed could increase the money supply to offset this decrease and thereby return the economy to its original equilibrium at point A, as in Figure 10-7.

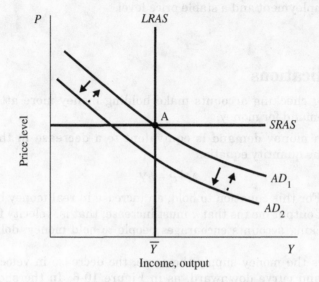

Figure 10-7

To the extent that the Fed can accurately measure changes in velocity, it has the ability to reduce or even eliminate the impact of such a demand shock on output. In particular, when a regulatory change causes money demand to change in a predictable way, the Fed should make the money supply respond to that change in order to prevent it from disrupting the economy.

e.   The decrease in velocity shifts the aggregate demand curve down and to the left. In the short run, the price level remains the same and the level of output falls below the natural rate. If the Fed wants to stabilize output and return it to the natural rate, they should increase the money supply. Note that increasing the money supply in this case will stabilize both output and the price level so that the answer here is the same as in part d.

2. a.   If the Fed reduces the money supply, then the aggregate demand curve shifts down, as in Figure 10-8. This result is based on the quantity equation $MV = PY$, which tells us that a decrease in money M leads to a proportionate decrease in nominal output PY (assuming that velocity V is fixed). For any given price level P, the level of output Y is lower, and for any given Y, P is lower.

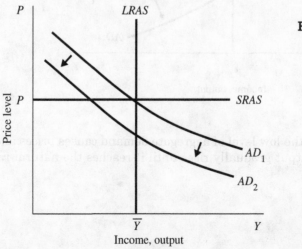

Figure 10-8

b. In the short run, we assume that the price level is fixed and that the aggregate supply curve is flat. As Figure 10-9 shows, in the short run, the leftward shift in the aggregate demand curve leads to a movement from point A to point B—output falls but the price level doesn't change. In the long run, prices are flexible. As prices fall, the economy returns to full employment at point C.

If we assume that velocity is constant, we can quantify the effect of the 5-percent reduction in the money supply. Recall from Chapter 5 that we can express the quantity equation in terms of percentage changes:

$$\%\Delta \text{ in } M + \%\Delta \text{ in } V = \%\Delta \text{ in } P + \%\Delta \text{ in } Y.$$

If we assume that velocity is constant, then the $\%\Delta$ in V = 0. Therefore,

$$\%\Delta \text{ in } M = \%\Delta \text{ in } P + \%\Delta \text{ in } Y.$$

We know that in the short run, the price level is fixed. This implies that the $\%\Delta$ in P = 0. Therefore,

$$\%\Delta \text{ in } M = \%\Delta \text{ in } Y.$$

Based on this equation, we conclude that in the short run a 5-percent reduction in the money supply leads to a 5-percent reduction in output. This is shown in Figure 10-9.

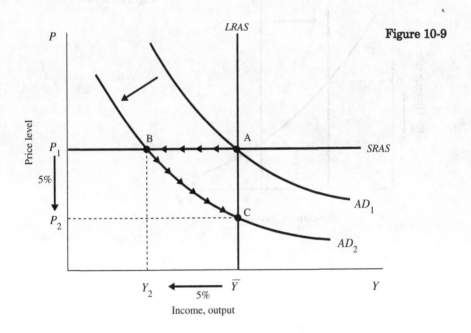

Figure 10-9

In the long run we know that prices are flexible and the economy returns to its natural rate of output. This implies that in the long run, the $\%\Delta$ in Y = 0. Therefore,

$$\%\Delta \text{ in } M = \%\Delta \text{ in } P.$$

Based on this equation, we conclude that in the long run a 5-percent reduction in the money supply leads to a 5-percent reduction in the price level, as shown in Figure 10-9.

c. Okun's law refers to the negative relationship that exists between unemployment and real GDP. Okun's law can be summarized by the equation:

$$\%\Delta \text{ in Real GDP} = 3\% - 2 \times [\Delta \text{ in Unemployment Rate}].$$

That is, output moves in the opposite direction from unemployment, with a ratio of 2 to 1. In the short run, when output falls, unemployment rises. Quantitatively, if velocity is constant, we found that output falls 5 percentage points relative to full employment in the short run. Okun's law states that output growth equals the full employment growth rate of 3 percent minus two times the change in the unemployment rate. Therefore, if output falls 5 percentage points relative to full-employment growth, then actual output growth is –2 percent. Using Okun's law, we find that the change in the unemployment rate equals 2.5 percentage points:

$$-2 = 3 - 2 \times [\Delta \text{ in Unemployment Rate}]$$

$$[-2 - 3]/[-2] = [\Delta \text{ in Unemployment Rate}]$$

$$2.5 = [\Delta \text{ in Unemployment Rate}]$$

In the long run, both output and unemployment return to their natural rate levels. Thus, there is no long-run change in unemployment.

d. The national income accounts identity tells us that saving $S = Y - C - G$. Thus, when Y falls, S falls (assuming the marginal propensity to consume is less than one). Figure 10-10 shows that this causes the real interest rate to rise. When Y returns to its original equilibrium level, so does the real interest rate.

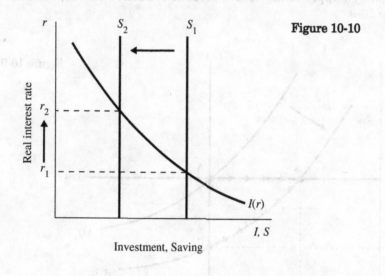

Figure 10-10

3. a. An exogenous decrease in the velocity of money causes the aggregate demand curve to shift downward, as in Figure 10-11. In the short run, prices are fixed, so output falls.

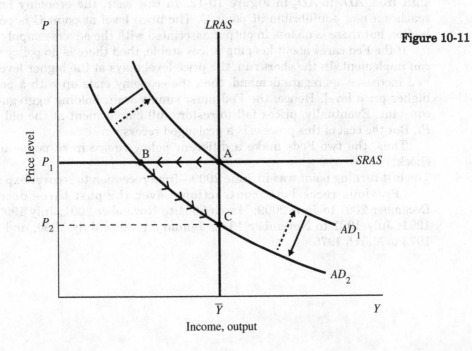

Figure 10-11

If the Fed wants to keep output and employment at their natural-rate levels, it must increase aggregate demand to offset the decrease in velocity. By increasing the money supply, the Fed can shift the aggregate demand curve upward, restoring the economy to its original equilibrium at point A. Both the price level and output remain constant.

If the Fed wants to keep prices stable, then it wants to avoid the long-run adjustment to a lower price level at point C in Figure 10-11. Therefore, it should increase the money supply and shift the aggregate demand curve upward, again restoring the original equilibrium at point A.

Thus, both Feds make the same choice of policy in response to this demand shock.

b. An exogenous increase in the price of oil is an adverse supply shock that causes the short-run aggregate supply curve to shift upward, as in Figure 10-12.

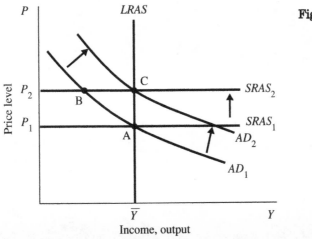

Figure 10-12

If the Fed cares about keeping output and employment at their natural-rate levels, then it should increase aggregate demand by increasing the money supply. This policy response shifts the aggregate demand curve upwards, as shown in the shift from AD_1 to AD_2 in Figure 10-12. In this case, the economy immediately reaches a new equilibrium at point C. The price level at point C is permanently higher, but there is no loss in output associated with the adverse supply shock.

If the Fed cares about keeping prices stable, then there is no policy response it can implement. In the short run, the price level stays at the higher level P_2. If the Fed increases aggregate demand, then the economy ends up with a permanently higher price level. Hence, the Fed must simply wait, holding aggregate demand constant. Eventually, prices fall to restore full employment at the old price level P_1. But the cost of this process is a prolonged recession.

Thus, the two Feds make a different policy choice in response to a supply shock.

4. The last turning point was in June 2009—from recession to recover/expansion.

Previous recessions (contractions) over the past three decades were December 2007 to June 2009; March 2001 to November 2001; July 1990 to March 1991; July 1981 to November 1982; January 1980 to July 1980; and November 1973 to March 1975.

CHAPTER **11** Aggregate Demand I: Building the *IS–LM* Model

Questions for Review

1. The Keynesian-cross model tells us that fiscal policy has a multiplied effect on income. The reason is that according to the consumption function, higher income causes higher consumption. For example, an increase in government purchases of ΔG raises expenditure and, therefore, income by ΔG. This increase in income causes consumption to rise by $MPC \times \Delta G$, where MPC is the marginal propensity to consume. This increase in consumption raises expenditure and income even further. This feedback from consumption to income continues indefinitely. Therefore, in the Keynesian-cross model, increasing government spending by one dollar causes an increase in income that is greater than one dollar: it increases by $1/(1 - MPC)$.

2. The theory of liquidity preference explains how the supply and demand for real money balances determine the interest rate. A simple version of this theory assumes that there is a fixed supply of money, which the Fed chooses. The price level P is also fixed in this model, so that the supply of real balances is fixed. The demand for real money balances depends on the interest rate, which is the opportunity cost of holding money. At a high interest rate, people hold less money because the opportunity cost is high. By holding money, they forgo the interest on interest-bearing deposits. In contrast, at a low interest rate, people hold more money because the opportunity cost is low. Figure 11-1 graphs the supply and demand for real money balances. Based on this theory of liquidity preference, the interest rate adjusts to equilibrate the supply and demand for real money balances.

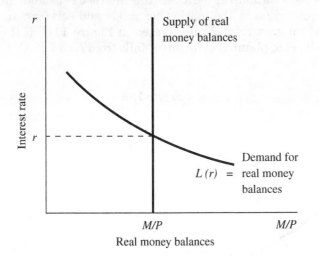

Figure 11-1

91

Why does an increase in the money supply lower the interest rate? Consider what happens when the Fed increases the money supply from M_1 to M_2. Because the price level P is fixed, this increase in the money supply shifts the supply of real money balances M/P to the right, as in Figure 11-2.

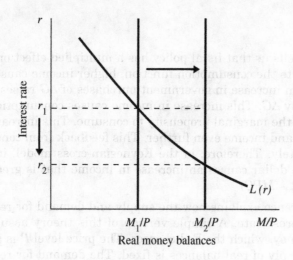

Figure 11-2

The interest rate must adjust to equilibrate supply and demand. At the old interest rate r_1, supply exceeds demand. People holding the excess supply of money try to convert some of it into interest-bearing bank deposits or bonds. Banks and bond issuers, who prefer to pay lower interest rates, respond to this excess supply of money by lowering the interest rate. The interest rate falls until a new equilibrium is reached at r_2.

3. The *IS* curve summarizes the relationship between the interest rate and the level of income that arises from equilibrium in the market for goods and services. Investment is negatively related to the interest rate. As illustrated in Figure 11-3, if the interest rate rises from r_1 to r_2, the level of planned investment falls from I_1 to I_2.

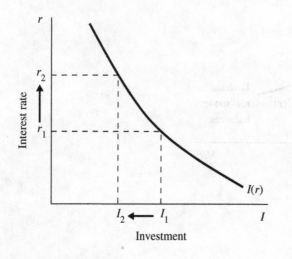

Figure 11-3

The Keynesian cross tells us that a reduction in planned investment shifts the expenditure function downward and reduces national income, as in Figure 11-4(A).

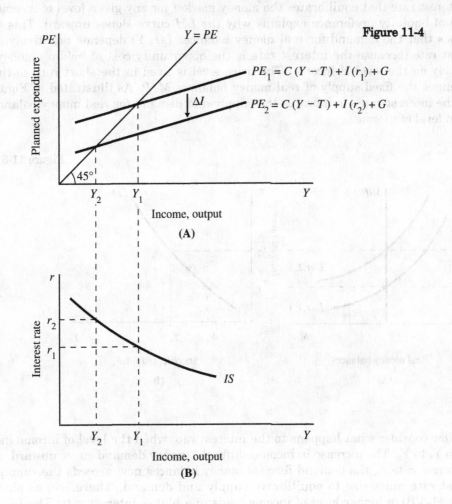

Figure 11-4

Thus, as shown in Figure 11-4(B), a higher interest rate results in a lower level of national income: the *IS* curve slopes downward.

4. The *LM* curve summarizes the relationship between the level of income and the interest rate that arises from equilibrium in the market for real money balances. It tells us the interest rate that equilibrates the money market for any given level of income. The theory of liquidity preference explains why the *LM* curve slopes upward. This theory assumes that the demand for real money balances $L(r, Y)$ depends negatively on the interest rate (because the interest rate is the opportunity cost of holding money) and positively on the level of income. The price level is fixed in the short run, so the Fed determines the fixed supply of real money balances M/P. As illustrated in Figure 11-5(A), the interest rate equilibrates the supply and demand for real money balances for a given level of income.

Figure 11-5

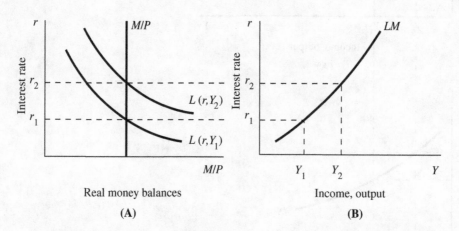

(A)

Real money balances

(B)

Income, output

Now consider what happens to the interest rate when the level of income increases from Y_1 to Y_2. The increase in income shifts the money demand curve upward. At the old interest rate r_1, the demand for real money balances now exceeds the supply. The interest rate must rise to equilibrate supply and demand. Therefore, as shown in Figure 11-5(B), a higher level of income leads to a higher interest rate: The *LM* curve slopes upward.

Problems and Applications

1. a.   The Keynesian cross illustrates an economy's planned expenditure function, $PE = C(Y - T) + I + G$, and the equilibrium condition that actual expenditure equals planned expenditure, $Y = PE$, as shown in Figure 11-6.

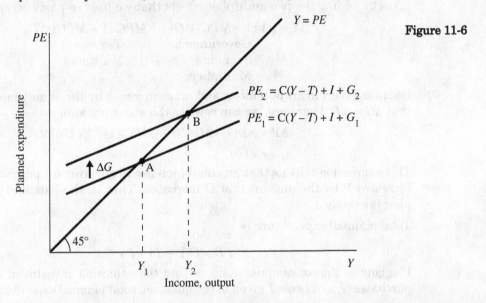

Figure 11-6

An increase in government purchases from G_1 to G_2 shifts the planned expenditure function upward. The new equilibrium is at point B. The change in equilibrium GDP, Y, equals the product of the government-purchases multiplier and the change in government spending: $\Delta Y = [1/(1 - MPC)]\Delta G$. Because we know that the marginal propensity to consume MPC is less than one, this expression tells us that a one-dollar increase in G leads to an increase in Y that is greater than one dollar.

b.   An increase in taxes ΔT reduces disposable income $Y - T$ by ΔT and, therefore, reduces consumption by $MPC \times \Delta T$. For any given level of income Y, planned expenditure falls. In the Keynesian cross, the tax increase shifts the planned-expenditure function down by $MPC \times \Delta T$, as in Figure 11-7.

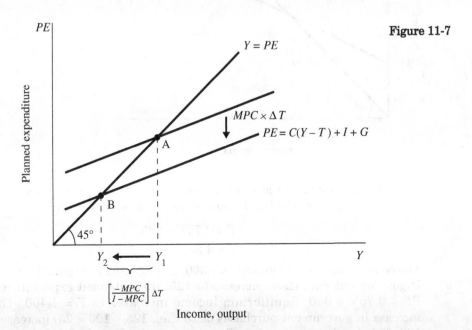

Figure 11-7

The amount by which equilibrium GDP falls is given by the product of the tax multiplier and the increase in taxes:

$$\Delta Y = [-MPC/(1 - MPC)]\Delta T.$$

c. We can calculate the effect of an equal increase in government expenditure and taxes by adding the two multiplier effects that we used in parts (a) and (b):

$$\Delta Y = [(1/(1 - MPC))\Delta G] - [(MPC/(1 - MPC))\Delta T].$$

Government	Tax
Spending	Multiplier
Multiplier	

Because government purchases and taxes increase by the same amount, we know that $\Delta G = \Delta T$. Therefore, we can rewrite the above equation as:

$$\Delta Y = [(1/(1 - MPC)) - (MPC/(1 - MPC))]\Delta G$$
$$= \Delta G.$$

This expression tells us that an equal increase in government purchases and taxes increases Y by the amount that G increases. That is, the balanced-budget multiplier is exactly 1.

2. a. Total planned expenditure is

$$PE = C(Y - T) + I + G.$$

Plugging in the consumption function and the values for investment I, government purchases G, and taxes T given in the question, total planned expenditure PE is

$$PE = 200 + 0.75(Y - 100) + 100 + 100$$
$$= 0.75Y + 325.$$

This equation is graphed in Figure 11-8.

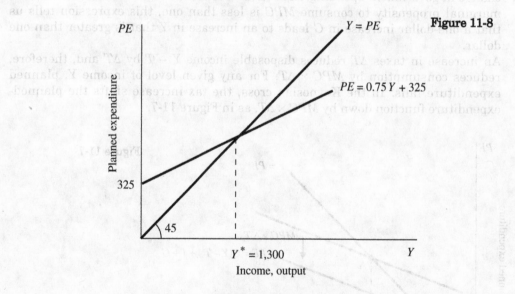

Figure 11-8

b. To find the equilibrium level of income, combine the planned-expenditure equation derived in part (a) with the equilibrium condition $Y = PE$:

$$Y = 0.75Y + 325$$
$$Y = 1,300.$$

The equilibrium level of income is 1,300, as indicated in Figure 11-8.

c. If government purchases increase to 125, then planned expenditure changes to $PE = 0.75Y + 350$. Equilibrium income increases to $Y = 1,400$. Therefore, an increase in government purchases of 25 (i.e., 125 − 100 = 25) increases income by 100. This is what we expect to find, because the formula for the government-purchases multiplier is $1/(1 - MPC)$, the *MPC* is 0.75, and the government-purchases multiplier therefore has a numerical value of 4.

d. An income level of 1,600 represents an increase of 300 over the original level of income. The government-purchases multiplier is $1/(1 - MPC)$: the *MPC* in this example equals 0.75, so the government-purchases multiplier is 4. This means that government purchases must increase by 75 (to a level of 175) for income to increase by 300.

3. a. When taxes do not depend on income, a one-dollar increase in income means that disposable income increases by one dollar. Consumption increases by the marginal propensity to consume *MPC*. When taxes do depend on income, a one-dollar increase in income means that disposable income increases by only $(1 - t)$ dollars. Consumption increases by the product of the *MPC* and the change in disposable income, or $(1 - t)MPC$. This is less than the *MPC*. The key point is that disposable income changes by less than total income, so the effect on consumption is smaller.

b. When taxes are fixed, we know that $\Delta Y/\Delta G = 1/(1 - MPC)$. We found this by considering an increase in government purchases of ΔG; the initial effect of this change is to increase income by ΔG. This in turn increases consumption by an amount equal to the marginal propensity to consume times the change in income, $MPC \times \Delta G$. This increase in consumption raises expenditure and income even further. The process continues indefinitely, and we derive the multiplier above.

When taxes depend on income, we know that the increase of ΔG increases total income by ΔG; disposable income, however, increases by only $(1 - t)\Delta G$—less than dollar for dollar. Consumption then increases by an amount $(1 - t)$ $MPC \times \Delta G$. Expenditure and income increase by this amount, which in turn causes consumption to increase even more. The process continues, and the total change in output is

$$\Delta Y = \Delta G \{1 + (1 - t)MPC + [(1 - t)MPC]^2 + [(1 - t)MPC]^3 + \dots.\}$$

$$= \Delta G [1/(1 - (1 - t)MPC)].$$

Thus, the government-purchases multiplier becomes $1/(1 - (1 - t)MPC)$ rather than $1/(1 - MPC)$. This means a much smaller multiplier. For example, if the marginal propensity to consume *MPC* is 3/4 and the tax rate *t* is 1/3, then the multiplier falls from $1/(1 - 3/4)$, or 4, to $1/(1 - (1 - 1/3)(3/4))$, or 2.

c. In this chapter, we derived the *IS* curve algebraically and used it to gain insight into the relationship between the interest rate and output. To determine how this tax system alters the slope of the *IS* curve, we can derive the *IS* curve for the case in which taxes depend on income. Begin with the national income accounts identity:

$$Y = C + I + G.$$

The consumption function is

$$C = a + b(Y - \overline{T} - tY).$$

Note that in this consumption function taxes are a function of income. The investment function is the same as in the chapter:

$$I = c - dr.$$

Substitute the consumption and investment functions into the national income accounts identity to obtain:

$$Y = [a + b(Y - \overline{T} - tY)] + c - dr + G.$$

Solving for *r*:

$$r = \frac{a - b\overline{T} + c + G}{d} + Y\left[\frac{b(1 - t) - 1}{d}\right].$$

The slope of the *IS* curve is therefore:

$$\frac{\Delta r}{\Delta y} = \frac{b(1 - t) - 1}{d}.$$

Recall that t is a number that is less than 1. As t becomes a bigger number, the slope of the IS curve increases in absolute value terms and the curve becomes steeper. Suppose, for example, that b is 0.80, t is 0.1, and d is 0.5. The slope of the IS curve is –0.56. If the tax rate increases to 0.2, then the slope becomes –0.72. Intuitively, if the tax rate is higher, then any given reduction in the interest rate has a smaller effect on real output Y because the multiplier will be smaller.

4. a. If society becomes more thrifty—meaning that for any given level of income people save more and consume less—then the planned-expenditure function shifts downward, as in Figure 11-9 (note that $C_2 < C_1$). Equilibrium income falls from Y_1 to Y_2.

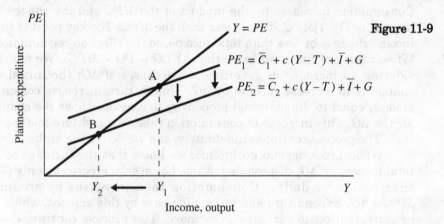

Figure 11-9

b. Equilibrium saving remains unchanged. The national accounts identity tells us that saving equals investment, or $S = I$. In the Keynesian-cross model, we assumed that desired investment is fixed. This assumption implies that investment is the same in the new equilibrium as it was in the old. We can conclude that saving is exactly the same in both equilibria.

c. The paradox of thrift is that even though thriftiness increases, saving is unaffected. Increased thriftiness leads only to a fall in income. For an individual, we usually consider thriftiness a virtue. From the perspective of the entire economy as represented by the Keynesian-cross model, however, thriftiness is a vice.

d. In the classical model of Chapter 3, the paradox of thrift does not arise. In that model, output is fixed by the factors of production and the production technology, and the interest rate adjusts to equilibrate saving and investment, where investment depends on the interest rate. An increase in thriftiness decreases consumption and increases saving for any level of output; since output is fixed, the saving schedule shifts to the right, as in Figure 11-10. At the new equilibrium, the interest rate is lower, and investment and saving are higher.

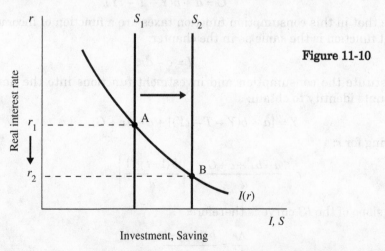

Figure 11-10

Thus, in the classical model, the paradox of thrift does not exist.

5. a.   The downward sloping line in Figure 11–11 represents the money demand function $(M/P)^d = 1,000 - 100r$. With $M = 1,000$ and $P = 2$, the real money supply $(M/P)^s = 500$. The real money supply is independent of the interest rate and is, therefore, represented by the vertical line in Figure 11-11.

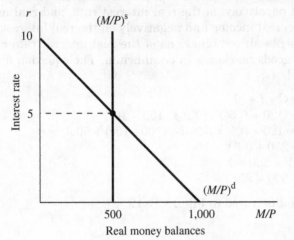

Figure 11-11

   b.   We can solve for the equilibrium interest rate by setting the supply and demand for real balances equal to each other:

$$500 = 1,000 - 100r$$

$$r = 5.$$

Therefore, the equilibrium real interest rate equals 5 percent.

   c.   If the price level remains fixed at 2 and the supply of money is raised from 1,000 to 1,200, then the new supply of real balances $(M/P)^s$ equals 600. We can solve for the new equilibrium interest rate by setting the new $(M/P)^s$ equal to $(M/P)^d$:

$$600 = 1,000 - 100r$$

$$100r = 400$$

$$r = 4.$$

Thus, increasing the money supply from 1,000 to 1,200 causes the equilibrium interest rate to fall from 5 percent to 4 percent.

   d.   To determine at what level the Fed should set the money supply to raise the interest rate to 7 percent, set $(M/P)^s$ equal to $(M/P)^d$:

$$M/P = 1,000 - 100r.$$

Setting the price level at 2 and substituting $r = 7$, we find:

$$M/2 = 1,000 - 100 \times 7$$

$$M = 600.$$

For the Fed to raise the interest rate from 5 percent to 7 percent, it must reduce the nominal money supply from 1,000 to 600.

6. a.   The variable Y represents real output or real income. From Chapter 2, we know that the value of the produced goods and services (real output) has to be equal to the value of the income earned in producing the goods and services (real income). The variable C represents the consumption of goods and services. The variable I represents investment by the firms. When firms purchase new capital goods, this counts as investment. When firms experience a change in their inventories, this

also counts in the investment category of GDP. The variable G represents the government's spending on newly produced goods and services. The variable T represents lump sum taxes, and $Y - T$ represents disposable income. The variable M represents the nominal money supply, P is the price level, and M/P is the real money supply. The variable r is the real interest rate. The variable $(M/P)^d$ represents real money demand. Consumption depends positively on disposable income, investment depends negatively on the real interest rate, and real money demand depends positively on real income and negatively on the real interest rate.

b. The IS curve represents all combinations of the real interest rate r and real output Y such that the goods market is in equilibrium. The equation for the IS curve can be derived as follows:

$$Y = C + I + G$$
$$Y = (120 + 0.5(Y - T)) + (100 - 10r) + 50$$
$$Y = (120 + 0.5(Y - 40)) + (100 - 10r) + 50$$
$$Y = 250 + 0.5Y - 10r$$
$$0.5Y = 250 - 10r$$
$$Y = 500 - 20r$$

The IS curve is illustrated in Figure 11-12.

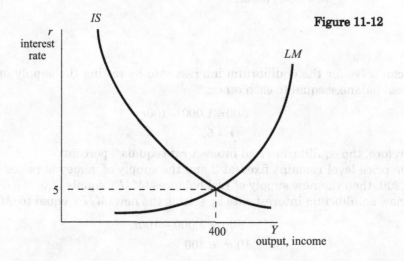

Figure 11-12

c. The LM curve represents all combinations of the real interest rate r and real output Y such that the money market is in equilibrium. The equation for the LM curve can be derived as follows:

$$\left(\frac{M}{P}\right)^d = \frac{M}{P}$$
$$Y - 20r = \frac{600}{2}$$
$$Y = 300 + 20r.$$

The LM curve is illustrated in Figure 11-12.

d. To find the equilibrium levels of the interest rate and output (or income), set the equation for the IS curve equal to the equation for the LM curve and solve for the interest rate r to get 5. Now substitute the interest rate of 5 back into either equation to solve for Y equal to 400.

CHAPTER 12

**Aggregate Demand II: Applying the
IS–LM Model**

Questions for Review

1. The aggregate demand curve represents the negative relationship between the price level and the level of national income. In Chapter 10, we looked at a simplified theory of aggregate demand based on the quantity theory. In this chapter, we explore how the *IS–LM* model provides a more complete theory of aggregate demand. We can see why the aggregate demand curve slopes downward by considering what happens in the *IS–LM* model when the price level changes. As Figure 12-1(A) illustrates, for a given money supply, an increase in the price level from P_1 to P_2 shifts the *LM* curve upward because real balances decline; this reduces income from Y_1 to Y_2. The aggregate demand curve in Figure 12-1(B) summarizes this relationship between the price level and income that results from the *IS–LM* model.

A. The *IS–LM* Model

Figure 12-1

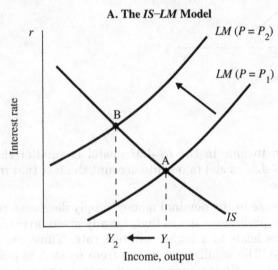

B. The Aggregate Demand Curve

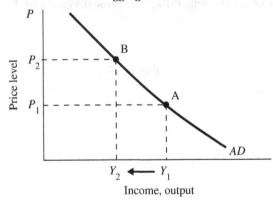

2. The tax multiplier in the Keynesian-cross model tells us that, for any given interest rate, the tax increase causes income to fall by $\Delta T \times [-MPC/(1 - MPC)]$. This *IS* curve shifts to the left by this amount, as in Figure 12-2. The equilibrium of the economy moves from point A to point B. The tax increase reduces the interest rate from r_1 to r_2 and reduces national income from Y_1 to Y_2. Consumption falls because disposable income falls; investment rises because the interest rate falls.

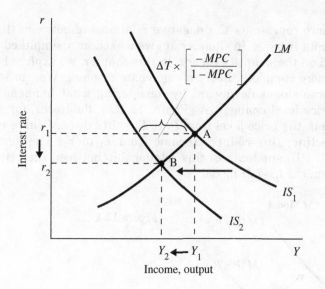

Figure 12-2

Note that the decrease in income in the *IS–LM* model is smaller than in the Keynesian cross, because the *IS–LM* model takes into account the fact that investment rises when the interest rate falls.

3. Given a fixed price level, a decrease in the nominal money supply decreases real money balances. The theory of liquidity preference shows that, for any given level of income, a decrease in real money balances leads to a higher interest rate. Thus, the *LM* curve shifts upward, as in Figure 12-3. The equilibrium moves from point A to point B. The decrease in the money supply reduces income and raises the interest rate. Consumption falls because disposable income falls, whereas investment falls because the interest rate rises.

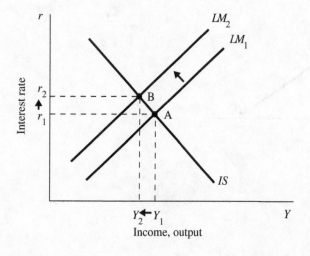

Figure 12-3

4. Falling prices can either increase or decrease equilibrium income. There are two ways in which falling prices can increase income. First, an increase in real money balances shifts the *LM* curve downward, thereby increasing income. Second, the *IS* curve shifts to the right because of the Pigou effect: real money balances are part of household wealth, so an increase in real money balances makes consumers feel wealthier and buy more. This shifts the *IS* curve to the right, also increasing income.

There are two ways in which falling prices can reduce income. The first is the debt-deflation theory. An unexpected decrease in the price level redistributes wealth from debtors to creditors. If debtors have a higher propensity to consume than creditors, then this redistribution causes debtors to decrease their spending by more than creditors increase theirs. As a result, aggregate consumption falls, shifting the *IS* curve to the left and reducing income. The second way in which falling prices can reduce income is through the effects of expected deflation. Recall that the real interest rate r equals the nominal interest rate i minus the expected inflation rate π^e: $r = i - \pi^e$. If everyone expects the price level to fall in the future (i.e., π^e is negative), then for any given nominal interest rate, the real interest rate is higher. A higher real interest rate depresses investment and shifts the *IS* curve to the left, reducing income.

Problems and Applications

1. a.   If the central bank increases the money supply, then the *LM* curve shifts downward, as shown in Figure 12-4. Income increases and the interest rate falls. The increase in disposable income causes consumption to rise; the fall in the interest rate causes investment to rise as well.

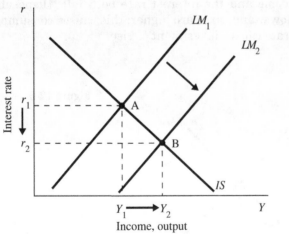

Figure 12-4

b.   If government purchases increase, then the government-purchases multiplier tells us that the *IS* curve shifts to the right by an amount equal to $[1/(1 - MPC)]\Delta G$. This is shown in Figure 12-5. Income and the interest rate both increase. The increase in disposable income causes consumption to rise, while the increase in the interest rate causes investment to fall.

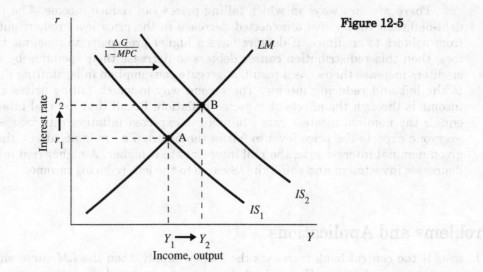

Figure 12-5

c.   If the government increases taxes, then the tax multiplier tells us that the *IS* curve shifts to the left by an amount equal to $[-MPC/(1 - MPC)]\Delta T$. This is shown in Figure 12-6. Income and the interest rate both fall. Disposable income falls because income is lower and taxes are higher; this causes consumption to fall. The fall in the interest rate causes investment to rise.

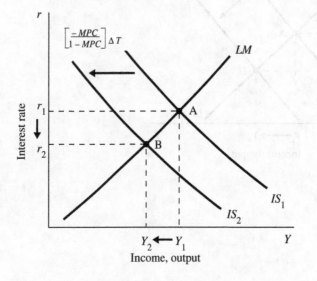

Figure 12-6

d. We can figure out how much the *IS* curve shifts in response to an equal increase in government purchases and taxes by adding together the two multiplier effects that we used in parts (b) and (c):

$$\Delta Y = [(1/(1 - MPC))]\Delta G] - [(MPC/(1 - MPC))\Delta T]$$

Because government purchases and taxes increase by the same amount, we know that $\Delta G = \Delta T$. Therefore, we can rewrite the above equation as:

$$\Delta Y = [(1/(1 - MPC)) - (MPC/(1 - MPC))]\Delta G$$

$$\Delta Y = \Delta G.$$

This expression tells us how output changes, holding the interest rate constant. It says that an equal increase in government purchases and taxes shifts the *IS* curve to the right by the amount that *G* increases.

This shift is shown in Figure 12-7. Output increases, but by less than the amount that *G* and *T* increase; this means that disposable income $Y - T$ falls. As a result, consumption also falls. The interest rate rises, causing investment to fall.

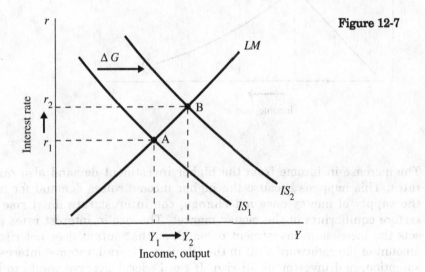

Figure 12-7

2. a.   The invention of the new high-speed chip increases investment demand, meaning that at every interest rate, firms want to invest more. The increase in the demand for investment goods shifts the *IS* curve out and to the right, raising income and employment. Figure 12-8 shows the effect graphically.

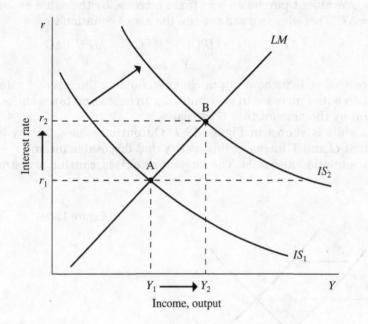

Figure 12-8

The increase in income from the higher investment demand also raises interest rates. This happens because the higher income raises demand for money; since the supply of money does not change, the interest rate must rise in order to restore equilibrium in the money market. The rise in interest rates partially off-sets the increase in investment demand, so that output does not rise by the full amount of the rightward shift in the *IS* curve. Overall, income, interest rates, consumption, and investment all rise. If the Federal Reserve wants to keep output constant, then it must decrease the money supply and increase interest rates fur-ther in order to offset the effect of the increase in investment demand. When the Fed decreases the money supply, the *LM* curve will shift up and to the left. Output will remain at the same level and the interest rate will be higher. There will be no change in consumption and no change in investment. The interest rate will increase by enough to completely offset the initial increase in investment demand.

b.   The increased demand for cash shifts the *LM* curve up. This happens because at any given level of income and money supply, the interest rate necessary to equili-brate the money market is higher. Figure 12-9 shows the effect of this *LM* shift graphically.

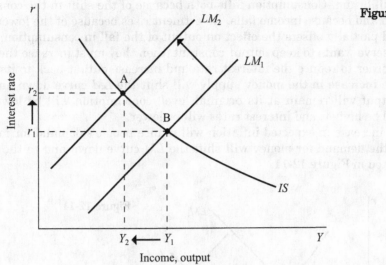

Figure 12-9

The upward shift in the *LM* curve lowers income and raises the interest rate. Consumption falls because income falls, and investment falls because the interest rate rises due to the increase in money demand. If the Federal Reserve wants to keep output constant, then they must increase the money supply in order to lower the interest rate and bring output back to its original level. The *LM* curve will shift down and to the right and return to its old position. In this case, nothing will change.

c.   At any given level of income, consumers now wish to save more and consume less. Because of this downward shift in the consumption function, the *IS* curve shifts inward. Figure 12-10 shows the effect of this *IS* shift graphically.

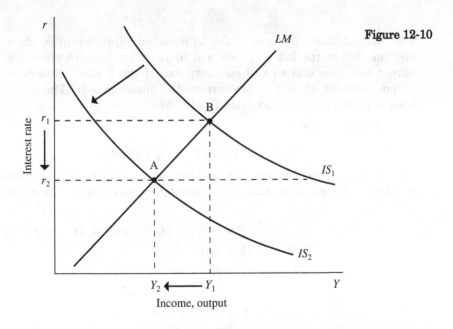

Figure 12-10

Income, interest rates, and consumption all fall, while investment rises. Income falls because at every level of the interest rate, planned expenditure falls. The interest rate falls because the fall in income reduces demand for money; since the supply of money is unchanged, the interest rate must fall to restore money-market equilibrium. Consumption falls both because of the shift in the consumption function and because income falls. Investment rises because of the lower interest rates and partially offsets the effect on output of the fall in consumption. If the Federal Reserve wants to keep output constant, then they must increase the money supply in order to reduce the interest rate and increase output back to its original level. The increase in the money supply will shift the *LM* curve down and to the right. Output will remain at its original level, consumption will be lower, investment will be higher, and interest rates will be lower.

d.   An increase in expected inflation will reduce people's demand for money. This fall in the demand for money will shift the *LM* curve down and to the right, as illustrated in Figure 12-11.

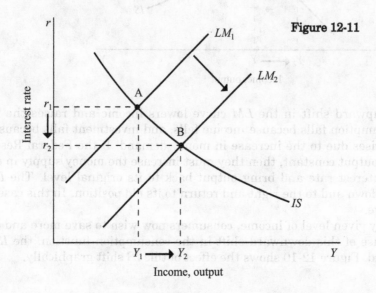

Figure 12-11

The interest rate will have to fall to maintain equilibrium in the money market and this fall in the interest rate will increase investment spending. Equilibrium output will rise, and so will consumption. If the Federal Reserve wants to keep output constant, then it must decrease the money supply. The *LM* curve will shift back to its old position and nothing will change.

3.   a.   The *IS* curve is given by:

$$Y = C(Y - T) + I(r) + G.$$

We can plug in the consumption and investment functions and values for G and T as given in the question and then rearrange to solve for the *IS* curve for this economy:

$$Y = 200 + 0.75(Y - 100) + 200 - 25r + 100$$
$$Y - 0.75Y = 425 - 25r$$
$$(1 - 0.75)Y = 425 - 25r$$
$$Y = (1/0.25)(425 - 25r)$$
$$Y = 1,700 - 100r.$$

This *IS* equation is graphed in Figure 12-12 for r ranging from 0 to 8.

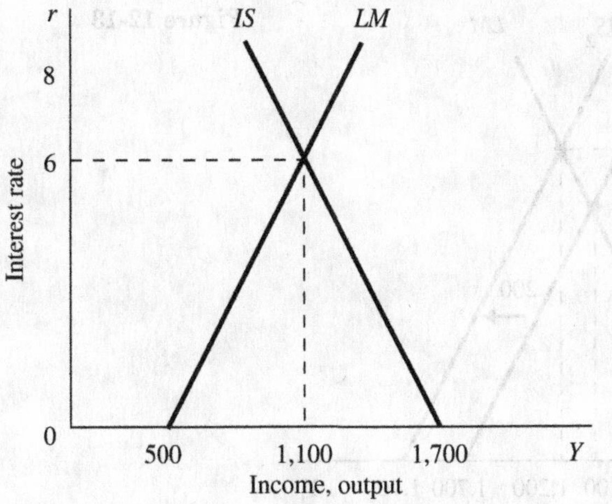

Figure 12-12

b. The *LM* curve is determined by equating the demand for and supply of real money balances. The supply of real balances is 1,000/2 = 500. Setting this equal to money demand, we find:

$$500 = Y - 100r.$$

$$Y = 500 + 100r.$$

This *LM* curve is graphed in Figure 12-11 for *r* ranging from 0 to 8.

c. If we take the price level as given, then the *IS* and the *LM* equations give us two equations in two unknowns, *Y* and *r*. We found the following equations in parts (a) and (b):

$$IS: Y = 1,700 - 100r.$$

$$LM: Y = 500 + 100r.$$

Equating these, we can solve for *r*:

$$1,700 - 100r = 500 + 100r$$

$$1,200 = 200r$$

$$r = 6.$$

Now that we know *r*, we can solve for *Y* by substituting it into either the *IS* or the *LM* equation. We find

$$Y = 1,100.$$

Therefore, the equilibrium interest rate is 6 percent and the equilibrium level of output is 1,100, as depicted in Figure 12-11.

d. If government purchases increase from 100 to 150, then the *IS* equation becomes:

$$Y = 200 + 0.75(Y - 100) + 200 - 25r + 150.$$

Simplifying, we find:

$$Y = 1,900 - 100r.$$

This *IS* curve is graphed as *IS*$_2$ in Figure 12-13. We see that the *IS* curve shifts to the right by 200.

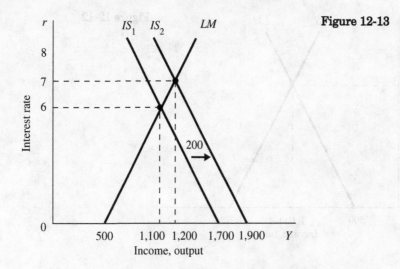

Figure 12-13

By equating the new *IS* curve with the *LM* curve derived in part (b), we can solve for the new equilibrium interest rate:

$$1,900 - 100r = 500 + 100r$$

$$1,400 = 200r$$

$$7 = r.$$

We can now substitute *r* into either the *IS* or the *LM* equation to find the new level of output. We find

$$Y = 1,200.$$

Therefore, the increase in government purchases causes the equilibrium interest rate to rise from 6 percent to 7 percent, while output increases from 1,100 to 1,200. This is depicted in Figure 12-13.

e.   If the money supply increases from 1,000 to 1,200, then the *LM* equation becomes:

$$(1,200/2) = Y - 100r,$$

or

$$Y = 600 + 100r.$$

This *LM* curve is graphed as LM_2 in Figure 12-14. We see that the *LM* curve shifts to the right by 100 because of the increase in real money balances.

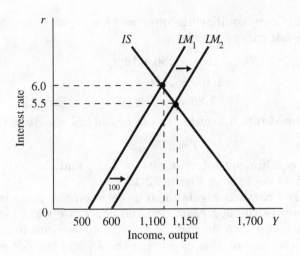

Figure 12-14

To determine the new equilibrium interest rate and level of output, equate the *IS* curve from part (a) with the new *LM* curve derived above:

$$1{,}700 - 100r = 600 + 100r$$

$$1{,}100 = 200r$$

$$5.5 = r.$$

Substituting this into either the *IS* or the *LM* equation, we find

$$Y = 1{,}150.$$

Therefore, the increase in the money supply causes the interest rate to fall from 6 percent to 5.5 percent, while output increases from 1,100 to 1,150. This is depicted in Figure 12–14.

f. If the price level rises from 2 to 4, then real money balances fall from 500 to $1{,}000/4 = 250$. The *LM* equation becomes:

$$Y = 250 + 100r.$$

As shown in Figure 12-15, the *LM* curve shifts to the left by 250 because the increase in the price level reduces real money balances.

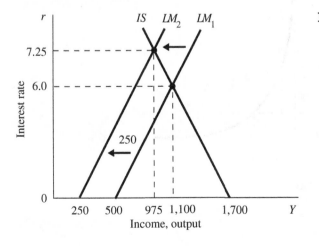

Figure 12-15

To determine the new equilibrium interest rate, equate the *IS* curve from part (a) with the new *LM* curve from above:

$$1,700 - 100r = 250 + 100r$$
$$1,450 = 200r$$
$$7.25 = r.$$

Substituting this interest rate into either the *IS* or the *LM* equation, we find

$$Y = 975.$$

Therefore, the new equilibrium interest rate is 7.25, and the new equilibrium level of output is 975, as depicted in Figure 12-15.

g. The aggregate demand curve is a relationship between the price level and the level of income. To derive the aggregate demand curve, we want to solve the *IS* and the *LM* equations for *Y* as a function of *P*. That is, we want to substitute out for the interest rate. We can do this by solving the *IS* and the *LM* equations for the interest rate:

$$IS: \qquad Y = 1,700 - 100r$$
$$100r = 1,700 - Y.$$

$$LM: \qquad (M/P) = Y - 100r$$
$$100r = Y - (M/P).$$

Combining these two equations, we find

$$1,700 - Y = Y - (M/P)$$
$$2Y = 1,700 + M/P$$
$$Y = 850 + M/2P.$$

Since the nominal money supply *M* equals 1,000, this becomes

$$Y = 850 + 500/P.$$

This aggregate demand equation is graphed in Figure 12-16.

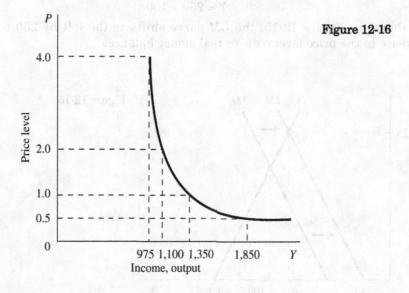

Figure 12-16

How does the increase in fiscal policy of part (d) affect the aggregate demand curve? We can see this by deriving the aggregate demand curve using the *IS* equation from part (d) and the *LM* curve from part (b):

$$IS: \quad Y = 1,900 - 100r$$
$$100r = 1,900 - Y.$$

$$LM: \quad (1,000/P) = Y - 100r$$
$$100r = Y - (1,000/P).$$

Combining and solving for Y:

$$1,900 - Y = Y - (1,000/P),$$

or

$$Y = 950 + 500/P.$$

By comparing this new aggregate demand equation to the one previously derived, we can see that the increase in government purchases by 50 shifts the aggregate demand curve to the right by 100.

How does the increase in the money supply of part (e) affect the aggregate demand curve? Because the AD curve is $Y = 850 + M/2P$, the increase in the money supply from 1,000 to 1,200 causes it to become

$$Y = 850 + 600/P.$$

By comparing this new aggregate demand curve to the one originally derived, we see that the increase in the money supply shifts the aggregate demand curve to the right.

4. a. This statement is false. Investment is part of planned expenditure, so changes in investment have an impact of the IS curve and not the LM curve.

   b. This statement is true. The IS curve represents the relationship between the interest rate and the level of income that arises from equilibrium in the market for goods and services. That is, it describes the combinations of income and the interest rate that satisfy the equation

$$Y = C(Y - T) + I(r) + G.$$

If investment does not depend on the interest rate, then *nothing* in the IS equation depends on the interest rate; income must adjust to ensure that the quantity of goods produced, Y, equals the quantity of goods demanded, $C + I + G$. Thus, the IS curve is vertical at this level, as shown in Figure 12-17.

Figure 12-17

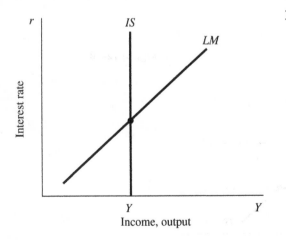

Monetary policy has no effect on output, because the IS curve determines Y. Monetary policy can affect only the interest rate. In contrast, fiscal policy is effective: output increases by the full amount that the IS curve shifts.

c. This statement is false. Money demand helps determine equilibrium in the money market, and this will have an impact on the *LM* curve and not the *IS* curve.

d. This statement is true. The *LM* curve represents the combinations of income and the interest rate at which the money market is in equilibrium. If money demand does not depend on the interest rate, then we can write the *LM* equation as

$$M/P = L(Y).$$

For any given level of real balances M/P, there is only one level of income at which the money market is in equilibrium. Thus, the *LM* curve is vertical, as shown in Figure 12-18.

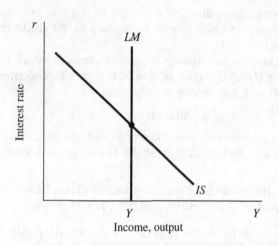

Figure 12-18

Fiscal policy now has no effect on output; it can affect only the interest rate. Monetary policy is effective: a shift in the *LM* curve increases output by the full amount of the shift.

e. This sentence is true. If money demand does not depend on income, then we can write the *LM* equation as

$$M/P = L(r).$$

For any given level of real balances M/P, there is only one level of the interest rate at which the money market is in equilibrium. Hence, the *LM* curve is horizontal, as shown in Figure 12-19.

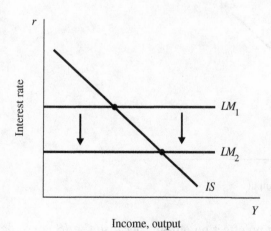

Figure 12-19

Fiscal policy is very effective: output increases by the full amount that the *IS* curve shifts. Monetary policy is also effective: an increase in the money supply causes the interest rate to fall, so the *LM* curve shifts down, as shown in Figure 12–19.

f. This statement is true. The *LM* curve gives the combinations of income and the interest rate at which the supply and demand for real balances are equal, so that the money market is in equilibrium. The general form of the *LM* equation is

$$M/P = L(r, Y).$$

Suppose income *Y* increases by $1. How much must the interest rate change to keep the money market in equilibrium? The increase in *Y* increases money demand. If money demand is extremely sensitive to the interest rate, then it takes a *very* small increase in the interest rate to reduce money demand and restore equilibrium in the money market. Hence, the *LM* curve is (nearly) horizontal, as shown in Figure 12-20.

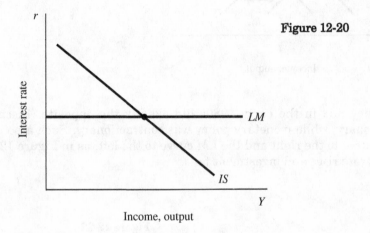

Figure 12-20

An example may make this clearer. Consider a linear version of the *LM* equation:

$$M/P = eY - fr.$$

Note that as *f* gets larger, money demand becomes increasingly sensitive to the interest rate. Rearranging this equation to solve for *r*, we find

$$r = (e/f)Y - (1/f)(M/P).$$

We want to focus on how changes in each of the variables are related to changes in the other variables. Hence, it is convenient to write this equation in terms of changes:

$$\Delta r = (e/f)\Delta Y - (1/f)\Delta(M/P).$$

The slope of the *LM* equation tells us how much *r* changes when *Y* changes, holding *M* fixed. If $\Delta(M/P) = 0$, then the slope is $\Delta r/\Delta Y = (e/f)$. As *f* gets very large, this slope gets closer and closer to zero.

If money demand is very sensitive to the interest rate, then fiscal policy is very effective: with a horizontal *LM* curve, output increases by the full amount that the *IS* curve shifts. Monetary policy is now completely ineffective: an increase in the money supply does not shift the *LM* curve at all. We see this in our example by considering what happens if *M* increases. For any given *Y* (so that we set $\Delta Y = 0$), $\Delta r/\Delta(M/P) = (-1/f)$; this tells us how much the *LM* curve shifts down. As *f* gets larger, this shift gets smaller and approaches zero. (This is in contrast to the horizontal *LM* curve in part (c), which does shift down.)

5. a.   To raise investment while keeping output constant, the government should adopt a loose monetary policy and a tight fiscal policy, as shown in Figure 12-21. In the new equilibrium at point B, the interest rate is lower, so that investment is higher. The tight fiscal policy—reducing government purchases, for example—offsets the effect of this increase in investment on output.

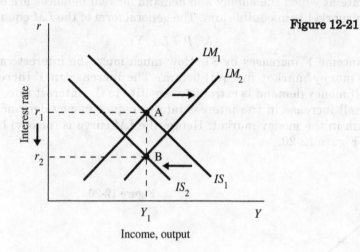

Figure 12-21

b.   The policy mix in the early 1980s did exactly the opposite. Fiscal policy was expansionary, while monetary policy was contractionary. Such a policy mix shifts the *IS* curve to the right and the *LM* curve to the left, as in Figure 12-22. The real interest rate rises and investment falls.

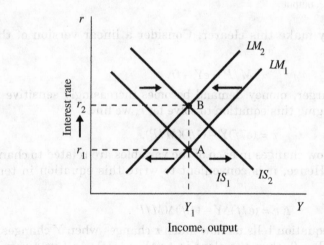

Figure 12-22

6. a.   An increase in the money supply shifts the *LM* curve to the right in the short run. This moves the economy from point A to point B in Figure 12-23: the interest rate falls from r_1 to r_2, and output rises from $\overline{Y}$ to Y_2. The increase in output occurs because the lower interest rate stimulates investment, which increases output.

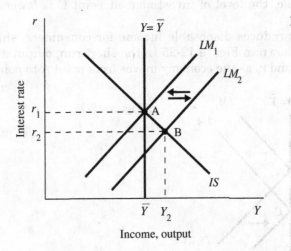

Figure 12-23

Since the level of output is now above its long-run level, prices begin to rise. A rising price level lowers real balances, which raises the interest rate. As indicated in Figure 12-23, the *LM* curve shifts back to the left. Prices continue to rise until the economy returns to its original position at point A. The interest rate returns to r_1, and investment returns to its original level. Thus, in the long run, there is no impact on real variables from an increase in the money supply. (This is what we called *monetary neutrality* in Chapter 5.)

b.   An increase in government purchases shifts the *IS* curve to the right, and the economy moves from point A to point B, as shown in Figure 12-24. In the short run, output increases from $\overline{Y}$ to Y_2, and the interest rate increases from r_1 to r_2.

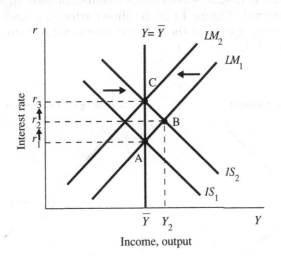

Figure 12-24

The increase in the interest rate reduces investment and "crowds out" part of the expansionary effect of the increase in government purchases. Initially, the *LM* curve is not affected because government spending does not enter the *LM* equation. After the increase, output is above its long-run equilibrium level, so prices begin to rise. The rise in prices reduces real balances, which shifts the *LM* curve to the left. The interest rate rises even more than in the short run. This process continues until the long-run level of output is again reached. At the new equilibrium, point C, interest rates have risen to r_3, and the price level is permanently higher. Note that, like monetary policy, fiscal policy cannot change the long-run level of output. Unlike monetary policy, however, it can change the *composition* of output. For example, the level of investment at point C is lower than it is at point A.

c. An increase in taxes reduces disposable income for consumers, shifting the *IS* curve to the left, as shown in Figure 12-25 In the short run, output and the interest rate decline to Y_2 and r_2 as the economy moves from point A to point B.

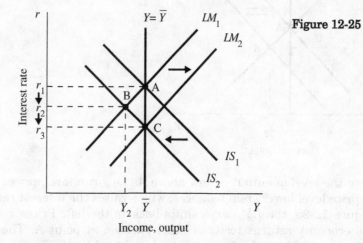

Figure 12-25

Initially, the *LM* curve is not affected. In the longer run, prices begin to decline because output is below its long-run equilibrium level, and the *LM* curve then shifts to the right because of the increase in real money balances. Interest rates fall even further to r_3 and, thus, further stimulate investment and increase income. In the long run, the economy moves to point C. Output returns to *Y*, the price level and the interest rate are lower, and the decrease in consumption has been offset by an equal increase in investment.

7. Figure 12-26(A) shows what the *IS–LM* model looks like for the case in which the Fed holds the money supply constant. Figure 12-26(B) shows what the model looks like if the Fed adjusts the money supply to hold the interest rate constant; this policy makes the effective *LM* curve horizontal.

Figure 12-26

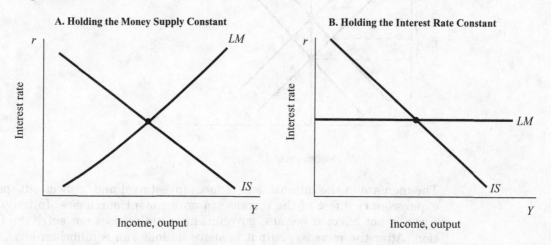

a. If all shocks to the economy arise from exogenous changes in the demand for goods and services, this means that all shocks are to the *IS* curve. Suppose a shock causes the *IS* curve to shift from IS_1 to IS_2. Figures 12-27(A) and (B) show what effect this has on output under the two policies. It is clear that output fluctuates less if the Fed follows a policy of keeping the money supply constant. Thus, if all shocks are to the *IS* curve, then the Fed should follow a policy of keeping the money supply constant.

Figure 12-27

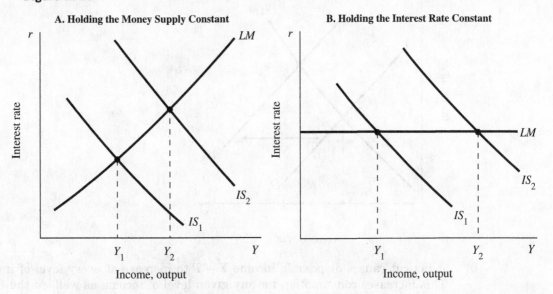

b. If all shocks in the economy arise from exogenous changes in the demand for money, this means that all shocks are to the *LM* curve. If the Fed follows a policy of adjusting the money supply to keep the interest rate constant, then the *LM* curve does not shift in response to these shocks—the Fed immediately adjusts the money supply to keep the money market in equilibrium. Figures 12-28(A) and (B) show the effects of the two policies. It is clear that output fluctuates less if the Fed holds the interest rate constant, as in Figure 12-28(B). If the Fed holds the interest rate constant and offsets shocks to money demand by changing the money supply, then all variability in output is eliminated. Thus, if all shocks are to the *LM* curve, then the Fed should adjust the money supply to hold the interest rate constant, thereby stabilizing output.

Figure 12-28

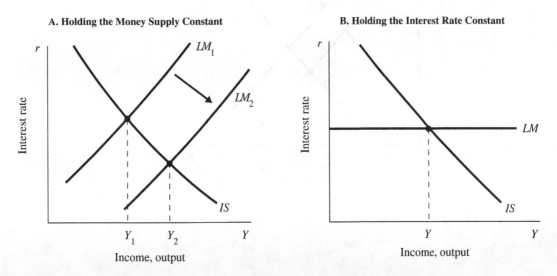

8. a. The analysis of changes in government purchases is unaffected by making money demand dependent on disposable income instead of total expenditure. An increase in government purchases shifts the *IS* curve to the right, as in the standard case. The *LM* curve is unaffected by this increase. Thus, the analysis is the same as it was before; this is shown in Figure 12-29.

Figure 12-29

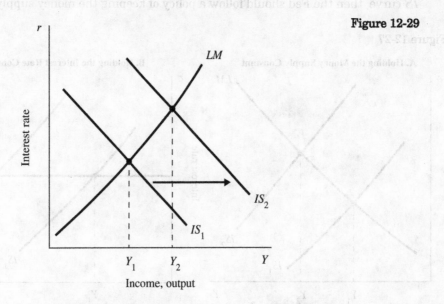

b. A tax cut causes disposable income $Y - T$ to increase at every level of income Y. This increases consumption for any given level of income as well, so the *IS* curve shifts to the right, as in the standard case. This is shown in Figure 12-30. If money demand depends on disposable income, however, then the tax cut increases money demand, so the *LM* curve shifts upward, as shown in the figure.

Thus, the analysis of a change in taxes is altered drastically by making money demand dependent on disposable income. As shown in the figure, it is possible for a tax cut to be contractionary.

Figure 12-30

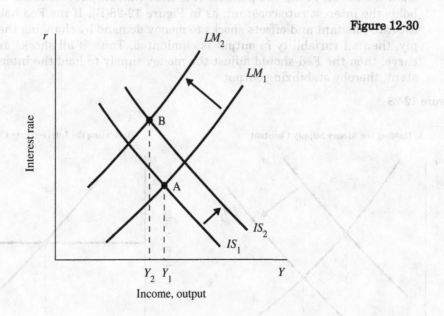

9.   a.   The goods market is in equilibrium when output is equal to planned expenditure, or $Y = PE$. Starting with this equilibrium condition, and making the substitutions from the information given in the problem, results in the following expression for equilibrium output Y:

$$Y = C + I + G$$

$$Y = C(Y - T) + I(r) + G$$

$$Y = a + b(Y - T) + c - dr + G$$

$$(1 - b)Y = a - bT + c - dr + G$$

$$Y = \frac{a - bT + c - dr + G}{1 - b}$$

b.   The slope of the *IS* curve is measured as

$$\frac{\Delta r}{\Delta Y}.$$

From the equation in part (a), the slope of the *IS* curve can be found as follows:

$$\frac{\Delta r}{\Delta y} = \frac{1}{(\Delta Y / \Delta r)} = \frac{1}{-(d/(1-b))} = -\frac{(1-b)}{d}.$$

Mathematically, as the parameter d becomes a larger number, the slope becomes a smaller number in absolute value terms and the *IS* curve becomes flatter. Intuitively, if the parameter d is a larger number, then investment is more responsive to changes in the interest rate. Any given decrease in the interest rate will cause a larger increase in investment and, via the multiplier effect, cause a larger increase in equilibrium output Y. This makes the *IS* curve flatter.

c.   A \$100 increase in government spending will cause a larger horizontal shift in the *IS* curve than a \$100 tax cut. From the equation for equilibrium output in part (a), note that the impact of the tax cut depends on the marginal propensity to consume, as given by the parameter b. If the *MPC* is 0.75, for example, then a \$100 tax cut will shift the *IS* curve by only \$75. Intuitively, this makes sense because the entire \$100 increase in government spending will be spent, whereas only a portion of the tax cut will be spent, and the rest will be saved depending on the size of the *MPC*.

d.   Money-market equilibrium occurs where the demand for real balances is equal to the supply of real balances. Using the given information about the demand for real balances, we can solve for the equilibrium interest rate:

$$\frac{M}{P} = L(r, Y) = eY - fr$$

$$fr = eY - \frac{M}{P}$$

$$r = \frac{eY}{f} - \frac{M}{fP}.$$

e. The slope of the *LM* curve is measured as

$$\frac{\Delta r}{\Delta Y}.$$

From the equation in part (d), the slope of the *LM* curve is *e/f*. As the parameter *f* becomes a larger number, the slope becomes smaller and the *LM* curve becomes flatter. Intuitively, as the parameter *f* becomes a larger number, money demand is more responsive to changes in the interest rate. This means that any increase in income that leads to an increase in money demand will require a relatively small increase in the interest rate to restore equilibrium in the money market.

f. The size of the horizontal shift in the *LM* curve caused by a change in the money supply *M* can be measured by looking at where the *LM* curve crosses the horizontal axis. From the equation in part (d), set *r* equal to zero and solve for *Y* to find the horizontal intercept: the *LM* curve crosses the horizontal axis where *Y = M/eP*. Mathematically, a $100 change in the money supply has a smaller effect on the horizontal intercept the larger the value of the parameter *e*. When the parameter *e* is larger, money demand is more responsive to changes in income *Y*, and the *LM* curve is steeper. Intuitively, if income increases and the parameter *e* is relatively larger, then money demand increases by a larger amount. This then requires a larger increase in the interest rate to restore money-market equilibrium and the *LM* curve becomes relatively steeper. Overall, the increase in the money supply will lower the interest rate and increase investment spending and output. When output rises, so does money demand, and if the parameter *e* is relatively large, then the interest rate will need to rise by a larger amount to restore equilibrium in the money market. The overall effect on equilibrium output is relatively smaller, as given by the smaller horizontal shift in the *LM* curve. The parameter *f* has no effect on the size of the horizontal shift in the *LM* curve caused by a change in the money supply. The parameter *f* affects the vertical shift and the slope of the *LM* curve but not the horizontal shift.

g. To derive the aggregate demand curve, substitute the result for part (d) into the result for part (a) and solve for *Y*:

$$Y = \frac{a - bT + c + G}{1 - b} - \frac{d}{1 - b}\left(\frac{eY}{f} - \frac{M}{fP}\right)$$

$$Y\left(1 + \frac{de}{f(1 - b)}\right) = \frac{1 - bT + c + G}{1 - b} + \frac{dM}{f(1 - b)P}$$

$$Y = \frac{f(a - bT + c + G)}{f(1 - b) + de} + \frac{dM}{\left[f(1 - b) + de\right]P}.$$

h. The aggregate demand curve has a negative slope, as can be seen from the equation in part (g) above. An increase in the price level *P* will decrease the value of the second term on the right-hand side, and therefore output *Y* will fall.

i. An increase in the money supply, an increase in government spending, and a decrease in taxes all shift the aggregate demand curve to the right, as can be seen from the equation for the aggregate demand curve found in part (g). Looking at the first term on the right-hand side, we see that an increase in *G* or a decrease in *T* will increase the value of this term and shift the aggregate demand curve to the right. Looking at the second term on the right-hand side, an increase in the money supply for any given value of the price level will increase the value of output and therefore shift the aggregate demand curve to the right. If the parameter f has a value of zero, then the first term on the right-hand side is zero and changes in government spending and taxes do not affect the aggregate demand curve. In this case, the *LM* curve is vertical and changes in fiscal policy that shift the *IS* curve have no effect on output. Monetary policy is still effective in this case, and an increase in the money supply will still shift the aggregate demand curve to the right. In this case, the aggregate demand curve is given by:

$$Y = \frac{M}{eP}.$$

CHAPTER 13 The Open Economy Revisited: The Mundell–Fleming Model and the Exchange-Rate Regime

Questions for Review

1. In the Mundell–Fleming model, an increase in taxes shifts the IS^* curve to the left. If the exchange rate floats freely, then the LM^* curve is unaffected. As shown in Figure 13-1, the exchange rate falls while aggregate income remains unchanged. The fall in the exchange rate causes the trade balance to increase.

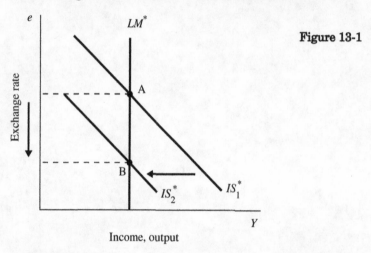

Figure 13-1

Now suppose there are fixed exchange rates. When the IS^* curve shifts to the left in Figure 13-2, the money supply has to fall to keep the exchange rate constant, shifting the LM^* curve from LM_1^* to LM_2^*. As shown in the figure, output falls while the exchange rate remains fixed.

Net exports can only change if the exchange rate changes or the net exports schedule shifts. Neither occurs here, so net exports do not change.

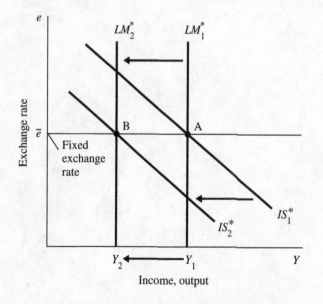

Figure 13-2

We conclude that in an open economy, fiscal policy is effective at influencing output under fixed exchange rates but ineffective under floating exchange rates.

2. In the Mundell–Fleming model with floating exchange rates, a reduction in the money supply reduces real balances M/P, causing the LM^* curve to shift to the left. As shown in Figure 13-3, this leads to a new equilibrium with lower income and a higher exchange rate. The increase in the exchange rate reduces the trade balance.

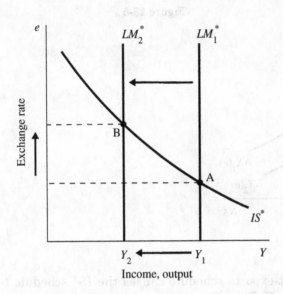

Figure 13-3

If exchange rates are fixed, then the upward pressure on the exchange rate forces the Fed to sell dollars and buy foreign exchange. This increases the money supply M and shifts the LM^* curve back to the right until it reaches LM_1^* again, as shown in Figure 13-4.

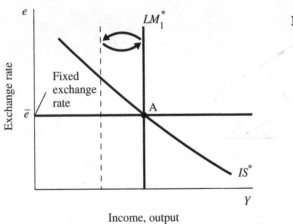

Figure 13-4

In equilibrium, income, the exchange rate, and the trade balance are unchanged.

We conclude that in an open economy, monetary policy is effective at influencing output under floating exchange rates but impossible under fixed exchange rates.

3. In the Mundell–Fleming model under floating exchange rates, removing a quota on imported cars shifts the net exports schedule inward, as shown in Figure 13-5. As in the figure, for any given exchange rate, such as e, net exports fall. This is because it now becomes possible for Americans to buy more Toyotas, Volkswagens, and other foreign cars than they could when there was a quota.

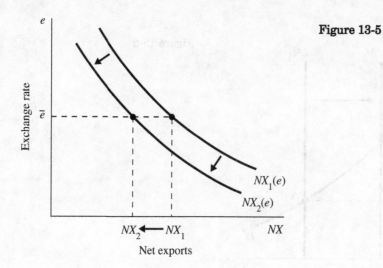

Figure 13-5

This inward shift in the net-exports schedule causes the IS^* schedule to shift inward as well, as shown in Figure 13-6.

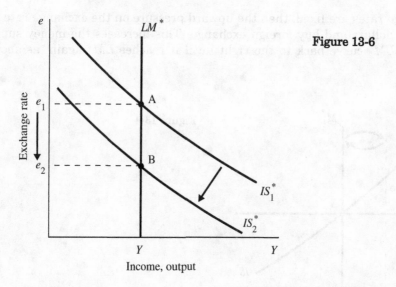

Figure 13-6

The exchange rate falls while income remains unchanged. The trade balance is also unchanged. We know this since

$$NX(e) = Y - C(Y - T) - I(r) - G.$$

Removing the quota has no effect on Y, C, I, or G, so it also has no effect on the trade balance. The decline in net exports caused by the removal of the quota is exactly offset by the increase in net exports caused by the decline in the value of the exchange rate.

If there are fixed exchange rates, then the shift in the IS^* curve puts downward pressure on the exchange rate, as above. In order to keep the exchange rate fixed, the

Fed is forced to buy dollars and sell foreign exchange. This shifts the LM^* curve to the left, as shown in Figure 13-7.

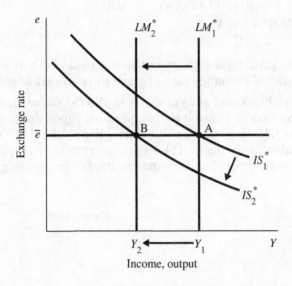

Figure 13-7

In equilibrium, income is lower and the exchange rate is unchanged. The trade balance falls; we know this because net exports are lower at any level of the exchange rate.

4. The following table lists some of the advantages and disadvantages of floating versus fixed exchange rates.

Table 13-1

Floating Exchange Rates

Advantages:	Allows monetary policy to pursue goals other than just exchange-rate stabilization, for example, the stability of prices and employment.
Disadvantages:	Exchange-rate uncertainty is higher, and this might make international trade more difficult.

Fixed Exchange Rates

Advantages:	Makes international trade easier by reducing exchange rate uncertainty.
	It disciplines the monetary authority, preventing excessive growth in M. As a monetary rule, it is easy to implement.
Disadvantages:	Monetary policy cannot be used to pursue policy goals other than maintaining the exchange rate.
	As a way to discipline the monetary authority, it may lead to greater instability in income and employment.

5. The impossible trinity states that it is impossible for a nation to have free capital flows, a fixed exchange rate, and independent monetary policy. In other words, you can only have two of the three. If you want free capital flows and an independent monetary policy, then you cannot also peg the exchange rate. If you want a fixed exchange rate and free capital flows, then you cannot have independent monetary policy. If you want to have independent monetary policy and a fixed exchange rate, then you need to restrict capital flows.

Problems and Applications

1. The following three equations describe the Mundell–Fleming model:

$$Y = C(Y - T) + I(r) + G + NX(e). \qquad (IS)$$
$$M/P = L(r, Y). \qquad (LM)$$
$$r = r^*.$$

In addition, we assume that the price level is fixed in the short run, both at home and abroad. This means that the nominal exchange rate e equals the real exchange rate .

a. If consumers decide to spend less and save more, then the IS^* curve shifts to the left. Figure 13-8 shows the case of floating exchange rates. Since the money supply does not adjust, the LM^* curve does not shift. Since the LM^* curve is unchanged, output Y is also unchanged. The exchange rate falls (depreciates), which causes an increase in the trade balance equal to the fall in consumption.

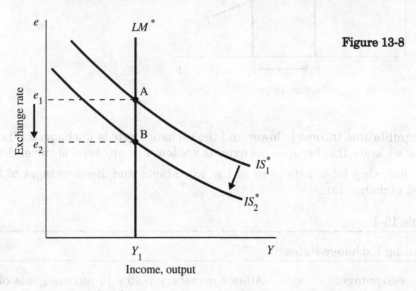

Figure 13-8

Figure 13-9 shows the case of fixed exchange rates. The IS^* curve shifts to the left, but the exchange rate cannot fall. Instead, output falls. Since the exchange rate does not change, we know that the trade balance does not change either.

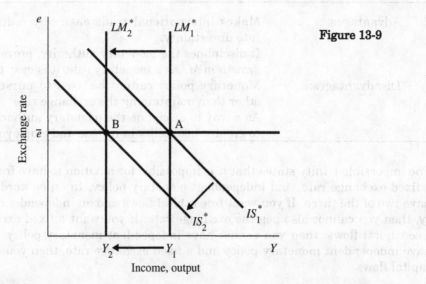

Figure 13-9

In essence, the fall in desired spending puts downward pressure on the interest rate and, hence, on the exchange rate. If there are fixed exchange rates, then the central bank buys the domestic currency that investors seek to exchange, and provides foreign currency, shifting LM^* to the left. As a result, the exchange rate does not change, so the trade balance does not change. Hence, there is nothing to offset the fall in consumption, and output falls.

b.   If some consumers decide they prefer stylish Toyotas to Fords and Chryslers, then the net-exports schedule, shown in Figure 13-10, shifts to the left. That is, at any level of the exchange rate, net exports are lower than they were before.

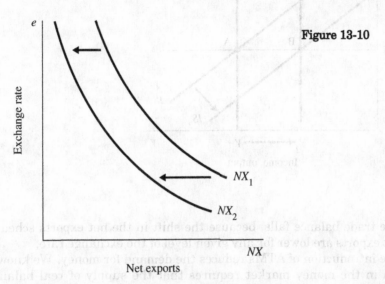

Figure 13-10

This shifts the IS^* curve to the left as well, as shown in Figure 13-11 for the case of floating exchange rates. Since the LM^* curve is fixed, output does not change, while the exchange rate falls (depreciates).

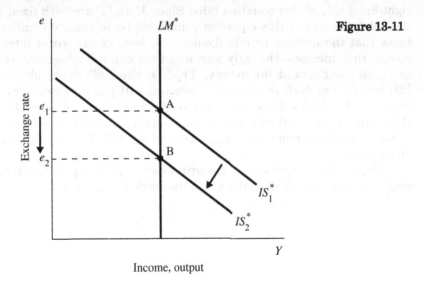

Figure 13-11

The trade balance does not change either, despite the fall in the exchange rate. We know this since $NX = S - I$, and both saving and investment remain unchanged. When consumers prefer to buy foreign cars, this will decrease net exports. The resulting decline in the value of the exchange rate will increase net exports and offset the decline, such that net exports remains unchanged

Figure 13-12 shows the case of fixed exchange rates. The leftward shift in the IS^* curve puts downward pressure on the exchange rate. The central bank buys dollars and sells foreign exchange to keep e fixed: this reduces M and shifts the LM^* curve to the left. As a result, output falls.

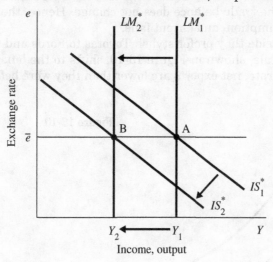

Figure 13-12

The trade balance falls, because the shift in the net exports schedule means that net exports are lower for any given level of the exchange rate.

c. The introduction of ATMs reduces the demand for money. We know that equilibrium in the money market requires that the supply of real balances M/P must equal demand:

$$M/P = L(r^*, Y).$$

A fall in money demand means that for unchanged income and interest rates, the right-hand side of this equation falls. Since M and P are both fixed, we know that the left-hand side of this equation cannot adjust to restore equilibrium. We also know that the interest rate is fixed at the level of the world interest rate. This means that income—the only variable that can adjust—must rise in order to increase the demand for money. That is, the LM^* curve shifts to the right. Intuitively, the decline in money demand will put downward pressure on the interest rate. This will cause capital outflow until balance is restored because in this model the interest rate will remain equal to the world interest rate. As capital flows out of the economy, the exchange rate will fall. This will increase net exports and output.

Figure 13-13 shows the case with floating exchange rates. Income rises, the exchange rate falls (depreciates), and the trade balance rises.

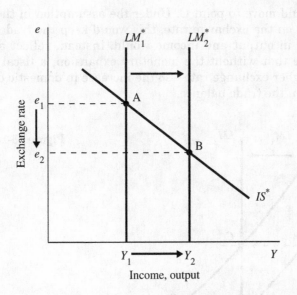

Figure 13-13

Figure 13-14 shows the case of fixed exchange rates. The LM^* schedule shifts to the right; as before, this tends to push domestic interest rates down and cause the currency to depreciate. However, the central bank buys dollars and sells foreign currency in order to keep the exchange rate from falling. This reduces the money supply and shifts the LM^* schedule back to the left. The LM^* curve continues to shift back until the original equilibrium is restored.

In the end, income, the exchange rate, and the trade balance are unchanged.

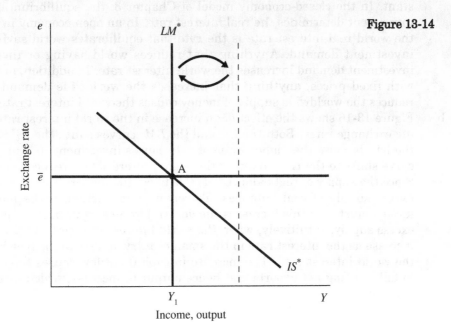

Figure 13-14

2. The economy is in recession, at point A in Figure 13-15. To increase income, the central bank should increase the money supply, thereby shifting the LM^* curve to the right. If only that happened, the economy would move to point B, with a depreciated exchange rate that would stimulate exports and raise the trade balance. To keep the exchange rate from depreciating and the trade balance from rising, the fiscal authorities should cut taxes or increase government spending. That would shift the IS^* curve to the right,

so that the economy would move to point C. Under the assumption in the chapter that net exports depend only on the exchange rate, this would keep the trade balance from changing. The increase in output and income would, instead, reflect an increase in domestic demand. (Note that without the monetary expansion, a fiscal expansion by itself would lead to a higher exchange rate—so the increase in domestic demand would be offset by a reduction in the trade balance.

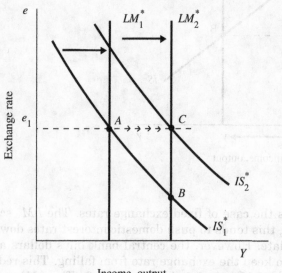

Figure 13-15

3. a.   The Mundell–Fleming model takes the world interest rate r^* as an exogenous variable. However, there is no reason to expect the world interest rate to be constant. In the closed-economy model of Chapter 3, the equilibrium of saving and investment determines the real interest rate. In an open economy in the long run, the world real interest rate is the rate that equilibrates world saving and world investment demand. Anything that reduces world saving or increases world investment demand increases the world interest rate. In addition, in the short run with fixed prices, anything that increases the worldwide demand for goods or reduces the worldwide supply of money causes the world interest rate to rise.

    b.   Figure 13-16 shows the effect of an increase in the world interest rate under floating exchange rates. Both the IS^* and the LM^* curves shift. The IS^* curve shifts to the left, because the higher interest rate causes investment $I(r^*)$ to fall. The LM^* curve shifts to the right because the higher interest rate reduces money demand. Since the supply of real balances M/P is fixed, the higher interest rate leads to an excess supply of real balances. To restore equilibrium in the money market, income must rise; this increases the demand for money until there is no longer an excess supply. Intuitively, when the world interest rate rises, capital outflow will increase as the interest rate in the small country adjusts to the new higher level of the world interest rate. The increase in capital outflow causes the exchange rate to fall, causing net exports and hence output to increase, which increases money demand.

Figure 13-16

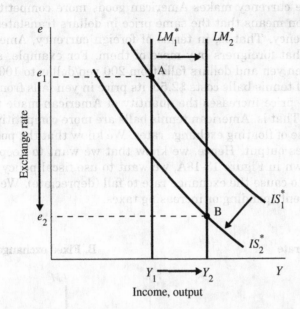

We see from the figure that output rises and the exchange rate falls (depreciates). Hence, the trade balance increases.

c. Figure 13-17 shows the effect of an increase in the world interest rate if exchange rates are fixed. Both the IS^* and LM^* curves shift. As in part (b), the IS^* curve shifts to the left since the higher interest rate causes investment demand to fall. The LM^* schedule, however, shifts to the left instead of to the right. This is because the downward pressure on the exchange rate causes the central bank to buy dollars and sell foreign exchange. This reduces the supply of money M and shifts the LM^* schedule to the left. The LM^* curve must shift all the way back to LM^*_2 in the figure, where the fixed-exchange-rate line crosses the new IS^* curve.

Figure 13-17

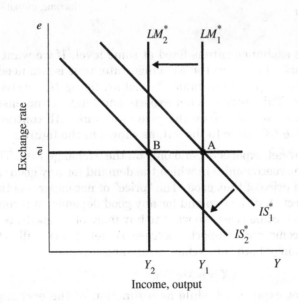

In equilibrium, output falls while the exchange rate remains unchanged. Since the exchange rate does not change, neither does the trade balance.

4. a. A depreciation of the currency makes American goods more competitive. This is because a depreciation means that the same price in dollars translates into fewer units of foreign currency. That is, in terms of foreign currency, American goods become cheaper so that foreigners buy more of them. For example, suppose the exchange rate between yen and dollars falls from 200 yen/dollar to 100 yen/dollar. If an American can of tennis balls costs $2.50, its price in yen falls from 500 yen to 250 yen. This fall in price increases the quantity of American-made tennis balls demanded in Japan. That is, American tennis balls are more competitive.

    b. Consider first the case of floating exchange rates. We know that the position of the LM^* curve determines output. Hence, we know that we want to keep the money supply fixed. As shown in Figure 13-18A, we want to use fiscal policy to shift the IS^* curve to the left to cause the exchange rate to fall (depreciate). We can do this by reducing government spending or increasing taxes.

Figure 13-18

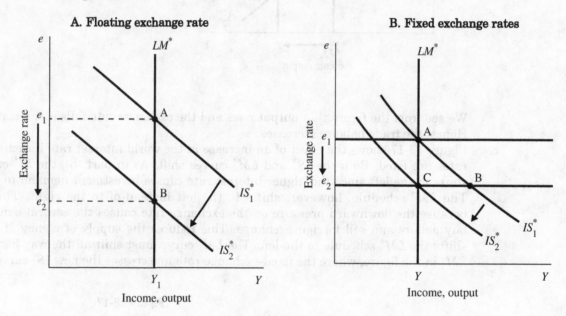

A. Floating exchange rate

B. Fixed exchange rates

Now suppose that the exchange rate is fixed at some level. If we want to increase competitiveness, we need to reduce the exchange rate; that is, we need to fix it at a lower level. The first step is to devalue the dollar, fixing the exchange rate at the desired lower level. This increases net exports and tends to increase output, as shown in Figure 13-18B. We can offset this rise in output with contractionary fiscal policy that shifts the IS^* curve to the left, as shown in the figure.

5. In the text, we assumed that net exports depend only on the exchange rate. This is analogous to the usual story in microeconomics in which the demand for any good (in this case, net exports) depends on the price of that good. The "price" of net exports is the exchange rate. However, we also expect that the demand for any good depends on income, and this may be true here as well: as income rises, we want to buy more of all goods, both domestic and imported. Hence, as income rises, imports increase, so net exports fall. Thus, we can write net exports as a function of both the exchange rate and income:

$$NX = NX(e, Y).$$

Figure 13-19 shows the net exports schedule as a function of the exchange rate. As before, the net exports schedule is downward sloping, so an increase in the exchange rate reduces net exports. We have drawn this schedule for a given level of income. If income increases from Y_1 to Y_2, the net exports schedule shifts inward from $NX(Y_1)$ to $NX(Y_2)$.

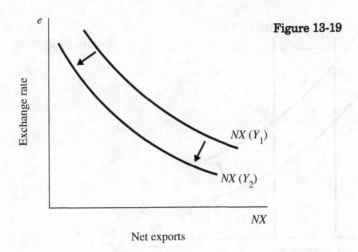

Figure 13-19

a. Figure 13-20 shows the effect of a fiscal expansion under floating exchange rates. The fiscal expansion (an increase in government expenditure or a cut in taxes) shifts the IS^* schedule to the right. But with floating exchange rates, if the LM^* curve does not change, neither does income. Since income does not change, the net-exports schedule remains at its original level $NX(Y_1)$.

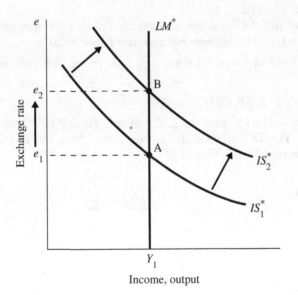

Figure 13-20

The final result is that income does not change, and the exchange rate appreciates from e_1 to e_2. Net exports fall because of the appreciation of the currency.

Thus, our answer is the same as that given in Table 12–1.

b. Figure 13-21 shows the effect of a fiscal expansion under fixed exchange rates. The fiscal expansion shifts the IS^* curve to the right, from IS_1^* to IS_2^*. As in part (a), for unchanged real balances, this tends to push the exchange rate up. To prevent this appreciation, however, the central bank intervenes in currency markets, selling dollars and buying foreign exchange. This increases the money supply and shifts the LM^* curve to the right, from LM_1^* to LM_2^*.

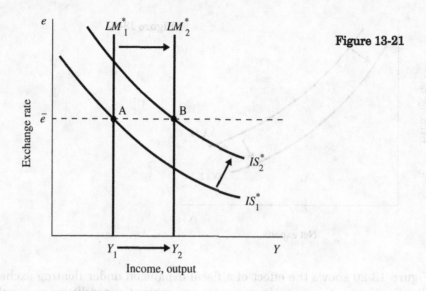

Figure 13-21

Output rises while the exchange rate remains fixed. Despite the unchanged exchange rate, the higher level of income reduces net exports because the net-exports schedule shifts inward.

Thus, our answer differs from the answer in Table 13-1 only in that under fixed exchange rates, a fiscal expansion reduces the trade balance.

6. We want to consider the effects of a tax cut when the LM^* curve depends on disposable income instead of income:

$$M/P = L[r, Y - T].$$

A tax cut now shifts both the IS^* and the LM^* curves. Figure 13-22 shows the case of floating exchange rates. The IS^* curve shifts to the right, from IS_1^* to IS_2^*. The LM^* curve shifts to the left, however, from LM_1^* to LM_2^*.

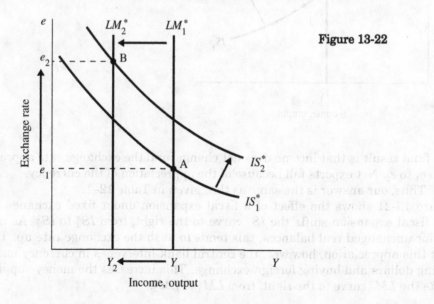

Figure 13-22

We know that real balances M/P are fixed in the short run, while the interest rate is fixed at the level of the world interest rate r^*. Disposable income is the only variable that can adjust to bring the money market into equilibrium: hence, the LM^* equation determines the level of disposable income. If taxes T fall, then income Y must also fall to keep disposable income fixed.

In Figure 13-22, we move from an original equilibrium at point A to a new equilibrium at point B. Income falls by the amount of the tax cut, and the exchange rate appreciates.

If there are fixed exchange rates, the IS^* curve still shifts to the right; but the initial shift in the LM^* curve no longer matters. That is, the upward pressure on the exchange rate causes the central bank to sell dollars and buy foreign exchange; this increases the money supply and shifts the LM^* curve to the *right*, as shown in Figure 13-23.

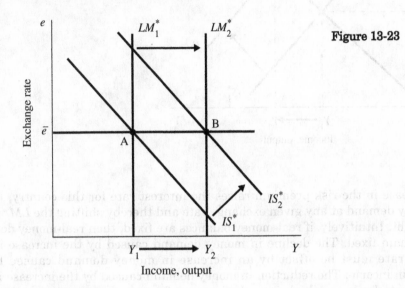

Figure 13-23

The new equilibrium, at point B, is at the intersection of the new IS^* curve, IS_2^*, and the horizontal line at the level of the fixed exchange rate. There is no difference between this case and the standard case where money demand depends on income.

7. Since people demand money balances in order to buy goods and services, it makes sense to think that the price level that is relevant is the price level of the goods and services they buy. This includes both domestic and foreign goods. But the dollar price of foreign goods depends on the exchange rate. For example, if the dollar rises from 100 yen/dollar to 150 yen/dollar, then a Japanese good that costs 300 yen falls in price from $3 to $2. Hence, we can write the condition for equilibrium in the money market as

$$M/P = L(r, Y),$$

where

$$P = \lambda P_d + (1 - \lambda)P_f/e.$$

a. A higher exchange rate makes foreign goods cheaper. To the extent that people consume foreign goods (a fraction $1 - \lambda$), this lowers the price level P that is relevant for the money market. This lower price level increases the supply of real balances M/P. To keep the money market in equilibrium, we require income to rise to increase money demand as well.

Hence, the LM^* curve is upward sloping.

b. In the standard Mundell–Fleming model, expansionary fiscal policy has no effect on output under floating exchange rates. As shown in Figure 13-24, this is no longer true here. A cut in taxes or an increase in government spending shifts the

IS^* curve to the right, from IS_1^* to IS_2^*. Since the LM^* curve is upward sloping, the result is an increase in output.

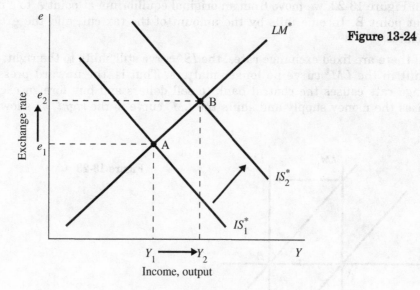

Figure 13-24

c. The increase in the risk premium raises the interest rate for this country, lowering money demand at any given exchange rate and thereby shifting the LM^* curve to the right. Intuitively, if real-money balances are fixed, then real-money demand must remain fixed. The decline in money demand caused by the increase in the interest rate must be offset by an increase in money demand caused by an increase in income. The reduction in money demand caused by the increase in the interest rate leads to a higher level of income for any given money supply. The higher interest rate also reduces investment spending at any given exchange rate, shifting the IS^* curve to the left. As shown in Figure 13-25, the exchange rate falls and output may either rise or fall depending on the size of the shifts.

Figure 13-25

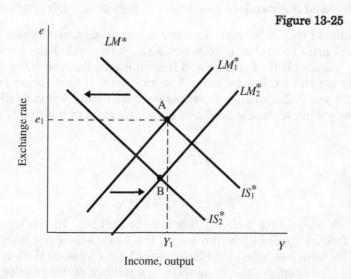

If money demand is not very sensitive to the interest rate and investment is very sensitive to the interest rate, then IS^* will shift by more than LM^* and output will decline. Compared to the traditional Mundell–Fleming model, where LM^* is vertical, output can fall here, whereas it does not fall in the traditional model but instead always rises. This model gives the more realistic result that both the exchange rate and output are likely to decline when the risk premium rises.

8. a. California is a small open economy, and we assume that it can print dollar bills. Its exchange rate, however, is fixed with the rest of the United States: one dollar can be exchanged for one dollar.

   b. In the Mundell–Fleming model with fixed exchange rates, California cannot use monetary policy to affect output, because this policy is already used to control the exchange rate. Hence, if California wishes to stimulate employment, it should use fiscal policy.

   c. In the short run, the import prohibition shifts the IS^* curve out. This increases demand for Californian goods and puts upward pressure on the exchange rate. To counteract this, the Californian money supply increases, so the LM^* curve shifts out as well. The new short-run equilibrium is at point K in Figures 13-26(A) and (B).

   Assuming that we started with the economy producing at its natural rate, the increase in demand for Californian goods tends to raise their prices. This rise in the price level lowers real money balances, shifting the short-run AS curve upward and the LM^* curve inward. Eventually, the Californian economy ends up at point C, with no change in output or the trade balance, but with a higher real exchange rate relative to Washington.

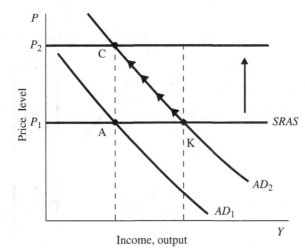

A. The Mundell–Fleming Model

Figure 13-26

B. The Model of Aggregate Supply and Aggregate Demand

d. Unlike Canada, California is part of a large monetary union where each of the 50 states readily accepts each other's currency. When a country chooses to be part of a monetary union, it is unable to conduct its own independent monetary policy. In the event of a recession, its only option is to use fiscal policy. Since Canada is not part of a monetary union, it has the option of maintaining a floating or fixed exchange rate, and it has the flexibility of using monetary or fiscal policy to influence economic activity.

More Problems and Applications to Chapter 13

1. a. Higher taxes shift the *IS* curve inward. To keep output unchanged, the central bank must increase the money supply, shifting the *LM* curve to the right. At the new equilibrium (point C in Figure 13-27), the interest rate is lower, the exchange rate has depreciated, and the trade balance has risen.

Figure 13-27

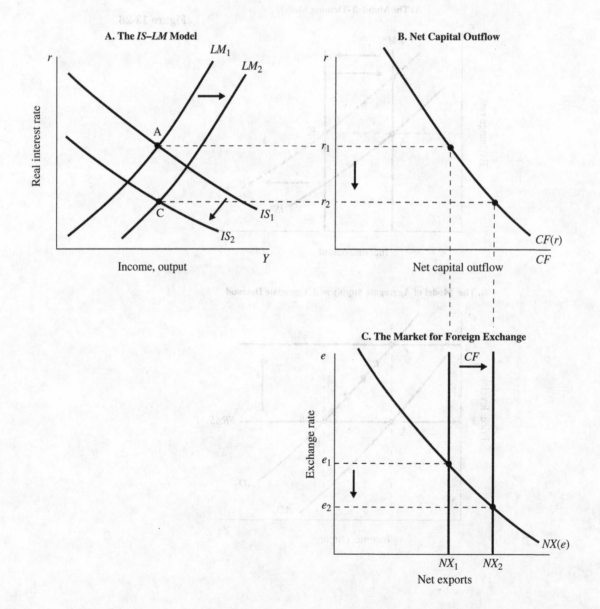

b. Restricting the import of foreign cars shifts the $NX(e)$ schedule outward [see panel (C)]. This has no effect on either the IS curve or the LM curve, however, because the CF schedule is unaffected. Hence, output doesn't change and there is no need for any change in monetary policy. As shown in Figure 13-28, interest rates and the trade balance don't change, but the exchange rate appreciates.

Figure 13-28

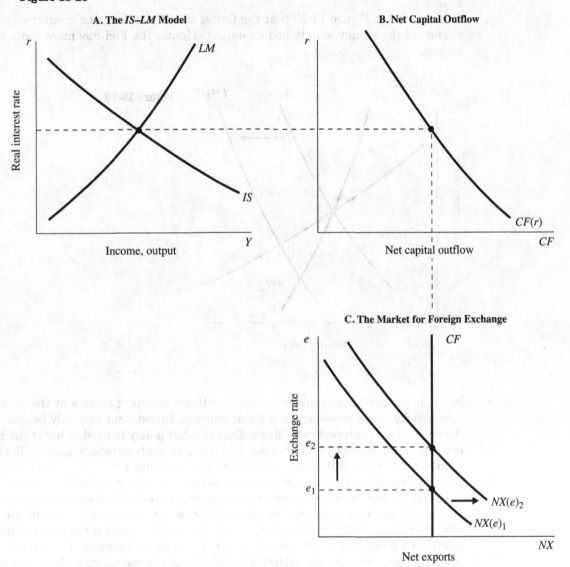

A. The IS–LM Model

B. Net Capital Outflow

C. The Market for Foreign Exchange

2. a.   The *CF* curve becomes flatter, because a small change in the interest rate now has a larger effect on capital flows.
    b.   As argued in the text, a flatter *CF* curve makes the *IS* curve flatter, as well.
    c.   Figure 13-29 shows the effect of a shift in the *LM* curve for both a steep and a flat *IS* curve. It is clear that the flatter the *IS* curve is, the less effect any change in the money supply has on interest rates. Hence, the Fed has less control over the interest rate when investors are more willing to substitute foreign and domestic assets.
    d.   It is clear from Figure 13-29 that the flatter the *IS* curve is, the greater effect any change in the money supply has on output. Hence, the Fed has more control over output.

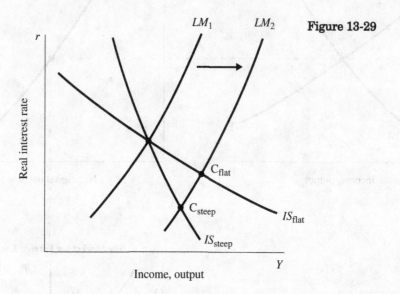

3. a.   No. It is impossible to raise investment without affecting income or the exchange rate just by using monetary and fiscal policies. Investment can only be increased through a lower interest rate. Regardless of what policy is used to lower the interest rate (e.g., expansionary monetary policy and contractionary fiscal policy), net foreign investment will increase, lowering the exchange rate.
    b.   Yes. Policymakers can raise investment without affecting income or the exchange rate with a combination of expansionary monetary policy and contractionary fiscal policy, and protection against imports can raise investment without affecting the other variables. Both the monetary expansion and the fiscal contraction would put downward pressure on interest rates and stimulate investment. It is necessary to combine these two policies so that their effects on income exactly offset each other. The lower interest rates will, as in part (a), increase net capital outflow, which will put downward pressure on the exchange rate. The protectionist policies, however, shift the net-exports curve out; this puts countervailing upward pressure on the exchange rate and offsets the effect of the fall in interest rates. Figure 13-30 shows this combination of policies.

Figure 13-30

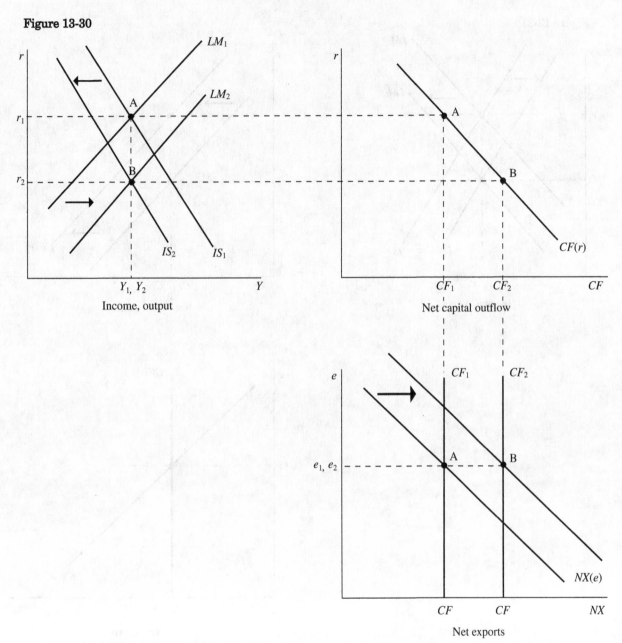

c.   Yes. Policymakers can raise investment without affecting income or the exchange rate through a home monetary expansion and fiscal contraction, combined with a lower foreign interest rate either through a foreign monetary expansion or fiscal contraction. The domestic policy lowers the interest rate, stimulating investment. The foreign policy shifts the *CF* curve inward. Even with lower interest rates, the quantity of capital outflow would be unchanged and there would be no pressure on the exchange rate. This combination of policies is shown in Figure 13-31.

Figure 13-31

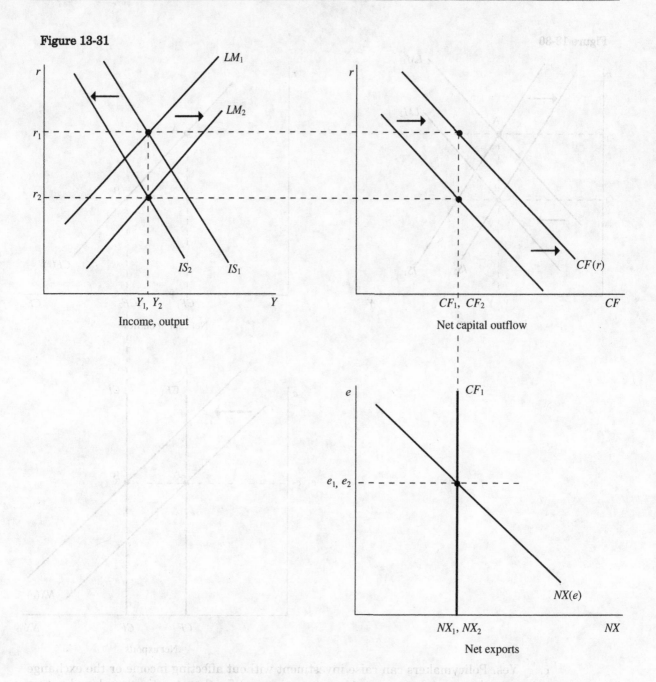

Income, output

Net capital outflow

Net exports

4. a. Figure 13-32 shows the effect of a fiscal expansion on a large open economy with a fixed exchange rate. The fiscal expansion shifts the *IS* curve to the right in panel (A), which puts upward pressure on the interest rate. This tends to decrease net capital outflow and cause the exchange rate to appreciate [see panels (B) and (C)]. To avoid this, the central bank intervenes and sells dollars. This keeps the exchange rate from appreciating; it also shifts the *LM* curve to the right. The new equilibrium, at point C, has an unchanged interest rate and exchange rate, but higher output.

   This effect is the same as in a small open economy.

Figure 13-32

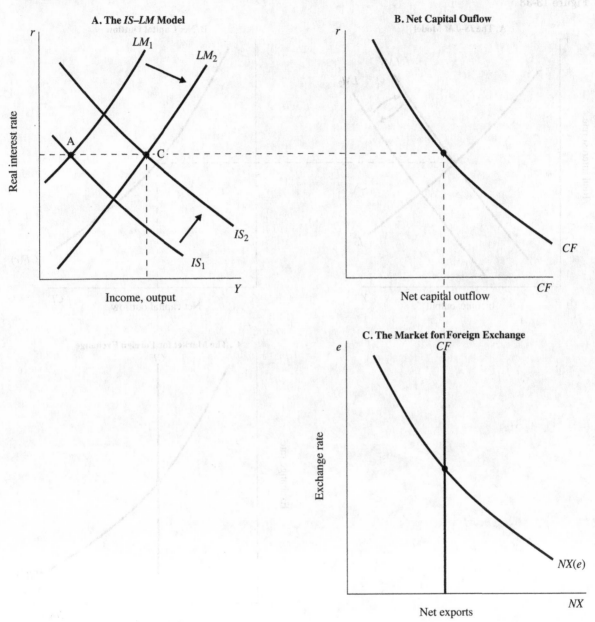

A. The *IS–LM* Model

B. Net Capital Ouflow

C. The Market for Foreign Exchange

b. A monetary expansion tends to shift the *LM* curve to the right, lowering the interest rate [panel (A) in Figure 13-33]. This tends to increase net capital outflow and cause the exchange rate to depreciate [see panels (B) and (C)]. To avoid this depreciation, the central bank must buy its currency and sell foreign exchange. This reduces the money supply and shifts the *LM* curve back to its original position. As in the model of a small open economy, monetary policy is ineffectual under a fixed exchange rate.

Figure 13-33

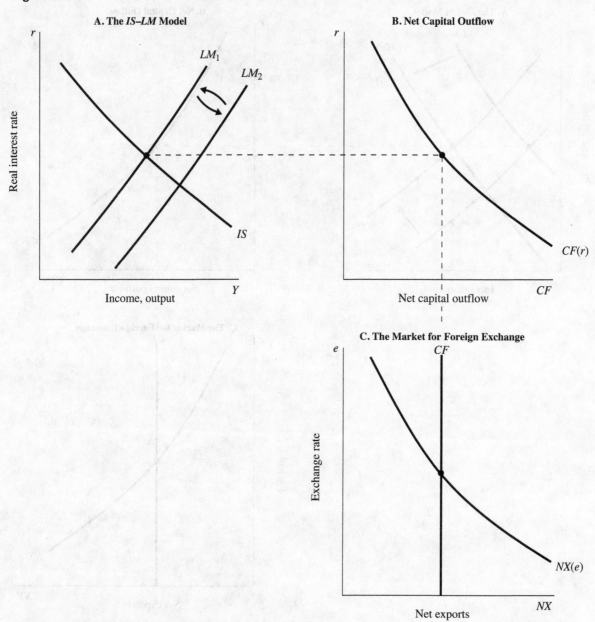

A. The *IS–LM* Model

B. Net Capital Outflow

C. The Market for Foreign Exchange

CHAPTER **14**   Aggregate Supply and the Short-Run Tradeoff Between Inflation and Unemployment

Questions for Review

1. In this chapter we looked at two models of the short-run aggregate supply curve. Both models attempt to explain why, in the short run, output might deviate from its long-run "natural rate"—the level of output that is consistent with the full employment of labor and capital. Both models result in an aggregate supply function in which output deviates from its natural rate $\overline{Y}$ when the price level deviates from the expected price level:

$$Y = \overline{Y} + \alpha(P - EP).$$

   The first model is the sticky-price model. The market imperfection in this model is that prices in the goods market do not adjust immediately to changes in demand conditions—the goods market does not clear instantaneously. If the demand for a firm's goods falls, some respond by reducing output, not prices.

   The second model is the imperfect-information model. This model assumes that there is imperfect information about prices, in that some suppliers of goods confuse changes in the price level with changes in relative prices. If a producer observes the nominal price of the firm's good rising, the producer attributes some of the rise to an increase in relative price, even if it is purely a general price increase. As a result, the producer increases production. In both models, there is a discrepancy between what is really happening and what firms think is happening. In the sticky-price model, some firms expect prices to be at one level and they end up at another level. In the imperfect-information model, some firms expect the relative price of their output has changed when it really has not.

2. In this chapter, we argued that in the short run, the supply of output depends on the natural rate of output and on the difference between the price level and the expected price level. This relationship is expressed in the aggregate-supply equation:

$$Y = \overline{Y} + \alpha(P - EP).$$

   The Phillips curve is an alternative way to express aggregate supply. It provides a simple way to express the tradeoff between inflation and unemployment implied by the short-run aggregate supply curve. The Phillips curve posits that inflation π depends on the expected inflation rate $E\pi$, on cyclical unemployment $u - u^n$, and on supply shocks v:

$$\pi = E\pi - \beta(u - u^n) + v.$$

   Both equations tell us the same information in a different way: both imply a connection between real economic activity and *unexpected* changes in prices. In addition, both the Phillips curve and the short-run aggregate supply curve show that inflation and unemployment move in opposite directions.

3. Inflation is inertial because of the way people form expectations. It is plausible to assume that people's expectations of inflation depend on recently observed inflation. These expectations then influence the wages and prices that people set. For example, if prices have been rising quickly, people will expect them to continue to rise quickly. These expectations will be built into the contracts people set, so that actual wages and prices will rise quickly. In addition, both the Phillips curve and the short-run aggregate supply curve show that inflation and unemployment move in opposite directions.

4. *Demand-pull inflation* results from high aggregate demand: the increase in demand "pulls" prices and output up. *Cost-push inflation* comes from adverse supply shocks that push up the cost of production—for example, the increases in oil prices in the mid- and late-1970s.

The Phillips curve tells us that inflation depends on expected inflation, the difference between unemployment and its natural rate, and a shock v:

$$\pi = E\pi - \beta(u - u^n) + v.$$

The term "$-\beta(u - u^n)$" is the demand-pull inflation, since if unemployment is below its natural rate ($u < u^n$), inflation rises. The supply shock v is the cost-push inflation.

5. The Phillips curve relates the inflation rate to the expected inflation rate and to the difference between unemployment and its natural rate. So one way to reduce inflation is to have a recession, raising unemployment above its natural rate. It is possible to bring inflation down without a recession, however, if we can costlessly reduce *expected* inflation.

According to the rational-expectations approach, people optimally use all of the information available to them in forming their expectations. So to reduce expected inflation, we require, first, that the plan to reduce inflation be announced before people form expectations (e.g., before they form wage agreements and price contracts); and second, that those setting wages and prices believe that the announced plan will be carried out. If both requirements are met, then expected inflation will fall immediately and without cost, and this in turn will bring down actual inflation.

6. One way in which a recession might raise the natural rate of unemployment is by affecting the process of job search, increasing the amount of frictional unemployment. For example, workers who are unemployed lose valuable job skills. This reduces their ability to find jobs after the recession ends because they are less desirable to firms. Also, after a long period of unemployment, individuals may lose some of their desire to work, and hence search less hard.

Second, a recession may affect the process that determines wages, increasing wait unemployment. Wage negotiations may give a greater voice to "insiders," those who actually have jobs. Those who become unemployed become "outsiders." If the smaller group of insiders cares more about high real wages and less about high employment, then the recession may permanently push real wages above the equilibrium level and raise the amount of wait unemployment.

This permanent impact of a recession on the natural rate of unemployment is called *hysteresis*.

Problems and Applications

1. In this question, we examine two special cases of the sticky-price model developed in this chapter. In the sticky-price model, all firms have a desired price p that depends on the overall level of prices P as well as the level of aggregate demand $Y - \overline{Y}$. We wrote this as

$$p = P + a(Y - \overline{Y}).$$

There are two types of firms. A proportion $(1 - s)$ of the firms have flexible prices and set prices using the above equation. The remaining proportion s of the firms have sticky prices—they announce their prices in advance based on the economic conditions that they expect in the future. We assume that these firms expect output to be at its natural rate, so $(EY - \overline{Y}) = 0$. Hence, these firms set their prices equal to the expected price level:

$$p = EP.$$

The overall price level is a weighted average of the prices set by the two types of firms:

$$P = sEP + (1 - s)[P + a(\overline{Y} - Y)].$$

Rearranging:

$$P = EP + [a(1 - s)/s](\overline{Y} - Y).$$

a. If no firms have flexible prices, then $s = 1$. The above equation tells us that

$$P = EP.$$

That is, the aggregate price level is fixed at the expected price level: the aggregate supply curve is horizontal in the short run, as assumed in Chapter 10.

b. If desired relative prices do not depend at all on the level of output, then $a = 0$ in the equation for the price level. Once again, we find $P = EP$: the aggregate supply curve is horizontal in the short run, as assumed in Chapter 10.

2. The economy has the Phillips curve:

$$\pi = \pi_{-1} - 0.5(u - 0.06).$$

a. The natural rate of unemployment is the rate at which the inflation rate does not deviate from the expected inflation rate. Here, the expected inflation rate is just last period's actual inflation rate. Setting the inflation rate equal to last period's inflation rate, that is, $\pi = \pi_{-1}$, we find that $u = 0.06$. Thus, the natural rate of unemployment is 6 percent.

b. In the short run (that is, in a single period) the expected inflation rate is fixed at the level of inflation in the previous period, π_{-1}. Hence, the short-run relationship between inflation and unemployment is just the graph of the Phillips curve: it has a slope of -0.5, and it passes through the point where $\pi = \pi_{-1}$ and $u = 0.06$. This is shown in Figure 14-1. In the long run, expected inflation equals actual inflation, so that $\pi = \pi_{-1}$, and output and unemployment equal their natural rates. The long-run Phillips curve thus is vertical at an unemployment rate of 6 percent.

Figure 14-1

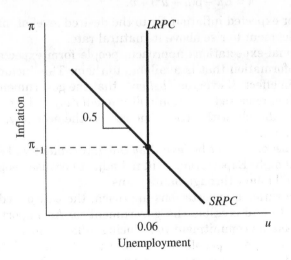

c. To reduce inflation, the Phillips curve tells us that unemployment must be above its natural rate of 6 percent for some period of time. We can write the Phillips curve in the form

$$\pi - \pi_{-1} = 0.5(u - 0.06).$$

Since we want inflation to fall by 5 percentage points, we want $\pi - \pi_{-1} = -0.05$. Plugging this into the left-hand side of the above equation, we find

$$-0.05 = -0.5(u - 0.06).$$

We can now solve this for u:

$$u = 0.16.$$

Hence, we need 10 percentage points of cyclical unemployment above the natural rate of 6 percent.

Okun's law says that a change of 1 percentage point in unemployment translates into a change of 2 percentage points in GDP. Hence, an increase in unemployment of 10 percentage points corresponds to a fall in output of 20 percentage points. The sacrifice ratio is the percentage of a year's GDP that must be forgone to reduce inflation by 1 percentage point. Dividing the 20 percentage-point decrease in GDP by the 5 percentage-point decrease in inflation, we find that the sacrifice ratio is $20/5 = 4$.

d. One scenario is to have very high unemployment for a short period of time. For example, we could have 16 percent unemployment for a single year. Alternatively, we could have a small amount of cyclical unemployment spread out over a long period of time. For example, we could have 8 percent unemployment for 5 years. Both of these plans would bring the inflation rate down from 10 percent to 5 percent, although at different speeds.

3. The cost of reducing inflation comes from the cost of changing people's expectations about inflation. If expectations can be changed costlessly, then reducing inflation is also costless. Algebraically, the Phillips curve tells us that

$$\pi = E\pi - \beta(u - u^n) + v.$$

If the government can lower expected inflation $E\pi$ to the desired level of inflation, then there is no need for unemployment to rise above its natural rate.

According to the rational-expectations approach, people form expectations about inflation using all of the information that is available to them. This includes information about current policies in effect. If everyone *believes* that the government is committed to reducing inflation, then expected inflation will immediately fall. In terms of the Phillips curve, $E\pi$ falls immediately with little or no cost to the economy. That is, the sacrifice ratio will be very small.

On the other hand, if people *do not* believe that the government will carry out its intentions, then $E\pi$ remains high. Expectations will not adjust because people are skeptical that the government will follow through on its plans.

Thus, according to the rational-expectations approach, the cost of reducing inflation depends on how resolute and credible the government is. An important issue is how the government can make its commitment to reducing inflation more credible. One possibility, for example, is to appoint people who have a reputation as inflation fighters. A second possibility is to have Congress pass a law requiring the Federal Reserve to lower inflation. Of course, people might expect the Fed to ignore this law, or expect Congress to change the law later. A third possibility is to pass a constitutional amendment limiting monetary growth. People might rationally believe that a constitutional amendment is relatively difficult to change.

4. a.   Beginning in long-run equilibrium, where output is at the natural level, if the Federal Reserve increases the money supply, this will cause the economy to go through an expansionary phase. Starting with the *IS–LM* model in Figure 14-2A, an increase in the money supply will shift the *LM* curve to the right, resulting in a lower interest rate and higher level of output at point B. In the long run, the price level will rise, real-money balances will decline, and the *LM* curve will shift back to its original position. There is no long-run change in the real interest rate or the level of output. Moving to the *AD–AS* model in Figure 14-2B, an increase in the money supply will shift the *AD* curve to the right, resulting in a higher level of output and a higher price level at point B. In the long run, expected inflation will rise, shifting the SRAS curve upward. The economy ends up at point C with output back at its natural level and the price level at a higher level. Moving to the Phillips curve graph in Figure 14-2C, the economy starts at point A, where unemployment is at the natural rate. The increase in the money supply pushes output above its natural level, and as a result, the unemployment rate falls below its natural level. This causes a movement along the short-run Phillips curve to point B, where inflation is higher and unemployment is lower. In the long run, expected inflation will rise, causing the Phillips curve to shift upward. The economy ends up at point C with higher inflation and no change in the unemployment rate. The economy moves through this expansionary cycle because the increase in the money supply does not immediately cause expected inflation to rise.

A. *IS–LM* Model   **Figure 14-2**

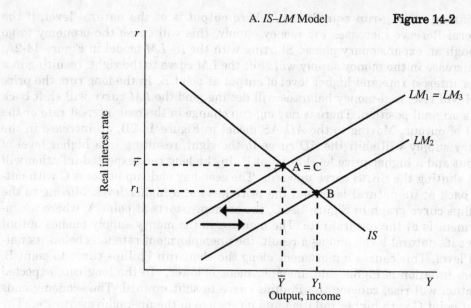

B. *AD–AS* Model

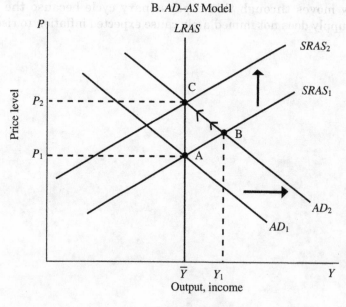

C. Phillips curve

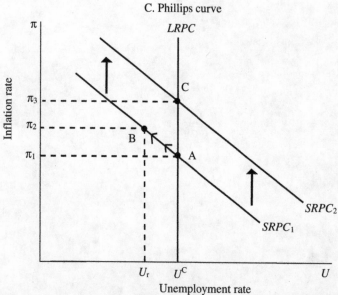

b. Beginning in long-run equilibrium with output at its natural level, if the Federal Reserve increases the money supply and people immediately expect inflation to rise, then nothing changes except for the price level and the inflation rate. In the *IS–LM* model, the increase in the money supply will cause the price level to rise at the same rate as the money supply such that there is no change in real balances. The economy stays at point A, as illustrated in Figure 14-3A. Moving to the *AD–AS* model, the increase in the money supply shifts the *AD* curve to the right, but at the same time, the increase in expected inflation shifts the *SRAS* curve up and to the left. The economy remains at the natural level of output and the price level is higher, as illustrated in Figure 14-3B. Moving to the Phillips curve, the immediate increase in expected inflation shifts the short-run Phillips curve upward, causing the inflation rate to rise with no change in the unemployment rate, as illustrated in Figure 14-3C. When the money supply increases and the public immediately expects higher inflation, the economy does not move through an expansionary cycle.

Figure 14-3

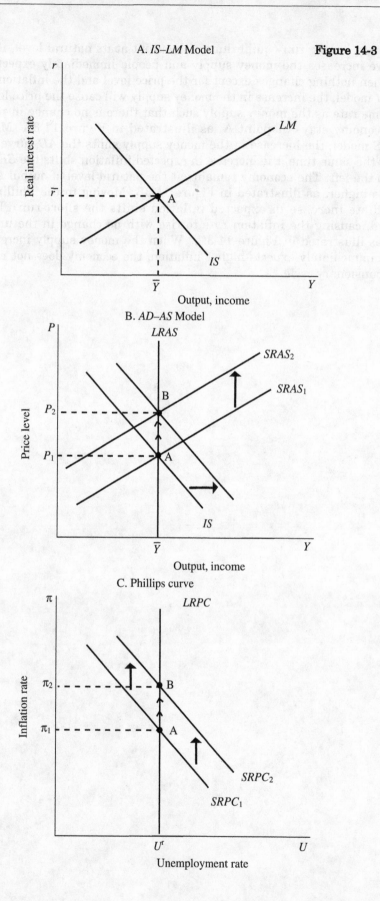

A. *IS–LM* Model

B. *AD–AS* Model

C. Phillips curve

5. In this question we consider several implications of rational expectations—the assumption that people optimally use all of the information available to them in forming their expectations—for the model of sticky prices that we considered in this chapter. This model implies an aggregate supply curve in which output varies from its natural rate only if the price level varies from its expected level:

$$\overline{Y} = Y + \alpha(P - EP).$$

Based on this model, monetary policy can affect real GDP only by affecting $(P - EP)$—that is, causing an unexpected change in the price level.

a. Only unanticipated changes in the money supply can affect real GDP. Since people take into account all of the information available to them, they already take into account the effects of anticipated changes in money when they form their expectations of the price level EP. For example, if people expect the money supply to increase by 10 percent and it actually does increase by 10 percent, then there is no effect on output since there is no price surprise—$(P - EP) = 0$. On the other hand, suppose the Fed increases the money supply more than expected, so that prices increase by 15 percent when people expect them to increase by only 10 percent. Since $P > EP$, output rises. But it is only the unanticipated part of money growth that increases output.

b. The Fed often tries to stabilize the economy by offsetting shocks to output and unemployment. For example, it might increase the money supply during recessions in an attempt to stimulate the economy, and it might reduce the money supply during booms in an attempt to slow it down. The Fed can only do this by surprising people about the price level: during a recession, they want prices to be higher than expected, and during booms, they want prices to be lower than expected. If people have rational expectations, however, they will *expect* the Fed to respond this way. So if the economy is in a boom, people expect the Fed to reduce the money supply; in a recession, people expect the Fed to increase the money supply. In either case, it is impossible for the Fed to cause $(P - EP)$ to vary systematically from zero. Since people take into account the systematic, anticipated movements in money, the effect on output of systematic, active policy is exactly the same as a policy of keeping the money supply constant, assuming the Fed chooses the level of the money supply at the same time people set prices so everyone has the same information.

c. If the Fed sets the money supply after people set wages and prices, then the Fed can use monetary policy systematically to stabilize output. The assumption of rational expectations means that people use all of the information available to them in forming expectations about the price level. This includes information about the state of the economy and information about how the Fed will respond to this state. This does not mean that people *know* what the state of the economy will be, nor do they know exactly how the Fed will act: they simply make their best guess.

As time passes, the Fed learns information about the economy that was unknown to those setting wages and prices. At this point, since contracts have already set these wages and prices, people are stuck with their expectations EP. The Fed can then use monetary policy to affect the actual price level P, and hence can affect output systematically.

6. In this model, the natural rate of unemployment is an average of the unemployment rates in the past two years. Hence, if a recession raises the unemployment rate in some year, then the natural rate of unemployment rises as well. This means that the model exhibits hysteresis: short-term cyclical unemployment affects the long-term natural rate of unemployment.

a. The natural rate of unemployment might depend on recent unemployment for at least two reasons, suggested by the theory of hysteresis. First, recent unemployment rates might affect the level of frictional unemployment. Unemployed workers lose job skills and find it harder to get jobs; also, unemployed workers might lose some of their desire to work, and hence search less hard for a job. Second, recent unemployment rates might affect the level of structural unemployment. If labor negotiations give a greater voice to "insiders" than "outsiders," then the insiders might push for high wages at the expense of jobs. This will be especially true in industries in which negotiations take place between firms and unions.

b. If the Fed seeks to reduce inflation permanently by 1 percentage point, then the Phillips curve tells us that in the first period we require

$$\pi_1 - \pi_0 = -1 = -0.5(u_1 - u_1^n),$$

or

$$(u_1 - u_1^n) = 2.$$

That is, we require an unemployment rate 2 percentage points above the original natural rate u. Next period, however, the natural rate will rise as a result of the cyclical unemployment. The new natural rate u will be

$$\begin{aligned} u &= 0.5[u_1 + u_0] \\ &= 0.5[(u_1^n + 2) + u_1^n] \\ &= u_1^n + 1. \end{aligned}$$

Hence, the natural rate of unemployment rises by 1 percentage point. If the Fed wants to keep inflation at its new level, then unemployment in period 2 must equal the new natural rate u. Hence,

$$u_2 = u_1^n + 1.$$

In every subsequent period, it remains true that the unemployment rate must equal the natural rate. This natural rate never returns to its original level: we can show this by deriving the sequence of unemployment rates:

$$u_3 = (1/2)u_2 + (1/2)u_1 = u + 1.5$$

$$u_4 = (1/2)u_3 + (1/2)u_2 = u + 1.25$$

$$u_5 = (1/2)u_4 + (1/2)u_3 = u + 1.375.$$

Unemployment always remains above its original natural rate. In fact, we can show that it is always *at least* 1 percent above its original natural rate. Thus, to reduce inflation by 1 percentage point, unemployment rises above its original level by 2 percentage points in the first year, and by 1 or more percentage points in every year after that.

c. Because unemployment is always higher than it started, output is always lower than it would have been. Hence, the sacrifice ratio is infinite.

d. Without hysteresis, we found that there was a short-run tradeoff but no long-run tradeoff between inflation and unemployment. With hysteresis, we find that there *is* a long-run tradeoff between inflation and unemployment: to reduce inflation, unemployment must rise permanently.

7. a. The natural level of output is determined by the production function, $\overline{Y} = F(\overline{K}, \overline{L})$. If a tax cut raises work effort, it increases L and, thus, increases the natural rate of output.

b. The tax cut shifts the aggregate demand curve outward for the normal reason that disposable income and, hence, consumption rise. It shifts the long-run aggregate supply curve outward because the natural rate of output rises.

The effect of the tax cut on the short-run aggregate supply (*SRAS*) curve depends on which model you use. The labor supply curve shifts outward because workers are willing to supply more labor at any given real wage while the labor demand curve is unchanged. In the sticky-price model the quantity of labor is demand-determined, so the *SRAS* curve does not move. By contrast, the imperfect-information model assumes that the labor market is always in equilibrium, so the greater supply of labor leads to higher employment immediately: the *SRAS* shifts out.

c. If you are using the sticky-price model, the short-run analysis is the same as the conventional model without the labor-supply effect. That is, output and prices both rise because aggregate demand rises while short-run aggregate supply is unchanged. If you use the imperfect-information model, short-run aggregate supply shifts outward, so that the tax cut is more expansionary and less inflationary than the conventional model. Figure 14-4 shows the effects in both models. Point A is the original equilibrium, point SW is the new equilibrium in the sticky-price model, and point II is the new equilibrium in the imperfect-information model.

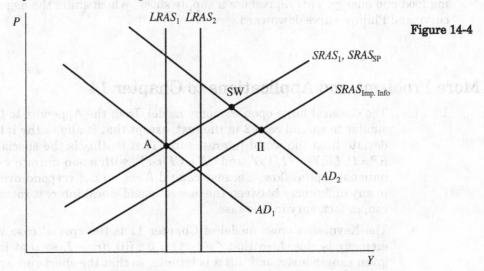

Figure 14-4

d. In the normal model, where the tax cut does not lead to a shift of labor supply that increases the natural level of output, the long-run price level will be higher as a result of the tax cut and output will return to the same natural level. The tax cut led to a rightward shift of the aggregate demand curve in the short run. In the long run, the short-run aggregate supply curve will shift up and to the left as the expected price level rises. In the alternative model, where the tax cut leads to an increase in the natural level of output, the long-run results depend on whether the horizontal shift in the aggregate demand curve is larger, smaller, or the same as the horizontal shift in the long-run aggregate supply curve. If the two shift horizontally by the same amount, then the price level is unaffected in the long run. If the shift in aggregate demand is greater than the shift in the long-run aggregate supply curve, then the price level will be higher in the long run.

8. In this quote, Alan Blinder argues that in low-inflation countries like the United States, the benefits of reducing inflation are small whereas the costs are large. That is, menu costs, shoeleather costs, and tax distortions simply do not add up to much, so eliminating inflation offers only small benefits. By contrast, the costs in terms of unemployment and lost output that are associated with lowering inflation are easily quantifiable and very large.

    The basic policy implication of these beliefs about the relative benefits and costs of reducing inflation is that policymakers should not tighten policy in order to lower inflation rates that are already relatively low. The statement leaves two other issues ambiguous. First, should policymakers concern themselves with rising inflation? Second, should policymakers concern themselves with making inflation more predictable around the level it has inherited? Blinder may feel that these issues should have little weight relative to output stabilization.

9. From the BLS Web site (www.bls.gov), there are various ways to get the CPI data. For the years 2007–2011, I obtained the following for "all urban consumers":

Year	2011	2010	2009	2008	2007
Overall CPI	3.2	1.6	−0.4	3.8	2.8
CPI excluding food and energy	2.4	1.8	2.3	2.7	2.6

The overall CPI was clearly more volatile than the CPI excluding food and energy. The difference reflects shocks to the price of food and energy—especially energy prices, which are highly variable.

When energy prices, say, go down, the total CPI will rise less than the CPI excluding food and energy. This represents a supply shock, which shifts the aggregate supply curve and Phillips curve downward.

More Problems and Applications to Chapter 14

1. a. The classical large open economy model (from the Appendix to Chapter 6) is similar to special case 2 in the text, except that it allows the interest rate to deviate from the world interest rate. That is, this is the special case where $EP = P$, $L(i,Y) = (1/V)Y$, and $CF = CF(r-r^*)$, with a non-infinitely elastic international capital flow. Because capital flows do not respond overwhelmingly to any differences between the domestic and world interest rates, these rates can, in fact, vary in this case.

b. The Keynesian cross model of Chapter 11 is the special case where (i) the economy is closed, so that $CF(r-r^*) = 0$; (ii) $I(r) = I$, so that investment is given exogenously; and (iii) α is infinite, so that the short-run aggregate-supply curve is horizontal. In this special case, output depends solely on the demand for goods and services.

c. The *IS–LM* model for the large open economy (from the appendix to Chapter 13) is the special case where α is infinite and $CF = CF(r-r^*)$ is not infinitely elastic. In this case, the short-run aggregate supply curve is horizontal, and capital flows do not respond too much to differences between the domestic and world interest rates.

CHAPTER 15 A Dynamic Model of Aggregate Demand and Aggregate Supply

Questions for Review

1. The equation for the dynamic aggregate supply curve is:

$$\pi_t = \pi_{t-1} + \phi(Y_t - \overline{Y}_t) + \upsilon_t.$$

Recall that ϕ is a positive parameter that measures how rapidly firms adjust their prices in response to output fluctuations. When output in the economy rises above its natural level, firms experience rising marginal costs and will increase prices. There is therefore a positive relationship between the level of output and inflation in the economy. The dynamic aggregate supply curve is upward sloping. The steepness of the dynamic aggregate supply curve depends on how quickly marginal costs rise when output is above its natural level and on how quickly firms respond to the rising marginal cost with an increase in prices. The dynamic aggregate supply curve will be steeper if marginal costs rise more quickly and if firms respond by increasing prices more quickly. The dynamic aggregate supply curve is illustrated in Figure 15-1.

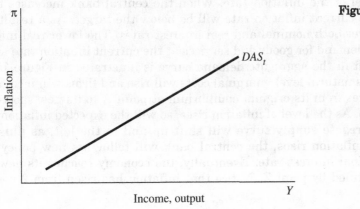

Figure 15-1

2. The equation for the dynamic aggregate demand curve is:

$$Y_t = \overline{Y} - \left[\frac{\alpha\theta_\pi}{1 + \alpha\theta_Y}\right](\pi_t - \pi_t^*) + \left[\frac{1}{(1 + \alpha\theta_y)}\right]\varepsilon_t.$$

The dynamic aggregate demand curve is defined by a given monetary policy rule and illustrates a negative relationship between the quantity of output demanded and inflation. When inflation changes, the central bank follows its monetary policy rule and changes the nominal interest rate. The monetary policy rule specifies that the nominal interest rate will change by more than the inflation rate so that there is a change in the real interest rate, and hence the demand for goods and services. If inflation rises, the central bank will follow its monetary policy rule, the real interest rate will rise, the amount of goods and services demanded will fall, and the level of output will fall. The dynamic aggregate demand curve is steeper if the central bank is more tolerant of high inflation (θ_π is smaller), if the central bank is less tolerant of deviations in output away from the natural level (θ_Y is larger), and if the public's spending is less responsive to changes in the real interest rate (α is smaller). The dynamic aggregate demand curve is illustrated in Figure 15-2.

159

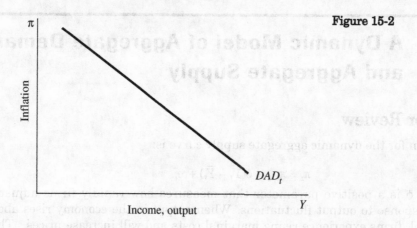

Figure 15-2

3. The dynamic aggregate demand curve is drawn for a given monetary policy rule. If the central bank changes the rule by increasing the target inflation rate, then the dynamic aggregate demand curve will shift to the right. Looking at the equation for the dynamic aggregate demand curve, an increase in the target inflation rate will increase output for any given level of the inflation rate. When the central bank increases the target inflation rate, the current inflation rate will be below the target. As a result, the central bank will lower both nominal and real interest rates. The lower real interest rate will increase the demand for goods and services at the current inflation rate and output will rise. The shift in the aggregate demand curve is illustrated in Figure 15-3. Since output is above its natural level, marginal costs will rise and firms will increase prices. The economy moves from its original equilibrium at point A to its new short-run equilibrium at point B. As the level of inflation rises, so will the expected inflation rate, and the dynamic aggregate supply curve will shift up and to the left, as illustrated in Figure 15-3. As inflation rises, the central bank will follow its new policy rule and increase the nominal interest rate. Eventually, the economy reaches its new long-run equilibrium, identified by point Z. Notice that inflation has risen from 2 percent to 3 percent.

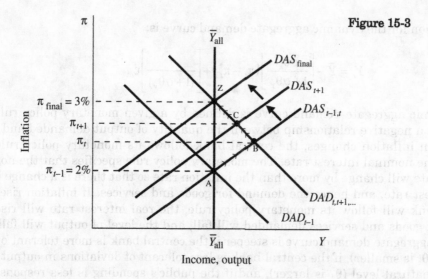

Figure 15-3

The nominal interest rate will be higher in the long run because there is no change in the long run real interest rate, and the nominal interest rate in the long run is equal to the real interest rate plus the target inflation rate.

4. If the central bank decides to increase the response of interest rates to changes in inflation (the parameter θ_π), then the central bank has become less tolerant of inflation. In
   this case, any increase in inflation will elicit a larger increase in nominal and real
   interest rates in an attempt to reduce the demand for goods and services and prevent
   further increases in inflation, such that the dynamic aggregate demand curve is flatter.
   Mathematically, the slope of the dynamic aggregate demand curve is given by:

   $$-\frac{1+\alpha\theta_Y}{\alpha\theta_\pi}.$$

   When the parameter θ_π increases in value, the slope becomes smaller in absolute-value
   terms and the dynamic aggregate demand curve becomes flatter. Intuitively, when the
   central bank is less tolerant of inflation, they are willing to put up with larger deviations of output from the natural rate, making the dynamic aggregate demand curve
   flatter. In this case, a supply shock that shifts the dynamic aggregate supply curve up
   and to the left will cause a larger reduction in the level of output and a smaller increase
   in the inflation rate, as illustrated in Figure 15-4. Under the new policy, the economy
   moves from A to C in response to the supply shock, as opposed to moving from A to B
   under the old policy. Note that, if the economy is in long-run equilibrium at the time of
   the central bank policy change, the economy will still remain in long-run equilibrium,
   but with a flatter dynamic aggregate demand curve.

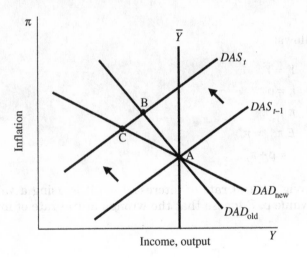

Figure 15-4

Problems and Applications

1. The five equations that make up the dynamic aggregate demand–aggregate supply
   model can be manipulated to derive long-run values for the variables. In this problem,
   it is assumed that there are no shocks to demand or supply and inflation has stabilized.
   Since inflation has stabilized, it must be true that inflation in time t is equal to inflation in time $t-1$ ($\pi_t = \pi_{t-1}$). We also know that expected inflation is equal to last period's
   inflation, or $E_{t-1}\pi_t = \pi_{t-1}$. Start with the Phillips curve equation on line 1 below and use
   these two facts to find the following:

   $$\pi_t = E_{t-1}\pi_t + \phi\left(Y_t - \bar{Y}_t\right) + \upsilon_t$$

   $$\pi_t = \pi_{t-1} + \phi\left(Y_t - \bar{Y}_t\right) + \upsilon_t$$

   $$\pi_t = \pi_t + \phi\left(Y_t - \bar{Y}_t\right) + \upsilon_t.$$

   From here, it follows that output must equal natural output since the supply shock
   parameter υ_t equals zero. Moving to the demand for goods and services equation next,

it now follows that the real interest rate equals the natural rate of interest since the demand shock parameter ε_t equals zero and $Y_t = \bar{Y}_t$:

$$Y_t = \bar{Y}_t - \alpha(r_t - \rho) + \varepsilon_t.$$

Turning to the Fisher equation on line 1 below, we can show the nominal interest rate is equal to the natural interest rate plus the current inflation rate. Since inflation has stabilized, expected inflation equals current inflation ($E_t\pi_{t+1} = \pi_t$) and we have just demonstrated that the real interest rate is equal to the natural rate of interest ($r_t = \rho$):

$$r_t = i_t - E_t\pi_{t+1}$$
$$r_t = i_t - \pi_t$$
$$i_t = r_t - \pi_t$$
$$i_t = \rho - \pi_t.$$

Moving now to the monetary policy rule equation on line 1 below, it must be true that current inflation equals the target inflation rate so that the third term on the right zeros out. Likewise, the fourth term on the right side will zero out since output is at the natural level:

$$i_t = \pi_t + \rho + \theta_\pi\left(\pi_t - \pi_t^*\right) + \theta_Y\left(Y_t - \bar{Y}_t\right)$$
$$i_t = \pi_t + \rho.$$

The final values are as follows:

$$Y_t = \bar{Y}_t$$
$$r_t = \rho$$
$$\pi_t = \pi_t^*$$
$$E_t\pi_{t+1} = \pi_t^*$$
$$i_t = \rho + \pi_t^*.$$

2. If the central bank has the wrong natural rate of interest, then it is using a value ρ' that is different from the real value ρ. Suppose that the wrong natural rate of interest is defined as follows:

$$\rho' = \rho + \Delta\rho$$

In this case, if $\Delta\rho$ equals zero, then the central bank has the correct natural rate of interest. If the natural rate of interest is wrong, then the long-run equilibrium values will change. The five equations that make up the dynamic aggregate demand–aggregate supply model can be manipulated to derive long-run values for the variables. In this problem, it is assumed that there are no shocks to demand or supply and inflation has stabilized. Since inflation has stabilized, it must be true that inflation in time t is equal to inflation in time $t - 1$ ($\pi_t = \pi_{t-1}$). We also know that expected inflation is equal to last period's inflation, or $E_{t-1}\pi_t = \pi_{t-1}$. Start with the Phillips curve on line 1 below and use these two facts to find the following:

$$\pi_t = E_{t-1}\pi_t + \phi\left(Y_t - \bar{Y}_t\right) + \upsilon_t$$
$$\pi_t = \pi_{t-1} + \phi\left(Y_t - \bar{Y}_t\right) + \upsilon_t$$
$$\pi_t = \pi_t + \phi\left(Y_t - \bar{Y}_t\right) + \upsilon_t.$$

From here it follows that output must equal natural output since the supply shock parameter υ_t equals zero. Moving to the demand for goods and services equation below it now follows that the real interest rate equals the natural rate of interest since the demand shock parameter ε_t equals zero and $Y_t = \bar{Y}_t$:

$$Y_t = \bar{Y}_t - \alpha(r_t - \rho) + \varepsilon_t.$$

Turning to the Fisher equation on line 1 below, we can show the natural interest rate is equal to the nominal interest rate minus the current inflation rate. Since inflation has stabilized, expected inflation equals current inflation ($E_t\pi_{t+1} = \pi_t$, and we have just demonstrated that the real interest rate is equal to the natural rate of interest ($r_t = \rho$):

$$r_t = i_t - E_t\pi_{t+1}$$
$$r_t = i_t - \pi_t$$
$$\rho = i_t - \pi_t.$$

The monetary policy rule equation on line 1 below has the wrong natural rate of interest ρ'. Substitute in the relationship between the correct and incorrect rates of natural interest and rearrange terms:

$$i_t = \pi_t + \rho' + \theta_\pi\left(\pi_t - \pi_t^*\right) + \theta_Y\left(Y_t - \bar{Y}_t\right)$$
$$i_t = \pi_t + \left(\rho + \Delta\rho\right) + \theta_\pi\left(\pi_t - \pi_t^*\right) + \theta_Y\left(Y_t - \bar{Y}_t\right)$$
$$i_t - \pi_t = \left(\rho + \Delta\rho\right) + \theta_\pi\left(\pi_t - \pi_t^*\right) + \theta_Y\left(Y_t - \bar{Y}_t\right).$$

The third term on the right side will zero out since output is at the natural level. Now, combine the rewritten Fisher equation with the rewritten monetary policy rule equation above:

$$i_t = \pi_t + \left(\rho + \Delta\rho\right) + \theta_\pi\left(\pi_t - \pi_t^*\right) + \theta_Y\left(Y_t - \bar{Y}_t\right)$$
$$\rho = \left(\rho + \Delta\rho\right) + \theta_\pi\left(\pi_t - \pi_t^*\right)$$
$$0 = \Delta\rho + \theta_\pi\pi_t - \theta_\pi\pi_t^*$$
$$\pi_t = \pi_t^* - \frac{\Delta\rho}{\theta_\pi}.$$

The final values are as follows:

$$Y_t = \bar{Y}_t$$
$$r_t = \rho$$
$$\pi_t = \pi_t^* - \frac{\Delta\rho}{\theta_\pi}$$
$$E_t\pi_{t+1} = \pi_t^* - \frac{\Delta\rho}{\theta_\pi}$$
$$i_t = \rho + \pi_t^* - \frac{\Delta\rho}{\theta_\pi}.$$

Intuitively, if the central bank thinks that the natural rate of interest is higher than it really is, then it will be setting interest rates higher than they should be set, and $\Delta\rho$ is greater than zero. The higher interest rates will result in lower demand for goods and services, and in the long run, this will result in an inflation rate that is lower than the target inflation rate. In the short run, higher interest rates will temporarily cause real interest rates to be higher than normal, causing the dynamic aggregate demand curve to shift down and to the left. In being wrong about the natural rate, the central bank has effectively forced the economy through a recessionary cycle, which has resulted in the inflation rate coming in below the target rate. As the lower inflation rate persists, the expected inflation rate will decrease and the dynamic aggregate supply curve will shift down and to the right until a new long run equilibrium is reached. This is illustrated in Figure 15-5. From the derived long-run values above, the inflation rate is below the target rate, expected inflation equals actual inflation and is also below the target rate, and the nominal interest rate is lower than it would otherwise be.

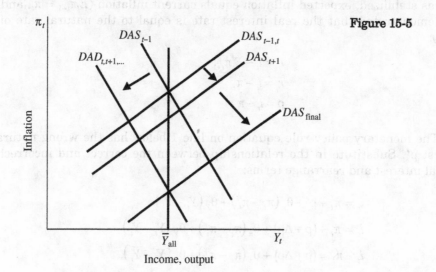

Figure 15-5

3. "If a central bank wants to achieve lower nominal interest rates, it has to raise the nominal interest rate." In long-run equilibrium, the nominal rate of interest is equal to the natural rate of interest plus the target inflation rate. To lower the long-run nominal interest rate, the central bank must lower the target inflation rate and, ultimately, the actual inflation rate. In the short run, the central bank must increase the nominal interest rate in order to reduce spending and output in the economy. This will reduce inflation and, ultimately, expected inflation. The economy will adjust to a new long-run equilibrium in which the nominal interest rate, the target inflation rate, and the actual inflation rate are all lower. Graphically, lowering the target inflation rate will shift the dynamic aggregate demand curve down and to the left, forcing the economy through a recessionary cycle, and in the short run, output and inflation will be lower. As expected inflation adjusts over the long run, the dynamic aggregate supply curve will shift down and to the right. In the long run, output is equal to the natural level and inflation is lower.

4. The sacrifice ratio measures the accumulated loss in output associated with a one-percentage-point reduction in the target inflation rate. Graphically, the reduction in the target inflation rate will shift the dynamic aggregate demand curve down and to the left, resulting in a short-run equilibrium with a lower level of output and a lower inflation rate. Over time, expected inflation will adjust and the dynamic aggregate supply curve will shift down and to the right until output again equals potential output. For each year that output remains below potential, the percentage deviation of actual output from potential output can be calculated, and these results can be summed to find the accumulated lost output in percentage terms. For the twelve years included in the text simulation, the accumulated lost output is 2.59 percent. During this same period, the inflation rate fell from 2 percent to 1.35 percent, which is a decrease of 0.65 percent. The implied sacrifice ratio is therefore 2.59/0.65 = 3.98. We can derive this same result directly from the dynamic aggregate demand–aggregate supply model. Start with the Phillips curve equation on line 1 below and use the adaptive expectations assumption to rewrite as follows:

$$\pi_t = E_{t-1}\pi_t + \phi\left(Y_t - \bar{Y}_t\right) + \upsilon_t$$

$$\pi_t = \pi_{t-1}\pi_t + \phi\left(Y_t - \bar{Y}_t\right) + \upsilon_t.$$

From this equation, we see that, in the absence of supply shocks ($\upsilon_\tau = 0$), a one-percentage-point decrease in output below its natural level causes inflation to decrease by θ percentage points. (Recall that the natural level of output is 100 so that a one-unit deviation of output from its natural level is equivalent to a one-percentage-point deviation.) Turning this result around, we find that, in order to reduce the inflation rate by one percentage point, output must decline by $1/\theta$. percentage points. From the simulation, the value of θ is 0.25 so that $1/\theta$ is equal to 4. Note that this is very close to the value of 3.98 that was obtained directly from the simulation results.

5. Follow the hint given in the problem and solve for the long-run equilibrium with the new assumption that the demand shock parameter ε_t is not zero. Since inflation has stabilized, it must be true that inflation in time t is equal to inflation in time $t-1$($\pi_t = \pi_{t-1}$). We also know that expected inflation is equal to last period's inflation, or $E_{t-1}\pi_t = \pi_{t-1}$. Start with the Phillips curve on line 1 below and use these two facts to find the following:

$$\pi_t = E_{t-1}\pi_t + \phi\left(Y_t - \bar{Y}_t\right) + \upsilon_t$$
$$\pi_t = \pi_{t-1} + \phi\left(Y_t - \bar{Y}_t\right) + \upsilon_t$$
$$\pi_t = \pi_t + \phi\left(Y_t - \bar{Y}_t\right) + \upsilon_t.$$

From here, it follows that output must equal natural output since the supply shock parameter υ_t equals zero. From the demand for goods and services equation on line 1 below, it now follows that the real interest rate equals the natural rate of interest plus a new term:

$$Y_t = \bar{Y}_t - \alpha\left(r_t - \rho\right) + \varepsilon_t$$
$$0 = -\alpha r_t + \alpha\rho + \varepsilon_t$$
$$\alpha r_t = \alpha\rho + \varepsilon_t$$
$$r_t = \rho + \frac{\varepsilon_t}{\alpha}.$$

Turning to the Fisher equation on line 1 below, we can show the nominal interest rate is equal to the natural interest rate plus the current inflation rate plus a new term. Since inflation has stabilized, expected inflation equals current inflation ($E_t\pi_{t+1} = \pi_t$, and we have just demonstrated that the real interest rate is equal to the natural rate of interest plus a new term:

$$\left(r_t = \rho + \frac{\varepsilon_t}{\alpha}\right):$$
$$r_t = i_t - E_t\pi_{t+1}$$
$$r_t = i_t - \pi_t$$
$$i_t = r_t + \pi_t$$
$$i_t = \rho + \pi_t + \frac{\varepsilon_t}{\alpha}.$$

Moving now to the monetary policy rule equation on line 1 below, substitute in for the nominal rate of interest from the rewritten Fisher equation above, and then note that the fourth term on the right side will zero out since output is at the natural level:

$$i_t = \pi_t + \rho + \theta_\pi\left(\pi_t - \pi_t^*\right) + \theta_Y\left(Y_t - \bar{Y}_t\right)$$
$$\rho + \frac{\varepsilon_t}{\alpha} + \pi_t = \pi_t + \rho + \theta_\pi\left(\pi_t - \pi_t^*\right)$$
$$\frac{\varepsilon_t}{\alpha} = \theta_\pi\pi_t^*$$
$$\pi_t = \pi_t^* + \frac{\varepsilon_t}{\theta_\pi\alpha}.$$

The final values are as follows:

$$Y_t = \overline{Y}_t$$

$$r_t = \rho + \frac{\varepsilon_t}{\alpha}$$

$$\pi_t = \pi_t^* + \frac{\varepsilon_t}{\theta_\pi \alpha}$$

$$E_t \pi_{t+1} = \pi_t^* + \frac{\varepsilon_t}{\theta_\pi \alpha}$$

$$i_t = \rho + \pi_t^* + \frac{\varepsilon_t}{\alpha}.$$

If the demand shock parameter ε_t were to increase permanently, such that it remained a constant positive number, the dynamic aggregate demand curve would shift to the right permanently. This would cause a short-run increase in output and inflation and a long-run increase in the inflation rate as the economy adjusted to its new long run equilibrium. This is consistent with the newly derived long-run values above, where the inflation rate is higher than the target inflation rate. Note that expected inflation is also higher, as is the nominal and the real interest rate. To deal with this issue, the central bank could decrease its target inflation rate. This would effectively offset the permanent increase in the demand shock parameter .t and shift the dynamic aggregate demand curve back to its original position.

6. The equation for the dynamic aggregate demand curve is given below:

$$Y_t = \overline{Y}_t - \left[\frac{\alpha \theta_\pi}{(1 + \alpha \theta_Y)} \right] (\pi_t - \pi_t^*) + \left[\frac{1}{(1 + \alpha \theta_Y)} \right] \varepsilon_t.$$

The parameter θ_π measures the central bank's responsiveness to changes in the inflation rate. When θ_π is large, the central bank aggressively responds to changes in the inflation rate. When θ_π is small but still positive, the central bank has a weak response to changes in the inflation rate, and the dynamic aggregate demand curve becomes very steep. If θ_π becomes negative, the dynamic aggregate demand curve actually has a positive slope, as can be seen in the equation above. In this case, a supply shock that shifts the dynamic aggregate supply curve up and to the left will lead to ever-increasing inflation, even if the shock is temporary. This is due to the fact that output remains above its natural level since the central bank's increase in nominal interest rates is not enough to increase real interest rates. The supply shock will shift the dynamic aggregate supply curve up and to the right as rising production costs increase the inflation rate. Since nominal interest rates rise by less than the inflation rate, real interest rates will fall and therefore output will rise. In Figure 15-6, this is shown as a movement from point A to point B. Since output is above the natural rate, inflation will continue to rise, and the dynamic aggregate supply curve will continue to shift up and to the left as people adjust their expectations about inflation. This analysis reinforces the Taylor principle as a guideline for the design of monetary policy in that the central bank wants to maintain low and stable inflation.

Figure 15-6

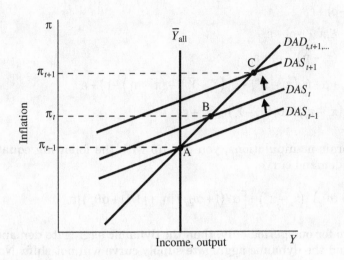

7. Suppose that the natural rate of interest is not a constant parameter but varies over time so that it is now written as ρ_t.

a. The equation for dynamic aggregate supply is not affected by this change because its derivation does not involve the natural rate of interest. The equation for dynamic aggregate demand is not affected by this change either because, although the variable ρ_t is involved in the derivation of the dynamic aggregate demand curve, it cancels out and does not end up as part of the final equation.

b. A shock to ρ_t would not cause a shift to either dynamic aggregate demand or dynamic aggregate supply because the variable does not appear in either equation. Output and inflation would not be affected. However, the real and nominal interest rates would both change by the amount of the change in ρ_t.

c. If the natural rate of interest varied over time, it would make the setting of monetary policy more difficult. If the central bank knows that the natural rate of interest is 4 percent, for example, and it is aiming for target inflation rate of 2 percent, then a nominal interest rate of 6 percent will be the long-run target. If, on the other hand, the natural rate of interest varies over time, then the target long-run interest rate will also vary over time. It is more difficult to hit a moving target than a target that is standing still. In particular, in contrast to what is implicitly assumed above, if the natural rate of interest is always moving, the central bank might have trouble knowing the natural rate of interest at every point in time.

8. Suppose people's expectations of inflation are subject to random shocks so that

$$E_{t-1}\pi_t = \pi_{t-1} + \eta_{t-1}.$$

a. The dynamic aggregate supply curve equation is derived from the Phillips curve and the expectations equation. In this case, start with the Phillips curve equation on line 1 below and substitute in for the expected inflation term using the expression above:

$$\pi_t = E_{t-1}\pi_t + \phi\left(Y_t - \bar{Y}_t\right) + \upsilon_t$$
$$\pi_t = \pi_{t-1} + \eta_{t-1} + \phi\left(Y_t - \bar{Y}_t\right) + \upsilon_t.$$

The dynamic aggregate demand curve is derived from the demand for goods and services equation, the Fisher equation, and the monetary policy rule equation. In this problem, the Fisher equation will be modified to include the new expected inflation equation. Start with the demand for goods and services equation on line 1 below, then use the Fisher equation and monetary policy rule equation to make the necessary substitutions:

$$Y_t = \bar{Y}_t - \alpha(r_t - \rho) + \varepsilon_t$$

$$Y_t = \bar{Y}_t - \alpha(i_t - E_t \pi_{t+1} - \rho) + \varepsilon_t$$

$$Y_t = \bar{Y}_t - \alpha(i_t - (\pi_t + \eta_t) - \rho) + \varepsilon_t$$

$$Y_t = \bar{Y}_t - \alpha((\pi_t + \rho + \theta_\pi(\pi_t - \pi_t^*) + \theta_Y(Y_t - \bar{Y}_t)) - (\pi_t + \eta_t) - \rho) + \varepsilon_t$$

$$Y_t = \bar{Y}_t - \alpha(\theta_\pi(\pi_t - \pi_t^*) + \theta_Y(Y_t - \bar{Y}_t) - \eta_t) + \varepsilon_t.$$

With a few more algebraic manipulations, you end up with the following equation for the dynamic aggregate demand curve:

$$Y_t = \bar{Y}_t - [\alpha\theta_\pi / (1 + \alpha\theta_Y)](\pi_t - \pi_t^*) + [\alpha / (1 + \alpha\theta_Y)]\eta_t + [1 / (1 + \alpha\theta_Y)]\varepsilon_t.$$

b. If η_t is greater than zero for one period only, then the dynamic aggregate demand curve will shift to the right and the dynamic aggregate supply curve will not shift. Note that the dynamic aggregate supply curve depends on the lagged value of this shock parameter so that it will be affected in period $t + 1$. As the dynamic aggregate demand curve shifts to the right, output and inflation will both rise. Based on the central bank's monetary policy rule, nominal and real interest rates will both increase. Intuitively, if people expect inflation to be higher next year, then they will increase purchases today to take advantage of the still-lower prices.

c. In period $t + 1$, the dynamic aggregate demand curve will shift back to its original position (because η_{t+1} is zero), and the dynamic aggregate supply curve will shift to the left (because η_t is positive and also because lagged inflation has increased). In comparison to long-run equilibrium, output will be lower and inflation will be higher. The economy is experiencing stagflation. Inflation is higher because of higher expectations of inflation, and output is lower because of the higher real interest rates that resulted from higher inflation.

d. In subsequent time periods, the dynamic aggregate supply curve will slowly shift back to its original position as the lower level of output reduces inflation, and hence expectations of future inflation. Although the parameter η_{t+1} was positive for only one time period, the dynamic aggregate supply curve does not immediately return to its original position because the short-run increase in inflation has caused expected inflation to rise above its long-run value.

e. This problem shows that inflation scares are self-fulfilling. When people believe inflation will rise, they act in such a way that inflation does actually rise, and the economy goes through a period of higher inflation.

9. Use the dynamic AD–AS model to solve for inflation as a function of only lagged inflation and the two shocks. Start with the dynamic aggregate supply curve and substitute in for Y_t using the dynamic aggregate demand curve equation as is done on line 1 below. Now, solve for inflation through a few algebraic manipulations:

$$\pi_t = \pi_{t-1} + \phi\left[\bar{Y}_t - [\alpha\theta_\pi / (1 + \alpha\theta_Y)](\pi_t - \pi_t^*) + [1 / (1 + \alpha\theta_Y)]\varepsilon_t - \bar{Y}_t\right] + \upsilon_t$$

$$\pi_t\left[1 + (\phi\alpha\theta_\pi / (1 + \alpha\theta_Y))\right] = \pi_{t-1} + (\phi\alpha\theta_Y)\pi_t^* + [\phi / (1 + \alpha\theta_Y)]\varepsilon_t + \upsilon_t$$

$$\pi_t = \frac{(1 + \alpha\theta_Y)}{(1 + \alpha\theta_Y + \phi\alpha\theta_\pi)}\pi_{t-1} + \frac{(\phi\alpha\theta_\pi)}{(1 + \alpha\theta_Y + \phi\alpha\theta_\pi)}\pi_t^* + \frac{\phi}{(1 + \alpha\theta_Y + \phi\alpha\theta_\pi)}\varepsilon_t + \frac{(1 + \alpha\theta_Y)}{(1 + \alpha\theta_Y + \phi\alpha\theta_\pi)}\upsilon_t.$$

a. A supply or demand shock will lead to an increase in current inflation. As the economy adjusts and returns to long-run equilibrium, the inflation rate will return to its target level. Note that the coefficient on the lagged inflation variable in the equation above is positive but less than 1. This means that inflation in time $t + 1$ will be less than inflation in time t, and that inflation will eventually return to its target rate.

b. If the central bank does not respond to changes in output so that θ_Y is zero, then the economy will still return to its target inflation rate after a supply or demand shock because the coefficient on the lagged inflation variable in the equation above is still positive but less than 1. In this case, inflation should return more quickly to its target rate. This is because the coefficient on lagged inflation has become smaller (the change in the numerator is larger in comparison to the change in the denominator). The dynamic aggregate demand curve is relatively flat when the central bank only cares about inflation.

c. If the central bank does not respond to changes in inflation so that θ_π is zero, then the coefficient on lagged inflation in the above inflation equation equals 1. In this case, the economy will not return to its target inflation rate after a demand or supply shock. The demand or supply shock will increase inflation in time t. When θ_π is zero, inflation in time $t + 1$ is equal to inflation in time t.

d. The Taylor rule says that a one-percentage-point increase in inflation will increase the nominal interest rate by $1 + \theta_\pi$ percentage points. If the central bank increases the nominal interest rate by only 0.8 percentage points for each one-percentage-point increase in the nominal interest rate, then this means θ_π is equal to -0.2. When θ_π is negative, the dynamic aggregate demand curve is upward sloping. A shock to demand or supply will set the economy on a path of ever-increasing inflation. This path of ever-increasing inflation will occur because real interest rates will continue to fall and output will remain above the natural level. You can see this phenomenon in the above equation for inflation: If θ_π is negative, the coefficient on lagged inflation is greater than 1. That larger-than-one coefficient is the mathematical manifestation of explosive inflation.

CHAPTER 16   Understanding Consumer Behavior

Questions for Review

1. First, Keynes conjectured that the marginal propensity to consume—the amount consumed out of an additional dollar of income—is between zero and one. This means that if an individual's income increases by a dollar, both consumption and saving increase.

   Second, Keynes conjectured that the ratio of consumption to income—called the *average propensity to consume*—falls as income rises. This implies that the rich save a higher proportion of their income than do the poor.

   Third, Keynes conjectured that income is the primary determinant of consumption. In particular, he believed that the interest rate does not have an important effect on consumption.

   A consumption function that satisfies these three conjectures is

   $$C = \overline{C} + cY.$$

   $\overline{C}$ is a constant level of "autonomous consumption," and Y is disposable income; c is the marginal propensity to consume, and is between zero and one.

2. The evidence that was consistent with Keynes's conjectures came from studies of household data and short time-series. There were two observations from household data. First, households with higher income consumed more and saved more, implying that the marginal propensity to consume is between zero and one. Second, higher-income households saved a larger fraction of their income than lower-income households, implying that the average propensity to consume falls with income.

   There were three additional observations from short time-series. First, in years when aggregate income was low, both consumption and saving were low, implying that the marginal propensity to consume is between zero and one. Second, in years with low income, the ratio of consumption to income was high, implying that the average propensity to consume falls as income rises. Third, the correlation between income and consumption seemed so strong that no variables other than income seemed important in explaining consumption.

   The first piece of evidence against Keynes's three conjectures came from the failure of "secular stagnation" to occur after World War II. Based on the Keynesian consumption function, some economists expected that as income increased over time, the saving rate would also increase; they feared that there might not be enough profitable investment projects to absorb this saving, and the economy might enter a long depression of indefinite duration. This did not happen.

   The second piece of evidence against Keynes's conjectures came from studies of long time-series of consumption and income. Simon Kuznets found that the ratio of consumption to income was stable from decade to decade; that is, the average propensity to consume did not seem to be falling over time as income increased.

3. Both the life-cycle and permanent-income hypotheses emphasize that an individual's time horizon is longer than a single year. Thus, consumption is not simply a function of current income.

   The life-cycle hypothesis stresses that income varies over a person's life; saving allows consumers to move income from those times in life when income is high to those times when it is low. The life-cycle hypothesis predicts that consumption should depend on both wealth and income, since these determine a person's lifetime resources. Hence, we expect the consumption function to look like

   $$C = \alpha W + \beta Y.$$

In the short run, with wealth fixed, we get a "conventional" Keynesian consumption function. In the long run, wealth increases, so the short-run consumption function shifts upward, as shown in Figure 16-1.

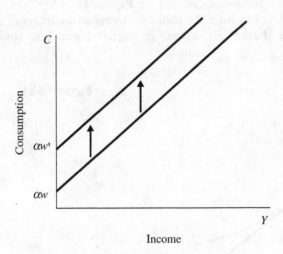

Figure 16-1

The permanent-income hypothesis also implies that people try to smooth consumption, though its emphasis is slightly different. Rather than focusing on the pattern of income over a lifetime, the permanent-income hypothesis emphasizes that people experience random and temporary changes in their income from year to year. The permanent-income hypothesis views current income as the sum of permanent income Y^p and transitory income Y^t. Milton Friedman hypothesized that consumption should depend primarily on permanent income:

$$C = \alpha Y^p.$$

The permanent-income hypothesis explains the consumption puzzle by suggesting that the standard Keynesian consumption function uses the wrong variable for income. For example, if a household has high transitory income, it will not have higher consumption; hence, if much of the variability in income is transitory, a researcher would find that high-income households had, on average, a lower average propensity to consume. This is also true in short time-series if much of the year-to-year variation in income is transitory. In long time-series, however, variations in income are largely permanent; therefore, consumers do not save any increases in income, but consume them instead.

4. Fisher's model of consumption looks at how a consumer who lives two periods will make consumption choices in order to be as well off as possible. Figure 16-2(A) shows the effect of an increase in second-period income if the consumer does not face a binding borrowing constraint. The budget constraint shifts outward, and the consumer increases consumption in both the first and the second period. In Figure 16-2(A), Y_1 is the first period income and Y_2 is second period income. In choosing to consume at point A or B, the consumer is consuming more than their income in period 1 and less than their income in period 2.

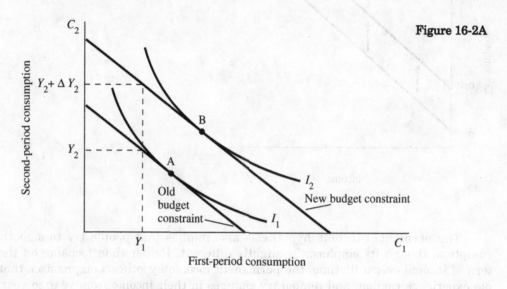

Figure 16-2A

Figure 16-2(B) shows what happens if there is a binding borrowing constraint. The consumer would like to borrow to increase first-period consumption but cannot. If income increases in the second period, the consumer is unable to increase first-period

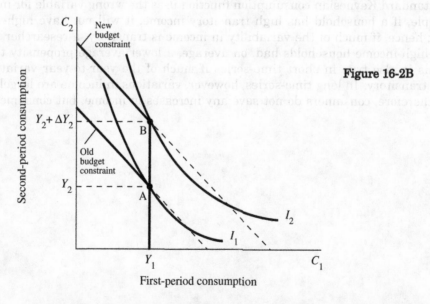

Figure 16-2B

consumption. Therefore, the consumer continues to consume his or her entire income in each period. That is, for those consumers who would like to borrow but cannot, consumption depends only on current income.

5. The permanent-income hypothesis implies that consumers try to smooth consumption over time, so that current consumption is based on current expectations about lifetime income. It follows that changes in consumption reflect "surprises" about lifetime income. If consumers have rational expectations, then these surprises are unpredictable. Hence, consumption changes are also unpredictable.

6. Section 16.6 included several examples of time-inconsistent behavior, in which consumers alter their decisions simply because time passes. For example, a person may legitimately want to lose weight, but decide to eat a large dinner today and eat a small dinner tomorrow and thereafter. But the next day, they may once again make the same choice—eating a large dinner that day while promising to eat less on following days.

Problems and Applications

1. Figure 16-3 shows the effect of an increase in the interest rate on a consumer who borrows in the first period. The increase in the real interest rate causes the budget line to rotate around the point (Y_1, Y_2), becoming steeper.

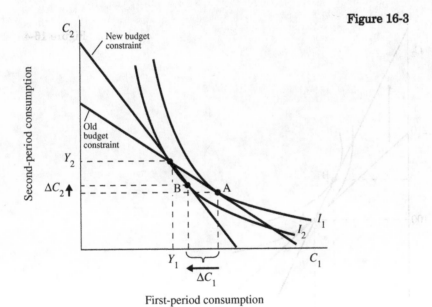

Figure 16-3

We can break the effect on consumption from this change into an income and substitution effect. The income effect is the change in consumption that results from the movement to a different indifference curve. Because the consumer is a borrower, the increase in the interest rate makes the consumer worse off—that is, he or she cannot achieve as high an indifference curve. If consumption in each period is a normal good, this tends to reduce both C_1 and C_2.

The substitution effect is the change in consumption that results from the change in the relative price of consumption in the two periods. The increase in the interest rate makes second-period consumption relatively less expensive; this tends to make the consumer choose more consumption in the second period and less consumption in the first period.

On net, we find that for a borrower, first-period consumption falls unambiguously when the real interest rate rises, since both the income and substitution effects push in the same direction. Second-period consumption might rise or fall, depending on which effect is stronger. In Figure 16-3, we show the case in which the substitution effect is stronger than the income effect, so that C_2 increases.

2. a.   We can use Jill's intertemporal budget constraint to solve for the interest rate:

$$C_1 + \frac{C_2}{1+r} = Y_1 + \frac{Y_2}{1+r}$$

$$\$100 + \frac{\$100}{1+r} = \$0 + \frac{\$210}{1+r}$$

$$r = 10\%.$$

Jill borrowed $100 for consumption in the first period and in the second period used her $210 income to pay $110 on the loan (principal plus interest) and $100 for consumption.

b.   The rise in interest rates leads Jack to consume less today and more tomorrow. This is because of the substitution effect: it costs him more to consume today than tomorrow, because of the higher opportunity cost in terms of forgone interest. This is shown in Figure 16-4.

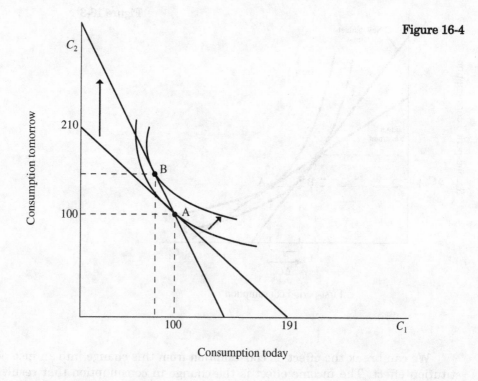

Figure 16-4

By revealed preference we know Jack is better off: at the new interest rate he could still consume $100 in each period, so the only reason he would change his consumption pattern is if the change makes him better off.

c.   Jill consumes less today, while her consumption tomorrow can either rise or fall. She faces both a substitution effect and income effect. Because consumption today is more expensive, she substitutes out of it. Also, since all her income is in the second period, the higher interest rate raises her cost of borrowing and, thus, lowers her income. Assuming consumption in period one is a normal good, this provides an additional incentive for lowering it. Her new consumption choice is at point B in Figure 16-5.

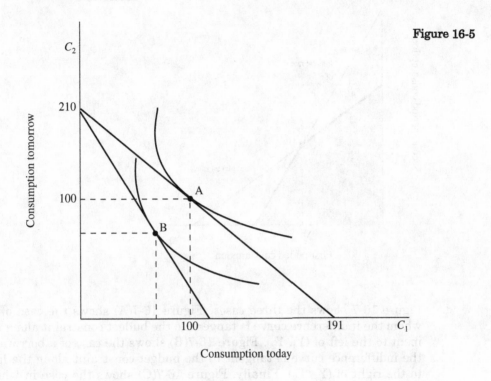

Figure 16-5

We know Jill is worse off with the higher interest rates because she could have consumed at point B before (by not spending all of her second-period money) but chose not to because point A had higher utility.

3. a.   A consumer who consumes less than his income in period one is a saver and faces an interest rate r_s. His budget constraint is

$$C_1 + C_2/(1 + r_s) = Y_1 + Y_2/(1 + r_s).$$

b.   A consumer who consumes more than income in period one is a borrower and faces an interest rate r_b. The budget constraint is

$$C_1 + C_2/(1 + r_b) = Y_1 + Y_2/(1 + r_b).$$

c.   Figure 16-6 shows the two budget constraints; they intersect at the point (Y_1, Y_2), where the consumer is neither a borrower nor a lender. The shaded area represents the combinations of first-period and second-period consumption that the consumer can choose. To the left of the point (Y_1, Y_2), the interest rate is r_b.

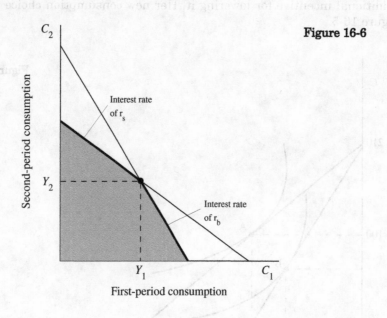

Figure 16-6

d.   Figure 16-7 shows the three cases. Figure 16-7(A) shows the case of a saver for whom the indifference curve is tangent to the budget constraint along the line segment to the left of (Y_1, Y_2). Figure 16-7(B) shows the case of a borrower for whom the indifference curve is tangent to the budget constraint along the line segment to the right of (Y_1, Y_2). Finally, Figure 16-7(C) shows the case in which the consumer is neither a borrower nor a lender: the highest indifference curve the consumer can reach is the one that passes through the point (Y_1, Y_2).

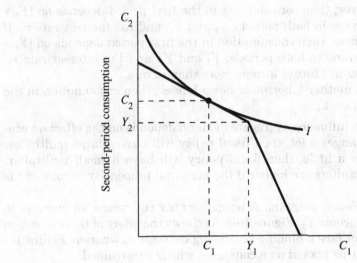

Figure 16-7A

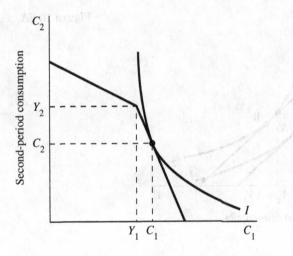

Figure 16-7B

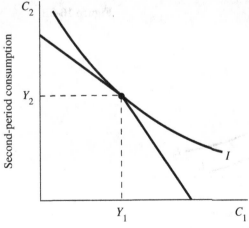

Figure 16-7C

e. If the consumer is a saver, then consumption in the first period depends on $[Y_1 + Y_2/(1 + r_s)]$—that is, income in both periods, Y_1 and Y_2, and the interest rate r_s. If the consumer is a borrower, then consumption in the first period depends on $[Y_1 + Y_2/(1 + r_b)]$—that is, income in both periods, Y_1 and Y_2, and the interest rate r_b. Note that borrowers discount future income more than savers.

If the consumer is neither a borrower nor a lender, then consumption in the first period depends just on Y_1.

4. The potency of fiscal policy to influence aggregate demand depends on the effect on consumption: if consumption changes a lot, then fiscal policy will have a large multiplier. If consumption changes only a little, then fiscal policy will have a small multiplier. That is, the fiscal-policy multipliers are higher if the marginal propensity to consume is higher.

a. Consider a two-period Fisher diagram. A temporary tax cut means an increase in first-period disposable income Y_1. Figure 16-8(A) shows the effect of this tax cut on a consumer who does not face a binding borrowing constraint, whereas Figure 16-8(B) shows the effect of this tax cut on a consumer who is constrained.

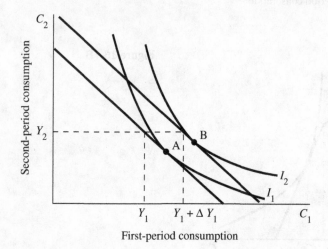

Figure 16-8A

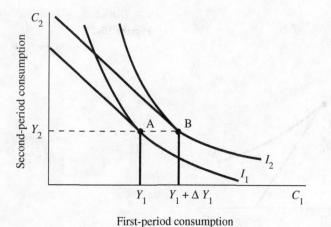

Figure 16-8B

The consumer with the constraint would have liked to get a loan to increase C_1, but could not. The temporary tax cut increases disposable income: as shown in the figure, the consumer's consumption rises by the full amount that taxes fall. The consumer who is constrained thus increases first-period consumption C_1 by more than the consumer who is not constrained—that is, the marginal propensity to consume is higher for a consumer who faces a borrowing constraint. Therefore, fiscal policy is more potent with binding borrowing constraints than it is without them.

b. Again, consider a two-period Fisher diagram. The announcement of a future tax cut increases Y_2. Figure 16-9(A) shows the effect of this tax cut on a consumer who does not face a binding borrowing constraint, whereas Figure 16-9(B) shows the effect of this tax cut on a consumer who is constrained.

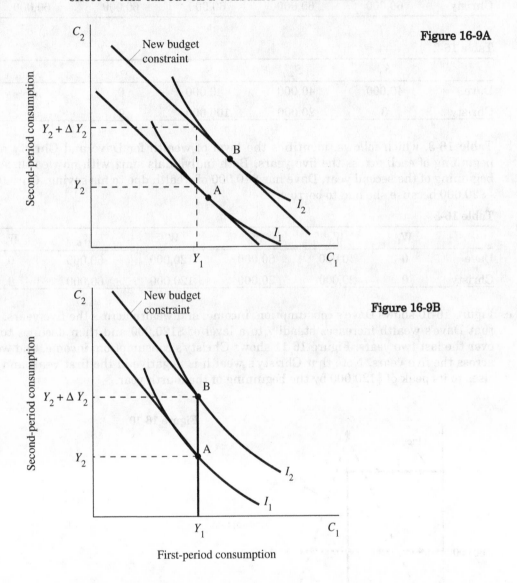

The consumer who is not constrained immediately increases consumption C_1. The consumer who is constrained cannot increase C_1, because disposable income has not changed. Therefore, the announcement of a future tax cut has no effect on consumption or aggregate demand if consumers face binding borrowing constraints: fiscal policy is less potent.

5. a. The life-cycle hypothesis states that individuals want to smooth their consumption as much as possible during their lifetime. People will add up their expected earnings and divide by the number of years they expect to live. Early in life they will save, and later in life they will dissave. Wealth will rise until they retire, and then will decline. Table 16-1, which follows, shows the consumption for Dave and Christy across five years, and Table 16-2, which follows, shows their saving across

the five years. Note that Christy saves nothing during the first year because her income is less than her consumption. In the second year, when her income rises, she consumes $60,000, pays off her debt of $20,000, and saves the remaining $20,000.

Table 16-1

	C_1	C_2	C_3	C_4	C_5
Dave	60,000	60,000	60,000	60,000	60,000
Christy	60,000	60,000	60,000	60,000	60,000

Table 16-2

	S_1	S_2	S_3	S_4	S_5
Dave	40,000	40,000	40,000	0	0
Christy	0	20,000	100,000	0	0

b. Table 16-3, which follows, identifies the level of wealth for Dave and Christy at the beginning of each across the five years. Both individuals start with no wealth. At the beginning of the second year, Dave has $40,000 of wealth due to his saving. Christy has −$20,000 because she had to borrow.

Table 16-3

	W_1	W_2	W_3	W_4	W_5	W_6
Dave	0	40,000	80,000	120,000	60,000	0
Christy	0	−20,000	20,000	120,000	60,000	0

c. Figure 16-10 shows Dave's consumption, income, and wealth across the five years. Note that Dave's wealth increases steadily to a level of $120,000 and then declines to zero over the last two years. Figure 16-11 shows Christy's consumption, income, and wealth across the five years. Note that Christy's wealth is negative in the first year, and then rises to its peak of $120,000 by the beginning of the fourth year.

Figure 16-10

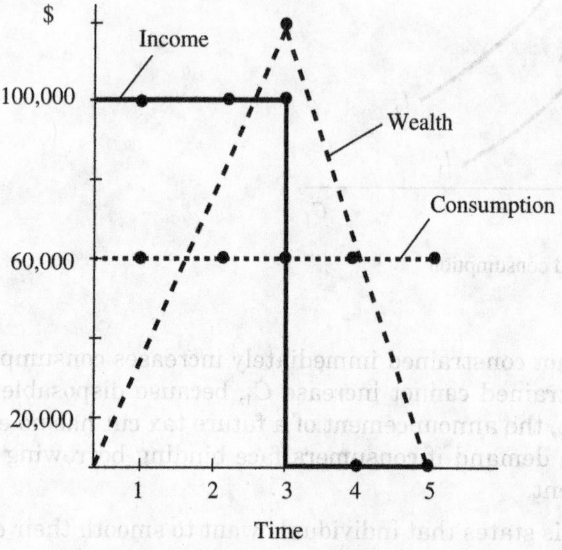

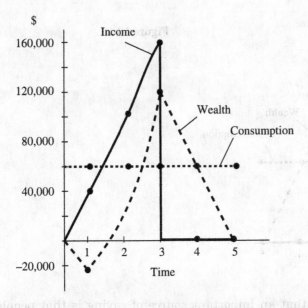

Figure 16-11

d. If there is no borrowing, then nothing changes for Dave because he never borrowed. Since Christy is unable to borrow in year 1 when her income is low, she will consume her entire income of $40,000. Her consumption in the remaining years is now higher than it was when she could borrow because her income is much higher in years 2 and 3. She spreads this higher income across the remaining 4 years and saves accordingly. Tables 16-4, 16-5, and 16-6, which follow, identify Dave's and Christy's consumption, saving, and wealth when there is no borrowing across the five years. Figure 16-12, which follows, illustrates Christy's new consumption, income, and wealth levels across the five years.

Table 16-4

	C_1	C_2	C_3	C_4	C_5
Dave	60,000	60,000	60,000	60,000	60,000
Christy	40,000	65,000	65,000	65,000	65,000

Table 16-5

	S_1	S_2	S_3	S_4	S_5
Dave	40,000	40,000	40,000	0	0
Christy	0	35,000	95,000	0	0

Table 16-6

	W_1	W_2	W_3	W_4	W_5	W_6
Dave	0	40,000	80,000	120,000	60,000	0
Christy	0	0	35,000	130,000	65,000	0

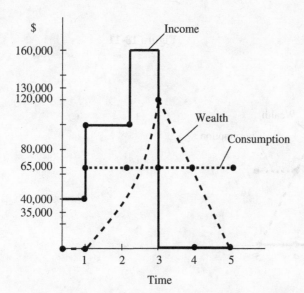

Figure 16-12

6. The life-cycle model predicts that an important source of saving is that people save while they work to finance consumption after they retire. That is, the young save, and the old dissave. If the fraction of the population that is elderly will increase over the next 20 years, the life-cycle model predicts that as these elderly retire, they will begin to dissave their accumulated wealth in order to finance their retirement consumption: thus, the national saving rate should fall over the next 20 years.

7. a. In this chapter, we discussed two explanations for why the elderly do not dissave as rapidly as the life-cycle model predicts. First, because of the possibility of unpredictable and costly events, they may keep some precautionary saving as a buffer in case they live longer than expected or have large medical bills. Second, they may want to leave bequests to their children, relatives, or charities, so again, they do not dissave all of their wealth during retirement.

   b. If the elderly who do not have children dissave at the same rate as the elderly who do have children, this seems to imply that the reason for low dissaving is the precautionary motive; the bequest motive is presumably stronger for people who have children than for those who don't. An alternative interpretation is that perhaps having children does not increase desired saving. For example, having children raises the bequest motive, but it may also lower the precautionary motive: you can rely on your children in case of financial emergency. Perhaps the two effects on saving cancel each other.

8. a. If you are a fully rational and time-consistent consumer, you would certainly prefer the saving account that lets you take the money out on demand. After all, you get the same return on that account, but in unexpected circumstances (e.g., if you suffer an unexpected, temporary decline in income), you can use the funds in the account to finance your consumption.

   b. By contrast, if you face the "pull of instant gratification," you may prefer the account that requires a 30-day notification before withdrawals. In this way, you precommit yourself to not using the funds to satisfy a desire for instant gratification. This precommitment offers a way to overcome the time-inconsistency problem. That is, some people would like to save more, but at any particular moment, they face such a strong desire for instant gratification that they always choose to consume rather than save.

   c. If you prefer the account that lets you take money out on demand, then you are the type of consumer described by the models of Irving Fisher, Franco Modigliani, and Milton Friedman. If you prefer the account that requires 30-day notice to withdraw funds, then you are the type of consumer described by the model of David Laibson.

9. a. According to Fisher's model, consumers allocate their income across time periods so that the marginal rate of substitution between consumption in any two periods is equal to $1 + r$, where r is the real interest rate. In this problem, the real interest rate is zero. The marginal rate of substitution is the ratio of the marginal utilities in any two periods. To find the marginal utility, differentiate the utility function with respect to C_i to find $MU_i = 1/C_i$. For time periods 1 and 2, we find:

$$\frac{1/C_1}{1/C_2} = 1$$
$$C_1 = C_2$$

For time periods 2 and 3, we find:

$$\frac{1/C_2}{1/C_3} = 1$$
$$C_2 = C_3$$

Therefore, $C_1 = C_2 = C_3 = \$40,000$.

b. David also sets his marginal rate of substitution between any two periods equal to 1. For time periods 1 and 2, we find:

$$\frac{2/C_1}{1/C_2} = 1$$
$$C_1 = 2C_2$$

For time periods 2 and 3, we find:

$$\frac{1/C_2}{1/C_3} = 1$$
$$C_2 = C_3$$

We also know $C_1 + C_2 + C_3 = \$120,000$. Substitute in for C_1 and C_3 from the preceding equations to find $2C_2 + C_2 + C_2 = \$120,000$, such that $C_1 = \$60,000$ and $C_2 = C_3 = \$30,000$. After period 1, David has $60,000 in wealth.

c. In period 2, David now gets twice as much utility as in period 3. Following the same process as in the preceding, we find $C_2 = 2C_3$, such that David will consume $40,000 in period 2 and $20,000 in period 3. David has revised his decision from period 1 because he values present consumption twice as high as future consumption.

d. If David could constrain his choices in period 2, he would prefer to consume $30,000 in period 2 and $30,000 in period 3. Given his utility function, he prefers to consume $60,000 in year 1 and $30,000 in each of the two next years. David's preferences are an example of Laibson's pull of instant gratification model. David may know he is an imperfect decision maker, so he may prefer to constrain his future decisions.

Questions for Review

1. In the neoclassical model of business fixed investment, firms will find it profitable to add to their capital stock if the marginal product of capital is greater than the cost of capital. The cost of capital depends on the real interest rate, the depreciation rate, and the relative price of capital goods.

2. Tobin's q is the ratio of the market value of installed capital to its replacement cost. Tobin reasoned that net investment should depend on whether q is greater or less than one. If q is greater than one, then the stock market values installed capital at more than it costs to replace. This creates an incentive to invest, because managers can raise the market value of their firms' stock by buying more capital. Conversely, if q is less than one, then the stock market values installed capital at less than its replacement cost. In this case, managers will not replace capital as it wears out.

   This theory provides an alternative way to express the neoclassical model of investment. If the marginal product of capital exceeds the cost of capital, for example, then installed capital earns profits. These profits make the firms desirable to own, which raises the market value of these firms' stock, implying a high value of q. Hence, Tobin's q captures the incentive to invest because it reflects the current and expected future profitability of capital.

3. An increase in the interest rate leads to a decrease in residential investment because it reduces housing demand. Many people take out mortgages to purchase their homes, and a rise in the interest rate increases the cost of the loan. Even for people who do not borrow to buy a home, the interest rate measures the opportunity cost of holding their wealth in housing rather than putting it in the bank.

   Figure 17-1 shows the effect of an increase in the interest rate on residential investment. The higher interest rate shifts the demand curve for housing to the left, as shown in Figure 17-1(A). This causes the relative price of housing to fall, and as shown in Figure 17-1(B), the lower relative price of housing decreases residential investment.

Figure 17-1

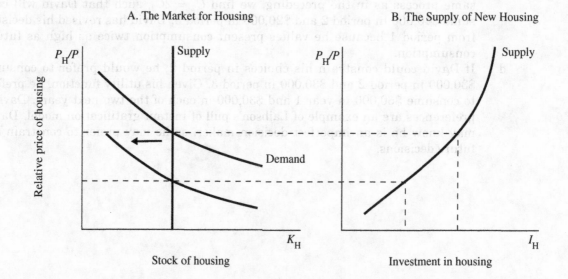

A. The Market for Housing

B. The Supply of New Housing

4. Reasons why firms might hold inventories include:
   a. **Production smoothing.** A firm may hold inventories to smooth the level of production over time. Rather than adjust production to match fluctuations in sales, it may be cheaper to produce goods at a constant rate. Hence, the firm increases inventories when sales are low and decreases them when sales are high.
   b. **Inventories as a factor of production.** Holding inventories may allow a firm to operate more efficiently. For example, a retail store may hold inventories so that it always has goods available to show customers. A manufacturing firm may hold inventories of spare parts to reduce the time an assembly line is shut down when a machine breaks.
   c. **Stock-out avoidance.** A firm may hold inventories to avoid running out of goods when sales are unexpectedly high. Firms often have to make production decisions before knowing how much customers will demand. If demand exceeds production and there are no inventories, the good will be out of stock for a period, and the firm will lose sales and profit.
   d. **Work in process.** Many goods require a number of steps in production and, therefore, take time to produce. When a product is not completely finished, its components are counted as part of a firm's inventory.

Problems and Applications

1. In answering parts (a) to (c), it is useful to recall the neoclassical investment function:

   $$I = I_n[MPK - (P_K/P)(r + \delta)] + \delta K.$$

   This equation tells us that business fixed investment depends on the marginal product of capital (MPK), the cost of capital $(P_K/P)(r + \delta)$, and the amount of depreciation of the capital stock (δK). Recall also that in equilibrium, the real rental price of capital equals the marginal product of capital.
   a. The rise in the real interest rate increases the cost of capital $(P_K/P)(r + \delta)$. Investment declines because firms no longer find it as profitable to add to their capital stock. Nothing happens immediately to the real rental price of capital, because the marginal product of capital does not change.
   b. If an earthquake destroys part of the capital stock, then the marginal product of capital rises because of diminishing marginal product. Hence, the real rental price of capital increases. Because the MPK rises relative to the cost of capital (which does not change), firms find it profitable to increase investment.
   c. If an immigration of foreign workers increases the size of the labor force, then the marginal product of capital and, hence, the real rental price of capital increase. Because the MPK rises relative to the cost of capital (which does not change), firms find it profitable to increase investment.
   d. Advances in computer technology that cause production to be more efficient will increase the marginal product of capital. The result will be an increase the real rental price of capital and investment. The cost of capital will not change.

2. Recall the equation for business fixed investment:

   $$I = I_n[MPK - (P_K/P)(r + \delta)] + \delta K.$$

   This equation tells us that business fixed investment depends on the marginal product of capital, the cost of capital, and the amount of depreciation of the capital stock.

   A one-time tax levied on oil reserves does not affect the MPK: the oil companies must pay the tax no matter how much capital they have. Because neither the benefit of owning capital (the MPK) nor the cost of capital are changed by the tax, investment does not change either.

   If the firm faces financing constraints, however, then the amount it invests depends on the amount it currently earns. Because the tax reduces current earnings, it also reduces investment.

3. a. There are several reasons why investment might depend on national income. First, from the neoclassical model of business fixed investment we know that an increase in employment increases the marginal product of capital. Hence, if national income is high because employment increases, then the MPK is high, and firms have an incentive to invest. Second, if firms face financing constraints, then an increase in current profits increases the amount that firms are able to invest. Third, increases in income raise housing demand, which increases the price of housing and, therefore, the level of residential investment. Fourth, the accelerator model of inventories implies that when output rises, firms wish to hold more inventories; this may be because inventories are a factor of production or because firms wish to avoid stock-outs.

   b. In the Keynesian cross model of Chapter 11, we assumed that $I = \bar{I}$. We found the government-purchases multiplier by considering an increase in government expenditure of ΔG. The immediate effect is an increase in income of ΔG. This increase in income causes consumption to rise by $MPC \times \Delta G$. This increase in consumption increases expenditure and income once again. This process continues indefinitely, so the ultimate effect on income is

$$\Delta Y = \Delta G[1 + mpc + mpc^2 + mpc^3 + \dots]$$
$$= (1/(1 - MPC))\Delta G.$$

Hence, the government spending multiplier we found in Chapter 11 is

$$\Delta Y/\Delta G = 1/(1 - MPC).$$

Now suppose that investment also depends on income, so that $I = \bar{I} + aY$. As before, an increase in government expenditure by ΔG initially increases income by ΔG. This initial increase in income causes consumption to rise by $MPC \times \Delta G$; now, it also causes investment to increase by $a \times \Delta G$. This increase in consumption and investment increases expenditure and income once again. The process continues until

$$\Delta Y = \Delta G[1 + (mpc + a) + (mpc + a)^2 + (mpc + a)^3 + \dots]$$
$$= (1/(1 - MPC - a))\Delta G.$$

Hence, the government-purchases multiplier becomes

$$\Delta Y/\Delta G = 1/(1 - MPC - a).$$

Proceeding the same way, we find that the tax multiplier becomes

$$\Delta Y/\Delta T = - MPC/(1 - MPC - a).$$

Note that the fiscal-policy multipliers are larger when investment depends on income.

c. The government-purchases multiplier in the Keynesian cross tells us how output responds to a change in government purchases, for a given interest rate. Therefore, it tells us how much the *IS* curve shifts out in response to a change in government purchases. If investment depends on both income and the interest rate, then we found in part (b) that the multiplier is larger, so that we know the *IS* curve shifts out farther than it does if investment depends on the interest rate alone. This is shown in Figure 17-2 by the shift from IS_1 to IS_2.

Figure 17-2

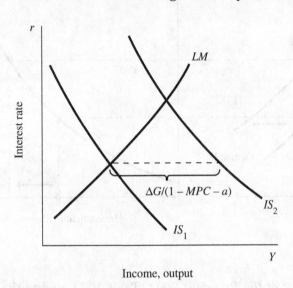

From the figure, it is clear that national income and the interest rate increase. Since income is higher, consumption is higher as well. We cannot tell whether investment rises or falls: the higher interest rate tends to make investment fall, whereas the higher national income tends to make investment rise.

In the standard model where investment depends only on the interest rate, an increase in government purchases unambiguously causes investment to fall. That is, government purchases "crowd out" investment. In this model, an increase in government purchases might instead increase investment in the short run through the temporary expansion in Y.

4. A stock market crash implies that the market value of installed capital falls. Tobin's q—the ratio of the market value of installed capital to its replacement cost—also falls. This causes investment and hence aggregate demand to fall.

   If the Fed seeks to keep output unchanged, it can offset this aggregate-demand shock by running an expansionary monetary policy.

5. If managers think the opposition candidate might win, they may postpone some investments that they are considering. If they wait, and the opposition candidate is elected, then the investment tax credit reduces the cost of their investment. Hence, the campaign promise to implement an investment tax credit next year causes current investment to fall. This fall in investment reduces current aggregate demand and output: the recession deepens.

   Note that this deeper recession makes it more likely that voters vote for the opposition candidate instead of the incumbent, making it more likely that the opposition candidate wins.

6. a. In the 1970s, the baby-boom generation reached adulthood and started forming their own households. This implies that in our model of residential investment, demand for housing rose. As shown in Figure 17-3, this causes housing prices and residential investment to rise.

Figure 17-3

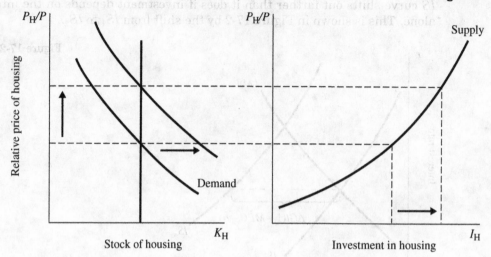

b. The *Economic Report of the President 2009* (Table B–7) reports that in 1970, the real price of housing—the ratio of the residential investment deflator to the GDP deflator—was 21.53/27.54, or 0.78. In 1980, this ratio had risen to 51.39/54.06, or 0.95. Thus, between 1970 and 1980 the real price of housing rose 22 percent. This finding is consistent with the prediction of our model.

7. Consider the Solow growth model from Chapters 8 and 9. The Solow model shows that the saving rate is a key determinant of the steady-state capital stock. If the tax laws encourage investment in housing but discourage investment in business capital, this implies that the fraction of output devoted to business investment is lower because of the tax consequences. Figure 17-4 shows the outcome of the Solow model for low and high saving rates. At the lower saving rate, business capital-per-worker and business output-per-worker is also lower. Thus, the tax system distorts the economy's choice of business output versus housing.

   An alternative way to see this effect is to think of the labor market. With less capital for each worker, the marginal product of labor is lower. Hence, in the long run, the real wage of workers is lower because of the distortions of the tax system.

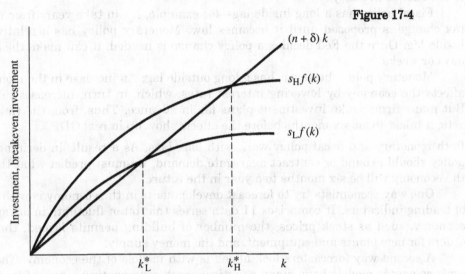

Figure 17-4

CHAPTER 18 Alternative Perspectives on Stabilization Policy

Questions for Review

1. The inside lag is the time it takes for policymakers to recognize that a shock has hit the economy and to put the appropriate policies into effect. Once a policy is in place, the outside lag is the amount of time it takes for the policy action to influence the economy. This lag arises because it takes time for spending, income, and employment to respond to the change in policy.

    Fiscal policy has a long inside lag—for example, it can take years from the time a tax change is proposed until it becomes law. Monetary policy has a relatively short inside lag. Once the Fed decides a policy change is needed, it can make the change in days or weeks.

    Monetary policy, however, has a long outside lag. An increase in the money supply affects the economy by lowering interest rates, which, in turn, increases investment. But many firms make investment plans far in advance. Thus, from the time the Fed acts, it takes about six months before the effects show up in real GDP.

2. Both monetary and fiscal policy work with long lags. As a result, in deciding whether policy should expand or contract aggregate demand, we must predict what the state of the economy will be six months to a year in the future.

    One way economists try to forecast developments in the economy is with the index of leading indicators. It comprises 11 data series that often fluctuate in advance of the economy, such as stock prices, the number of building permits issued, the value of orders for new plants and equipment, and the money supply.

    A second way forecasters look ahead is with models of the economy. These large-scale computer models have many equations, each representing a part of the economy. Once we make assumptions about the path of the exogenous variables—taxes, government spending, the money supply, the price of oil, and so forth—the models yield predictions about the paths of unemployment, inflation, output, and other endogenous variables.

3. The way people respond to economic policies depends on their expectations about the future. These expectations depend on many things, including the economic policies that the government pursues. The Lucas critique of economic policy argues that traditional methods of policy evaluation do not adequately take account of the way policy affects expectations.

    For example, the sacrifice ratio—the number of percentage points of GDP that must be forgone to reduce inflation by 1 percentage point—depends on individuals' expectations of inflation. We cannot simply assume that these expectations will remain constant, or will adjust only slowly, no matter what policies the government pursues; instead, these expectations will depend on what the Fed does.

4. A person's view of macroeconomic history affects his or her view of whether macroeconomic policy should play an active role or a passive role. If one believes that the economy has experienced many large shocks to aggregate supply and aggregate demand, and if policy has successfully insulated the economy from these shocks, then the case for active policy is clear. Conversely, if one believes that the economy has experienced few large shocks, and if the fluctuations we observe can be traced to inept economic policy, then the case for passive policy is clear.

5. The problem of time inconsistency arises because expectations of future policies affect how people act today. As a result, policymakers may want to announce today the policy they intend to follow in the future, in order to influence the expectations held by private decisionmakers. Once these private decisionmakers have acted on their expectations, the policymakers may be tempted to renege on their announcement.

   For example, your professor has an incentive to announce that there will be a final exam in your course, so that you study and learn the material. On the morning of the exam, when you have already studied and learned all the material, the professor might be tempted to cancel the exam so that he or she does not have to grade it.

   Similarly, the government has an incentive to announce that it will not negotiate with terrorists. If terrorists believe that they have nothing to gain by kidnapping hostages, then they will not do so. However, once hostages are kidnapped, the government faces a strong temptation to negotiate and make concessions.

   In monetary policy, suppose the Fed announces a policy of low inflation, and everyone believes the announcement. The Fed then has an incentive to raise inflation, because it faces a favorable tradeoff between inflation and unemployment.

   The problem with situations in which time inconsistency arises is that people are led to distrust policy announcements. Then students do not study for their exams, terrorists kidnap hostages, and the Fed faces an unfavorable tradeoff. In these situations, a rule that commits the policymaker to a particular policy can sometimes help the policymaker achieve his or her goals—students study, terrorists do not take hostages, and inflation remains low.

6. One policy rule that the Fed might follow is to allow the money supply to grow at a constant rate. Monetarist economists believe that most large fluctuations in the economy result from fluctuations in the money supply; hence, a rule of steady money growth would prevent these large fluctuations.

   A second policy rule is a nominal GDP target. Under this rule, the Fed would announce a planned path for nominal GDP. If nominal GDP were below this target, for example, the Fed would increase money growth to stimulate aggregate demand. An advantage of this policy rule is that it would allow monetary policy to adjust to changes in the velocity of money.

   A third policy rule is an inflation target. The Fed would announce a target for the inflation rate and adjust the money supply when actual inflation deviated from its target. This rule helps insulate the economy from changes in velocity and is easy to explain to the public.

Problems and Applications

1. Suppose the economy has a Phillips curve

$$u = u^n - \alpha(\pi - E\pi).$$

As usual, this implies that if inflation is lower than expected, then unemployment rises above its natural rate, and there is a recession. Similarly, if inflation is higher than expected, then unemployment falls below its natural rate, and there is a boom. Also, suppose that the Democratic party always follows a policy of high money growth and high inflation (call it π^D), whereas the Republican party always follows a policy of low money growth and low inflation (call it π^R).

a. The pattern of the political business cycle we observe depends on the inflation rate people expect at the beginning of each term. If expectations are perfectly rational and contracts can be adjusted immediately when a new party comes into power, then there will be no political business cycle pattern to unemployment. For example, if the Democrats win the coin flip, people immediately expect high inflation. Because $\pi = \pi^D = E\pi$, the Democrats' monetary policy will have no effect on the real economy. We do observe a political business cycle pattern to inflation, in which Democrats have high inflation and Republicans have low inflation.

Now suppose that contracts are long enough that nominal wages and prices cannot be adjusted immediately. Before the result of the coin flip is known, there is a 50-percent chance that inflation will be high and a 50-percent chance that inflation will be low. Thus, at the beginning of each term, if people's expectations are rational, they expect an inflation rate of

$$E\pi = 0.5\pi^D + 0.5\pi^R.$$

If Democrats win the coin toss, then $\pi > \pi^e$ initially, and unemployment falls below its natural rate. Hence, there is a boom at the beginning of Democratic terms. Over time, inflation rises to π^D, and unemployment returns to its natural rate.

If Republicans win, then inflation is lower than expected, and unemployment rises above its natural rate. Hence, there is a recession at the beginning of Republican terms. Over time, inflation falls to π^R, and unemployment returns to its natural rate.

b. If the two parties take turns, then there will be no political business cycle to unemployment, since everyone knows which party will be in office, so everyone knows whether inflation will be high or low. Even long-lasting contracts will take the actual inflation rate into account, since all future inflation rates are known with certainty. Inflation will alternate between a high level and a low level, depending on which party is in power.

c. The advantage of having an independent central bank set monetary policy is that this bypasses the political business cycle. If elected officials are responsible for setting monetary policy, then they can in theory use policy to their advantage and randomly or arbitrarily set policy in order to help themselves get reelected. If the two parties in this example agree to take turns setting policy, then the result will be some of the same advantages of having monetary policy set by an independent central bank. By taking turns, people know exactly what to expect and so can plan and act accordingly. Inflation will still alternate between a high level and a low level, but it would be predictable and therefore less costly. An independent central bank would have the added advantage of being able at least in theory to always maintain a low and stable inflation rate.

2. There is a time-inconsistency problem with an announcement that new buildings will be exempt from rent-control laws. Before new housing is built, a city has an incentive to promise this exemption: landlords then expect to receive high rents from the new housing they provide. Once the new housing has been built, however, a city has an incentive to renege on its promise not to extend rent control. That way, many tenants gain while a few landlords lose. The problem is that builders might expect the city to renege on its promise; as a result, they may not build new buildings.

3. a. If the central bank commits to a target 5-percent inflation rate, then the expected inflation rate will be equal to 5 percent. If it follows through and actual inflation is equal to 5 percent, then the unemployment rate will be 5 percent. Plugging these values into the loss function results in a loss of 6.25.

b. If the central bank commits to a target zero inflation rate, then the expected inflation rate will be equal to 0 percent. If it follows through and actual inflation is equal to 0 percent, then the unemployment rate will be 5 percent. Plugging these values into the loss function results in a loss of 5.

c. The zero inflation rate target results in a smaller loss, so this would be the better choice.

d. If the central bank commits to a target zero inflation rate, then the expected inflation rate will be equal to 0 percent. If it does not follow through and actual inflation is equal to 5 percent, then the unemployment rate will be 2.5 percent. Plugging these values into the loss function results in a loss of 3.75.

e. This example illustrates the problem of time inconsistency. The central bank may want to announce a zero inflation rate target so that people will form their expectations based on this announced target. Later, the central bank may be tempted to change this policy and allow higher inflation so that the unemployment rate will fall. If the central bank does this frequently, then its announcements will no longer be credible.

4. The Federal Reserve Web site (www.federalreserve.gov) has many items that are relevant to a macroeconomics course. For example, following the links to "Monetary Policy" (http://www.federalreserve.gov/policy.htm) take you to material from the Federal Open Market Committee meetings and to testimony given by the Federal Reserve Chairman twice a year to Congress. Other links take you to speeches or testimony by the Chairman or members of the Board of Governors of the Federal Reserve System. Note that the web site also contains many items that are not related to macroeconomics. (For example, if you check the "Press Release" link on the web site, you are likely to find many items that concern regulatory matters, since the Federal Reserve plays an important role in regulating the banking system.)

More Problems and Applications to Chapter 18

1. a. In the model so far, nothing happens to the inflation rate when the natural rate of unemployment changes.

   b. The new loss function is

   $$L(u, \pi) = u^2 + \gamma\pi^2.$$

   The first step is to solve for the Fed's choice of inflation, for any given inflationary expectations. Substituting the Phillips curve into the loss function, we find:

   $$L(u, \pi) = [u^n - \alpha(\pi - E\pi)]^2 + \gamma\pi^2.$$

   We now differentiate with respect to inflation π, and set this first-order condition equal to zero:

   $$dL/d\pi = 2\alpha^2(\pi - E\pi) - 2\alpha u^n + 2\gamma\pi = 0$$

   or,

   $$\pi = (\alpha^2 E\pi + \alpha u^n)/(\alpha^2 + \gamma).$$

   Of course, rational agents understand that the Fed will choose this level of inflation. Expected inflation equals actual inflation, so the above equation simplifies to:

   $$\pi = \alpha u^n/\gamma.$$

   c. When the natural rate of unemployment rises, the inflation rate also rises. Why? The Fed's dislike for a marginal increase in unemployment now rises as unemployment rises. Hence, private agents know that the Fed has a greater incentive to inflate when the natural rate is higher. Hence, the equilibrium inflation rate also rises.

   d. Appointing a conservative central banker means that γ rises. Hence, the equilibrium inflation rate falls. What happens to unemployment depends on how quickly inflationary expectations adjust. If they adjust immediately, then there is no change in unemployment, which remains at the natural rate. If expectations adjust slowly, however, then, from the Phillips curve, the fall in inflation causes unemployment to rise above the natural rate.

CHAPTER **19**   Government Debt and Budget Deficits

Questions for Review

1. What is unusual about U.S. fiscal policy since 1980 is that government debt increased sharply during a period of peace and prosperity. Over the course of U.S. history, the indebtedness of the federal government relative to GDP has varied substantially. Historically, the debt–GDP ratio generally increased sharply during major wars and fell slowly during peacetime. The 1980s and 1990s are the only instance in U.S. history of a large increase in the debt–GDP ratio during peacetime.

2. Many economists project increasing budget deficits and government debt over the next several decades because of changes in the age profile of the population. Life expectancy has steadily increased, and birth rates have fallen. As a result, the elderly are becoming a larger share of the population. As more people become eligible for "entitlements" of Social Security and Medicare, government spending will rise automatically over time. Without changes in tax and expenditure policies, government debt will also rise sharply.

3. Standard measures of the budget deficit are imperfect measures of fiscal policy for at least four reasons. First, they do not correct for the effects of inflation. The measured deficit should equal the change in the government's real debt, not the change in the nominal debt. Second, such measures do not offset changes in government liabilities with changes in government assets. To measure the government's overall indebtedness, we should subtract government assets from government debt. Hence, the budget deficit should be measured as the change in debt minus the change in assets. Third, standard measures omit some liabilities altogether, such as the pensions of government workers and accumulated future Social Security benefits. Fourth, they do not correct for the effects of the business cycle.

4. Public saving is the difference between taxes and government purchases, so a debt-financed tax cut reduces public saving by the full amount that taxes fall. The tax cut also increases disposable income. According to the traditional view, since the marginal propensity to consume is between zero and one, both consumption and private saving increase. Because consumption rises, private saving increases by less than the amount of the tax cut. National saving is the sum of public and private saving; because public saving falls by more than private saving increases, national saving falls.

5. According to the Ricardian view, a debt-financed tax cut does not stimulate consumption because it does not raise permanent income—forward-looking consumers understand that government borrowing today means higher taxes in the future. Because the tax cut does not change consumption, households save the extra disposable income to pay for the future tax liability that the tax cut implies: private saving increases by the full amount of the tax cut. This increase in private saving exactly offsets the decrease in public saving associated with the tax cut. Therefore, the tax cut has no effect on national saving.

6. Which view of government debt you hold depends on how you think consumers behave. If you hold the traditional view, then you believe that a debt-financed tax cut stimulates consumer spending and lowers national saving. You might believe this for several reasons. First, consumers may be shortsighted or irrational, so that they think their permanent income has increased even though it has not. Second, consumers may face binding borrowing constraints, so that they are only able to consume their current income. Third, consumers may expect that the implied tax liability will fall on future

generations, and these consumers may not care enough about their children to leave them a bequest to offset this tax liability.

If you hold the Ricardian view, then you believe that the preceding objections are not important. In particular, you believe that consumers have the foresight to see that government borrowing today implies future taxes to be levied on them or their descendants. Hence, a debt-financed tax cut gives consumers transitory income that eventually will be taken back. As a result, consumers will save the extra income they receive in order to offset that future tax liability.

7. A budget deficit might be good policy for the following reasons. First, it can help stabilize the economy if output is below full employment. Second, it can allow the country to keep tax rates relatively smooth despite fluctuations in government spending (e.g., temporary wars) or in output (namely, in recessions). Third, it can shift a tax burden from current to future generations. For example, some expenditures might benefit future generations, and some economists argue that those generations should bear some of the costs of financing the expenditures.

8. The level of government debt might affect the government's incentives regarding money creation because the government debt is specified in nominal terms. A higher price level reduces the real value of the government's debt. Hence, a high level of debt might encourage the government to print money in order to raise the price level and reduce the real value of its debt.

Problems and Applications

1. The budget deficit is defined as government purchases minus government revenues. Selling the Liberty Bell to Taco Bell would raise revenue for the U.S. government and, hence, reduce the deficit. A smaller budget deficit would lead the government to borrow less, and as a result the measured national debt would fall.

   If the United States adopted capital budgeting, the net national debt would be defined as the assets of the government (its schools, armies, parks, and so forth) minus the liabilities of the government (principally outstanding public debt). By selling the Liberty Bell the government would be reducing its assets by the value of the Liberty Bell and reducing its liabilities by its purchase price. Assuming Taco Bell paid a fair price, these reductions would be the same amount and the net national debt would be unchanged.

   Before you worry too much about the Taco Liberty Bell, you might want to notice that this ad appeared on April Fools Day.

2. Here is one possible letter:

   Dear Senator:

   In my previous letter, I assumed that a tax cut financed by government borrowing would stimulate consumer spending. Many economists make this assumption because it seems sensible that if people had more current income, then they would consume more. As a result of this increase in consumption, national saving would fall.

   Ricardian economists argue that the seemingly sensible assumption that I made is incorrect. Although a debt-financed tax cut would increase current disposable income, it would also imply that at some point in the future, the government must raise taxes to pay off the debt and accumulated interest. As a result, the tax cut would merely give consumers a transitory increase in income that would eventually be taken back. If consumers understand this, then they would know that their permanent, or lifetime, resources had not changed. Hence, the tax cut would have no effect on consumption, and households would save all of their extra disposable income to pay for the future tax liability. Because there would be no effect on consumption, there would also be no effect on national saving.

If national saving did not change, then as pointed out by the prominent economist you heard from yesterday, the budget deficit would not have the effects I listed. In particular, output, employment, foreign debt, and interest rates would be unaffected in both the short run and the long run. The tax cut would have no effect on economic well-being.

There are several reasons the Ricardian argument may fail. First, consumers might not be rational and forward-looking: they may not fully comprehend that the current tax cut means a future tax increase. Second, some people may face constraints on their borrowing: in essence, the tax cut would give these taxpayers a loan that they are unable to obtain now. Third, consumers may expect the implied future taxes to fall not on them, but on future generations whose consumption they do not care about.

Your committee must decide how you think consumers would behave in response to this debt-financed tax cut. In particular, would they consume more, or not?

Your faithful servant,
CBO Economist.

3. a. The tax on the workers will reduce their disposable income. When their disposable income falls, they will reduce consumption by an amount that depends on their marginal propensity to consume and will reduce savings by the remaining amount. When the elderly receive the temporary benefit, they will increase their consumption by an amount that depends on their marginal propensity to consume. Since elderly people will tend to have a larger marginal propensity to consume than working people, the net effect on the economy is an increase in consumption.

   b. The answer to part (a) does depend on whether generations are altruistically linked. If generations are altruistically linked, then the elderly may not feel any better off because of the Social Security benefit, since the tax and benefit increase has no effect on a typical family's permanent income; it simply transfers resources from one generation of the family to another. If the elderly do not want to take advantage of this opportunity to consume at their children's expense, they may try to offset the effect of the tax increase on the young by giving them a gift or leaving a bequest. To the extent that this takes place, it mitigates the impact of the tax change on consumption and saving.

4. A rule requiring a cyclically adjusted balanced budget has the potential to overcome, at least partially, the first two objections to a balanced-budget rule that were raised in this chapter. First, this rule allows the government to run countercyclical fiscal policy in order to stabilize the economy. That is, the government can run deficits during recessions, when taxes automatically fall and expenditures automatically rise. These automatic stabilizers affect the deficit but not the cyclically adjusted deficit. Second, this rule allows the government to smooth tax rates across years when income is especially low or high—it is not necessary to raise tax rates in recessions or to cut them in booms.

On the other hand, this rule only partially overcomes these two objections, since the government can only run a deficit of a certain size, which might not be big enough. Also, a cyclically adjusted balanced budget does not allow the government to smooth tax rates across years when *expenditure* is especially high or low, as in times of war or peace. (We might take account of this by allowing an exemption from the balanced budget rule in special circumstances such as war.) This rule does not allow the government to overcome the third objection raised in the chapter, since the government cannot shift the burden of expenditure from one generation to another when this is warranted.

Finally, a serious problem with a rule requiring a balanced cyclically adjusted budget is that we do not directly *observe* this budget. That is, we need to estimate how far we are from full employment; then we need to estimate how expenditures and taxes would differ if we were at this full-employment level. None of these estimates can be made precisely.

5. The Congressional Budget Office (www.cbo.gov) regularly provides budget forecasts. One excellent CBO publication that summarizes these forecasts is the "The Budget and Economic Outlook." For example, in the March 2009 update of this publication, the CBO projected that the debt held by the public would rise from 41 percent of GDP at the end of 2008 to a peak of 62 percent by the end of 2011 and then decline to 56 percent at the end of 2019. Under current rules for producing baseline projections of the debt, the CBO makes several assumptions.

First, the CBO assumes that so-called discretionary government spending (items such as defense, administration, and the like, amounting to about one-third of federal spending) will grow at only the rate of inflation. Since nominal GDP generally grows faster than inflation, this implies that the CBO builds in a steady decline in discretionary government spending relative to GDP.

Second, the CBO assumes that the growth of both Medicare and Medicaid averages about 7 percent per year under the rate setting system that constrains fees paid for physician's services. But if Congress overrides these limits in the future, as it has every year since 2003, federal spending on these health programs will be much greater than projected.

Third, the CBO assumes that the taxes in the future will be whatever legislation currently says they will be (i.e., the CBO does not take a stand on what changes legislators might pass in the future).

Fourth, the CBO makes educated guesses about future potential economic growth, now projected at 2.3 percent over the next decade, and other economic indicators. As discussed in the January 2009 issue of the "Budget and Economic Outlook," the CBO justifies these assumptions by noting "CBO's baseline projections are not intended to be a forecast of future budgetary outcomes; rather, they serve as a neutral benchmark that legislators and others can use to assess the potential effects of policy decisions. As such, CBO's baseline budget projections, like its economic projections, do not incorporate potential changes in policy."

These assumptions, which serve the purpose of providing a neutral benchmark, are unlikely to hold in practice. Policymakers probably will increase real spending on discretionary programs as the economy grows over time. They may also change taxes, although the direction is harder to predict. If the United States experiences a productivity slowdown, this will reduce output growth and hence growth in tax revenue. As a consequence, future government debt likely will be somewhat different than currently projected.

Questions for Review

1. When a company raises funds by issuing bonds, this is called debt finance. The company borrows funds to buy needed capital and then repays the loan at a later date. When a company raises funds by issuing stock, this is called equity finance. The company acquires the funds it needs to by selling stock, or ownership, in its company.

2. The main advantage of holding a stock mutual fund over an individual stock is that stock mutual funds are less risky. Mutual funds are financial intermediaries that sell shares to savers and then use the funds to buy a diversified pool of assets. When you buy a small share of many different stocks, it is less risky than buying stock in only one company because the many companies in the pool are likely to be performing differently at any given time.

3. Adverse selection exists when the person who is borrowing the funds has information about her situation that is unobservable to the person who is lending the funds. Sometimes, those most eager to borrow funds possess characteristics that make them the least desirable party to lend to. Banks can reduce the problem of adverse selection by screening potential borrowers and thereby evaluating the odds that the borrower will be successful in using the funds. Moral hazard is the risk that one party to a transaction will act in a way that harms the other party. In financial markets, it exists when the borrower of the funds uses the funds in ways that do not enhance the profitability of the business. The borrower may misuse the funds and therefore earn lower profits that reduce the value of the company. Banks can reduce the problem of moral hazard by including covenants in the loan contract that effectively restrict the borrower's behavior. This form of monitoring by the bank helps guarantee that the borrowed funds are used for their intended purpose.

4. The leverage ratio is the ratio of a bank's assets to its bank capital. A leverage ratio of 20 means that the bank assets are 20 times as great as the bank capital. In this case, every \$1 of bank capital allows the bank to borrow \$19. The higher its leverage ratio, the less stable the financial institution during a time of bad economic news. For example, suppose a bank's capital is \$10 and its assets are \$200. If bad economic news reduces the value of the bank assets by 5%, this is equivalent to the \$10 of bank capital. Beyond this point, the financial institution has no funds with which to pay off future creditors.

5. During a financial crisis, it becomes difficult for consumers and firms to obtain loans and financing for new investment projects. The reduction in loans will reduce spending and the overall demand for goods and services in the economy, causing a leftward shift of the aggregate demand curve.

6. When a central bank acts as a lender of last resort, it helps to alleviate a liquidity crisis. A liquidity crisis occurs when the financial institution has insufficient funds to satisfy the claims of its creditors. In this case, if the central bank lends funds to the financial institution, the creditors' claims can be met. These actions help to restore and maintain the public's confidence in the banking system.

7. The benefit of using public funds to help prop up a financial system in crisis is that it helps to maintain confidence in the financial system. A well-functioning financial system helps to facilitate future economic growth. A problem with using public funds to rescue the financial system is that it is unfair to taxpayers since they are paying for the

mistakes of others. In addition, if the government offers a bailout, then this can lead to a moral hazard problem in the future. People may believe they can engage in risky behavior because the government will bail them out in a crisis.

Problems and Applications

1. a. This is a problem of moral hazard. Once Rick obtains the loan, he changes his behavior and does not follow through on his commitment to write the book. This problem could be dealt with by having Rick commit to a series of deadlines.

   b. This is a problem of adverse selection. David knows something about himself that the publisher does not know. David's poor score on the writing portion of the SAT may impact his ability to write a book. The problem could be dealt with by having the publisher assess David's writing ability prior to giving him the advance.

   c. This is a problem of adverse selection. Brenda knows something about her family history that the insurance company does not know. The problem could be dealt with by having the insurance company ask Brenda for a history of her family's health.

   d. This is a problem of moral hazard. Maria changes her behavior after she gets the life insurance policy. The problem could be dealt with by restricting payment under certain conditions. There could, for example, be stipulations that limit the amount paid if Maria dies while engaging in risky behavior.

2. a. Nation A will have a higher level of total factor productivity. Total factor productivity measures the effect of any change that results in the same quantity of inputs (labor and capital) yielding a higher level of output. In channeling funds from savers to borrowers, a well-functioning financial system can, all else the same, cause higher levels of economic growth. Entrepreneurs with ideas about how to improve and enhance the production process will be able to acquire needed funds if there is a well-developed financial system. Their ability to do so will lead to a higher level of total factor productivity. In a country, like Nation B, with a less-developed financial system, some good investment projects may not happen because the funds to finance them cannot be raised.

   b. The Solow growth model assumes there is only one type of capital. In this case, if the two countries have the same rates of saving, depreciation, and technological progress, then they will be converging toward the same steady state, assuming they have the same rates of population growth. The levels of output per worker, capital per worker, and the capital-output ratio will be the same between the two countries. But, if there are different types of capital, then Nation A, with the more developed financial system, will be better able to channel funds to projects that lead to higher total factor productivity. As a result, output per worker and capital per worker will be higher in Nation A.

   c. Assume the Cobb–Douglas production function is given by $Y = AL^{1-\alpha}K^{\alpha}$, where Y represents output, L is labor, K is the capital stock, and A is total factor productivity. From Chapter 3, we know that real factor prices are equal to the marginal product of the corresponding factor. Therefore,

$$MPL = (1 - \alpha)AL^{-\alpha}K^{\alpha} = W$$
$$MPK = \alpha AL^{1-\alpha}K^{\alpha-1} = R.$$

   Nation A, with its well-developed financial system, will have higher total factor productivity and therefore higher levels of the real wage and the real rental price of capital.

   d. Labor and the owners of capital both benefit from having a well-developed financial system because they earn higher income.

3. If people believe that the government will take steps to rescue firms when a financial crisis strikes, then they have an incentive to engage in relatively more risky behavior. This is the moral hazard problem. If, however, the government does not rescue the equity holders, and as a result they lose all of the assets they put into the firm, then this will solve some of the moral hazard problem. If you are an equity holder and you know the government will not bail you out in the event of a financial crisis, then you have an incentive to make sure the financial firm does not engage in overly risky behavior. A firm's creditors may also engage in overly risky behavior if they believe the government will bail them out if there is a crisis. Creditors can be overly optimistic in deciding which assets to buy. It could, for example, be argued that some buyers of mortgage-backed securities were overly confident in the return that these assets would provide. It is therefore not only the equity holders, but also the creditors that can engage in overly risky behavior.

4. The economic downturns that occurred in both the United States and Greece had similar causes. In the United States, the decline in housing prices led to a string of foreclosures and the subsequent decline in the value of the assets of many financial firms. As people lost confidence in the mortgage-backed securities, the value of these securities fell even further. The result was more stress to the financial system. In Greece, the government had been issuing sovereign debt, which for some time was perceived as risk free. When it became known that Greek debt had increased to 116 percent of GDP, people lost confidence in holding this debt. As the value of the Greek bonds fell, this pushed some financial institutions toward insolvency. In both countries, the credit rating was reduced as a result of the financial crisis, though the reduction in Greece's credit rating was much more severe than that of the United States. The financial crisis that occurred in both countries resulted in reduced expenditure and, therefore, reduced output.

A difference between the two situations involves which party or parties in each country was responsible for the financial crisis. In Greece, the financial crisis was a result of the government's actions, whereas in the United States it was the result of the actions of private financial firms. Also, the increase in government debt in Greece was a cause of the financial crisis, whereas in the United States the increase in government debt was a result of efforts to help alleviate the crisis. In addition, the two nations had different policy options available to deal with their respective crises because the United States controls its own monetary policy, while Greece does not because they are part of the European Union. The Federal Reserve in the United States has been able to use monetary policy to help control the severity of the crisis by, for example, buying up many of the financial assets that had been losing value. Greece's only option has been to appeal to the European Union for help in resolving its financial crisis, through loans and/or debt forgiveness.

Answers to Selected
Student Guide Problems*

*Note to instructors: The answers to most of the data questions were taken from the *2012 Economic Report of the President*, which is available at http://www.gpoaccess.gov/eop/ and at http://www.gpo.gov/fdsys/. Some of the data for 2011 are preliminary and may be revised in later publications.

Data Questions

1. a. The following preliminary data may be revised in future publications.

   Table 2-7

(1)	(2)
Gross Domestic Product	$15,088 billion
EQUALS	
Consumption	$10,723
+Investment	$ 1,914
+Government Purchases of Goods and Services	$ 3,030
+Exports	$ 2,087
–Imports	$ 2,660

   b. GDP = $10,723 + $1,914 + $3,030 + $2,087 – $2,660 = $15,088 (billion)

2. a. **Table 2-8**

(1) Year	(2) CPI	(3) % Change in CPI from Preceding Year	(4) GDP Deflator	(5) % Change in GDP Deflator from Preceding Year
2007	207.34		106.23	
		3.8		2.2
2008	215.30		108.58	

   b. Imported oil is not part of U.S. GDP. Therefore, it is not included in the calculation of the GDP deflator, although it is included in the calculation of the CPI when it is purchased by consumers. Because the United States imports, rather than produces, a large portion of the oil households consume, the oil price increase had a greater effect on the CPI than on the GDP deflator in 2007–2008.

3. a. **Table 2-9**

(1) Year	(2) Real GDP ($ in billions)	(3) Total U.S. Population (in millions)	(4) Real GDP per Capita	(5) % Change in Real GDP per Capita from Preceding Decade
1981	5,982	230	$26,009	
				21.7
1991	8,008	253	$31,652	
				25.7
2001	11,338	285	$39,782	
				7.3
2011	13,313	312	$42,670	

   b. U.S. real GDP per capita grew the fastest from 1991 to 2001; it grew the slowest from 2001 to 2011.

4. a. and c.

Table 2-10

(1) Year	(2) GDP Deflator (P)	(3) % Change in P	(4) Real GDP (Y) ($ in billions)	(5) % Change in Y ($ in billions)	(6) Nominal GDP (PY) ($ in billions)	(7) % Change in PY ($ in billions)
2010	111.0		13,088		14,527	
		2.1		1.7		3.9
2011	113.3		13,313		15,088	

b. 3.8

CHAPTER **4**   **The Monetary System: What It Is, and How It Works**

Data Questions

1. a. and b.

Table 4-2

(1) Year	(2) Monetary Base ($ in billions)	(3) M1 (in Dec.) ($ in billions)	(4) M1 Money Multiplier	(5) M2 (in Dec.) ($ in billions)	(6) M2 Money Multiplier
1987	240	750	3.1	2,831	11.8
1997	480	1,073	2.2	4,029	8.4
2007	825	1,375	1.7	7,485	9.1

c. If the Fed had preset targets for $M1$, it would have had to continually increase its target for the monetary base after 1987 to offset the decline in the $M1$ money multiplier. If the Fed had preset targets for $M2$, it would have had to increase its target for the monetary base between 1987 and 1997 to offset the decrease in the $M2$ money multiplier.

d. **Table 4-3**

(1) Year	(2) Monetary Base ($ in billions)	(3) M1 (in Dec.) ($ in billions)	(4) M1 Money Multiplier	(5) M2 (in Dec.) ($ in billions)	(6) M2 Money Multiplier
2007	825	1,375	1.7	7,485	9.1
2011	2,611	2,174	0.8	9,640	3.7

e. The increase in the monetary base was the result of the Fed's quantitative easing, which was designed to increase liquidity in the banking system and help the economy recover from the financial crisis of 2008–2009. Although the monetary base and bank reserves soared, banks were reluctant to increase their loans. As a result, banks increased their reserve-deposit ratio, which decreased the money multiplier.

2. The average federal funds rate was 5.02 percent in 2007, 0.16 percent in 2009, and 0.10 percent in 2011. As of February, 2012, the Fed was keeping it close to zero in order to bolster a fragile economic recovery.

CHAPTER **5**   **Inflation: Its Causes, Effects, and Social Costs**

Problems

10. a.   The costs of expected inflation are the shoeleather costs of inflation, the menu costs of changing prices, the cost of unindexed taxes, the cost of greater variability in prices, and the costs to people who receive incomes fixed in nominal terms (such as private pensions) that were contracted before the inflation was expected.

   b.   Although federal income taxes are now indexed for inflation, taxes on capital gains and interest income are not. Consequently, if inflation were to fall from 2 percent to 0 percent and, according to the Fisher effect, nominal interest rates were to fall by 2 percentage points, the after-tax real return to saving and investment would increase.

   c.   3 percent, assuming a constant velocity of money

   d.   Expected inflation would fall; the nominal interest rate would fall; real money demand would increase by more than the 3-percent growth in output; real money balances would increase by the same amount; the price level would fall; actual inflation would temporarily be negative.

   e.   With 0 percent inflation, real wages can fall only if nominal wages decline, and workers vigorously resist reductions in nominal wages.

Data Questions

1. a.   **Table 5-9**

(1)	(2)	(3)	(4)	(5)	(6)	(7)
			Consumer Price Indices			
			CPI			
Year	CPI All items	% Change	Medical Care	% Change	CPI Energy	% Change
1969	36.7		31.9		24.8	
		171.4		215.4		302.8
1983	99.6		100.6		99.9	
		61.1		133.2		11.6
1997	160.5		234.6		111.5	
		40.1		70.6		118.7
2011	224.9		400.3		243.9	

   b. $6.27

   c.   1969–1983

   d.   1997–2011

   e.   The OPEC oil shocks in 1973–1974 and 1979 and the more recent oil price shocks in 2002–2005 account for the increase in the relative price of oil during those periods.

2. a. **Table 5-10**

(1) Year	(2) Nominal GDP ($ in billions)	(3) GDP Deflator	(4) % Change in GDP Deflator	(5) M1 (Dec.) ($ in billions)	(6) % Change in M1	(7) M2 (Dec.) ($ in billions)	(8) % Change in M2
1978	2,294	40.4		357		1,366	
			66.1		120.4		119.1
1988	5,100	67.1		787		2,993	
			27.6		39.3		46.0
1998	8,794	85.6		1,096		4,370	
			26.9		46.6		88.4
2008	14,292	108.6		1,607		8,232	

   b. If the long-run growth rate of real GDP is 3 percent per year, or about 34 percent per decade, and velocity were constant, the quantity theory would predict that

$$\pi = \% \text{ Change in } M - 34\% \text{ per decade.}$$

   If we use $M1$ as our measure of the money supply, the simple quantity theory predicts 10-year inflation rates of 86.4 percent from 1978 to 1988; 5.3 percent from 1988 to 1998, and 12.6 percent from 1998 to 2008.

   c. Using $M1$, the quantity theory is a fairly good predictor of inflation in the first and third decades and a poor predictor in the middle decade.

   d. If we use $M2$ as our measure of the money supply, the simple quantity theory predicts 10-year inflation rates of 85.1 percent, 12.0 percent, and 54.4 percent for the three decades, respectively. It is a fairly good predictor for the first two decades, but not for the most recent decade.

3. a. V for $M2$ in 1978 = 1.68; V for $M2$ in 2008 = 1.74; obviously, $M2$ velocity has risen a bit, contrary to the assumption of the simple quantity theory, but not much.

   b. V for $M1$ in 1978 = 6.43, V for $M1$ in 2008 = 8.89; $M1$ velocity has risen a lot, contrary to the assumption of the simple quantity theory.

   c. Even if velocity changes, $MV = PY$ and the % change in M + % change in V approximately equals the % change in P + % change in Y. Thus, if both velocity and real GDP change steadily over time, % change in P = % change in M + % change in Y – % change in V, and any increase in the money supply will be accompanied by an equal increase in the price level.

   d. **Table 5-11**

(1) Year	(2) Real GDP ($ in billions)	(3) % Change in Real GDP	(4) M1 (Dec.) $ in billions	(5) % Change in M1	(6) M2 (Dec.) $ in billions	(7) % Change in M2
2008	$13,162		$1,607		$8,232	
		1.2		35.3		17.1
2011	$13,313		$2,174		$9,640	

   e. Predicted percentage change in the GDP deflator using $M1$ = 34.1 percent

   f. Predicted percentage change in the GDP deflator using $M2$ = 15.9 percent

   g. GDP deflator for 2008 = 108.6; GDP deflator for 2011 = 113.3; % change in GDP deflator = 4.3 percent

   h. The income velocities of both $M1$ and $M2$ increased dramatically during this three-year period.

CHAPTER **6**   **The Open Economy**

Problems

12. a.   If the deficit were eliminated, public saving would rise. If taxes were cut, in the long run private saving would also rise. Thus, national saving would rise.

   b.   In a closed economy, the S curve shifts right (as saving increases), the real rate of interest falls, and the amount of investment increases although the investment curve does not shift:

Graph for Problem 12(b)

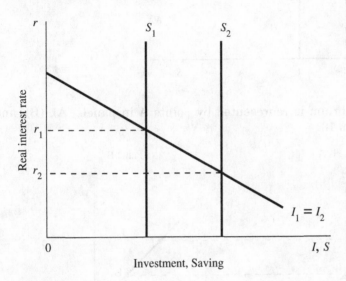

   c.   Graph for Problems 12(c) and 12(d)

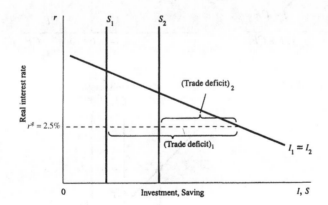

   d.   Treating the United States as a small open economy, we once again shift the S curve to the right as national saving increases. The real interest rate, however, remains fixed at r^*. Consequently, investment does not change, but $S - I$ increases.

e.   As the $S - I$ curve shifts right below, the U.S. real exchange rate falls and net exports rise.
Graph for Problem 12(e)

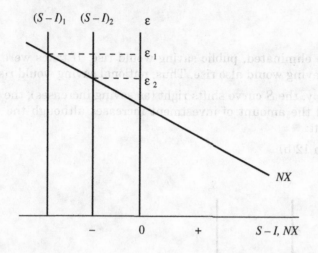

18. The initial equilibrium is represented by points A in panels (A), (B), and (C) below.
Graph for Problem 18

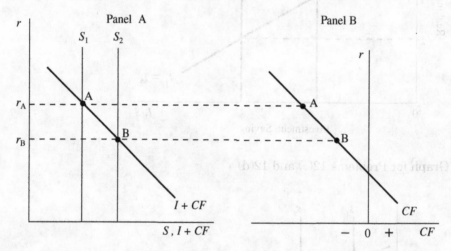

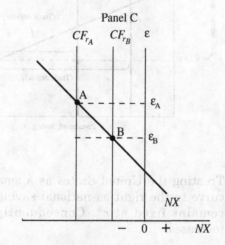

The reduction in taxes and government spending would increase national saving and shift the S curve right to S_2 in panel (A). The $I + CF$ curve would not shift, so the domestic real interest rate would fall to point B. Consequently, the level of net capital outflow would rise in panel (B). Since net capital outflow equals the trade surplus, the latter would also rise, implying a decrease in the trade deficit. As NX rises, the real exchange rate will fall. As the domestic real interest rate falls, investment will rise.

Data Questions

1. a. **Table 6-8**

(1) Year	(2) Nominal GDP ($ in billions)	(3) Exports of Goods and Services ($ in billions)	(4) Exports as % of Nominal GDP	(5) Imports of Goods and Services ($ in billions)	(6) Imports as % of Nominal GDP
1971	1,127	63	5.6	62	5.5
1991	5,992	597	10.0	624	10.4
2011	15,088	2,088	13.8	2,666	17.7

   b. increased; more
   c. **Table 6-9**

(1) Year	(2) Net Exports of Goods and Services ($ in billions)	(3) Net Exports as % of Nominal GDP
1971	1	0.1
1991	−27	−0.5
2011	−578	−3.8

   d. 1; 1
   e. −578; −578

CHAPTER **7** **Unemployment**

Problems

3. a. The Western European natural rate of unemployment in the 1960s was 2.5 percent, compared with the U.S. natural rate in the textbook of 4.76 percent.
   b. 8 percent
6. a. $E/POP = E/L \times L/POP$, where POP = the noninstitutional population
   b. E/POP indicates the portion of the population that has a job. In a healthy economy, this will be large. Furthermore, many of the unemployed may not really want to work at the jobs that area available to them. While it may be difficult to measure true unemployment accurately, it is easier to measure E and POP.
   c. The unemployment rate represents the portion of those who desire to work who cannot find work. Even if the employment-to-population ratio is high, a high unemployment rate will signify an economy that is producing much less than its potential. Furthermore, if leisure is a normal good, the goal of society may well be a low employment-to-population ratio coupled with a low unemployment rate.

Data Questions

Labor Force Participation Rate (in percent)

1. a. **Table 7-1**

(1) Year	(2) Male and Female Total Civilian	(3) Civilian Males	(4) Civilian Females
1971	60.2	79.1	43.4
1991	66.2	75.8	57.4
2011	64.1	70.5	58.1

   b. The labor-force participation rate among civilian females has increased as more married women have entered the labor market. The labor-force participation rate among civilian males has fallen because of earlier retirement and greater disability, among other reasons.

   c. Real GDP has risen by the amount of extra output women produce in their new jobs. "Total production" does not rise as much as measured real GDP because the reduction in household production that was formerly performed by these women must be subtracted from the extra output produced in paid employment, especially between 1971 and 1991. If we consider the fact that many of these women now pay others to do some of this household production, the difference between the change in real GDP and the change in "total production" is even greater.

2. a. The median of a group of numbers is the "middle" number. Half of the numbers are greater than the median, and half are less than the median. The mean or average is equal to the sum of all the numbers divided by the number of numbers.

   b. **Table 7-2**

(1) Year	(2) Unemployment Rate	(3) Mean (Average) Duration of Unemployment (weeks)	(4) Median Duration of Unemployment (weeks)
2006	4.6	16.8	8.3
2011	8.9	39.4	21.4

   c. In 2006, unemployment in the United States was characterized by many short spells and a smaller number of very long spells. Hence, the median duration of unemployment was only about 2 months while the mean duration was twice that.

   d. Barro believes that the increases are largely due to the extension of unemployment insurance benefits to 99 weeks. Krugman (and others) believe that the increase is due to a lack of jobs. According to the model presented in Chapter 7 of the textbook, this might occur if there was an increase in real wage rigidity, resulting in greater structural unemployment.

3. a., b., and c.
   Table 7-3

(1) Year	(2) Unemployment Rate	(3) Inflation Rate (Year to Year)	(4) Conventional Misery Index	(5) New Misery Index
2008	5.8%	3.8%	9.6	13.7
2010	9.6%	1.6%	11.2	17.9
2011	8.9%	3.2%	12.1	18.3

   d. Economic suffering has increased more rapidly using the new misery index.

CHAPTER **8** **Economic Growth I: Capital Accumulation and Population Growth**

Data Questions

1. a. Approximate Average Annual Percentage Growth Rates of Real GDP

	1993–2002	2002–2011
United States	3.4	1.6
Germany	1.4	1.2
Japan	0.8	0.7
China	9.8	10.7
India	5.8	8.1
Sub-Saharan Africa	3.7	5.6

b. Real GDP per capita in China would surpass real GDP in the United States in the year 2061.

CHAPTER **10** **Introduction to Economic Fluctuations**

Problems

4. The short-run aggregate supply curve would shift downward, while the aggregate demand curve would be unaffected. Output would rise, and the aggregate price level would fall.

Data Questions

1. a. **Table 10-4**

	(1) 2007 (in 1,000s)	(2) 2010 (in 1,000s)	(3) % Change 2007–2010
Civilian noninstitutional population	231,867	237,830	2.6
Civilian labor force	153,124	153,889	0.5
Civilian employment	146,047	139,064	–4.8
Civilian unemployment	7,078	14,825	109.5

b. During the recession the labor force grew significantly less than the noninstitutional population, but employment actually fell by about 5 percent. Unemployment more than doubled.

c. The actual unemployment rate would eventually return to its natural rate of 6 percent.

2. a. and b.

Table 10-5

(1) Year	(2) Unemployment Rate (%)	(3) Change in Unemployment Rate	(4) Predicted % Change in Real GDP	(5) Real GDP ($ in billions)	(6) Actual % Change in Real GDP
2008	5.8			13,162	
		3.5	−4.0		−3.5
2009	9.3			12,703	
		0.3	2.4		3.0
2010	9.6			13,088	
		−0.7	4.4		1.7
2011	8.9			13,313	

b. Okun's law worked reasonably well between 2008 and 2010, but it over-predicted economic growth substantially between 2010 and 2011.

3. The Conference Board's leading economic indicator rose by 0.5 percent in December, 2011, and by 0.4 percent in January, 2012, implying that real GDP will increase moderately in the future.

CHAPTER **11**   **Aggregate Demand I**

Problems

4. a.   0.75

   b.   Graph for Problem 4(b)

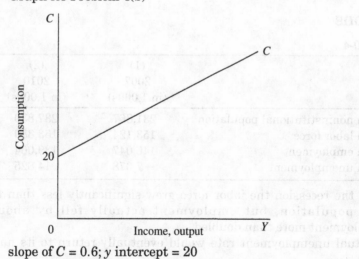

slope of $C = 0.6$; y intercept = 20

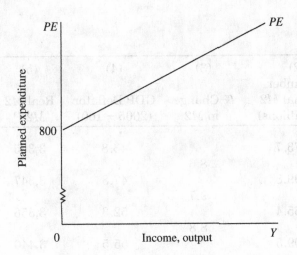

slope of $PE = 0.6$; y intercept = 800

   c.   2,000

   d.   0

   e.   The government-purchases multiplier is 2.5. When G rises, the multiplier is smaller than $1/(1 - MPC)$ because any increase in income will be accompanied by an increase in taxes. Hence, the increase in disposable income in each round will be smaller than the increase in income. Alternatively, the slope of the planned expenditure curve becomes $MPC(1 - t)$, where t equals the income tax rate. Hence, the multiplier becomes $1/[1 - MPC(1 - t)]$.

6. a.   Planned investment might increase as Y rises (leading to the positively sloped line below) if investment depends on profits or sales expectations (along with r) and either or both of these rise along with Y.

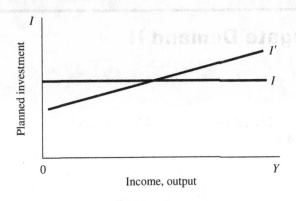

   b.   i. The slope of the planned-expenditure curve would increase.

       ii. The government-purchases multiplier would increase.

       iii.The IS curve would be flatter, and the LM curve would be unaffected.

Data Questions

1. a. **Table 11-7**

(1)	(2)	(3)	(4)	(5)	(6)
Year	December Nominal $M2$ ($ in billions)	% Change in $M2$	GDP Deflator (2005 = 100)	Real $M2$ $M2/P$	% Change in $M2/P$
1979	1,473.7		43.8	3,365	
		8.6			−0.5
1980	1,599.8		47.8	3,347	
		9.7			0.3
1981	1,755.4		52.3	3,356	
		8.8			2.5
1982	1,909.3		55.5	3,440	
		11.3			7.1
1983	2,125.7		57.7	3,684	

b. The *LM* curve implies that changes in the real money supply are the appropriate measures of monetary conditions. Using this measure, the Fed pursued mildly contractionary monetary policy between 1979 and 1980, neutral policy between 1980 and 1981, expansionary policy between 1981 and 1982, and very expansionary policy between 1982 and 1983. A better measure might be changes in the real money supply in excess of the long-run growth rate of natural GDP of 3 percent. Using this measure, monetary policy was contractionary during the first three periods and expansionary in the fourth.

CHAPTER **12**   **Aggregate Demand II**

Problems

4. a. The deficit would fall. The *IS* curve would shift to the left.
   Graph for Problem 4(a)

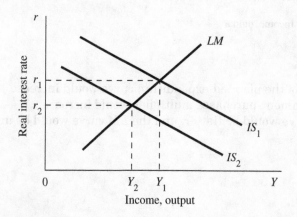

As a result, the interest rate would fall, but so would real GDP. This last change is contrary to some economists' predictions.

b. If expansionary monetary policy is pursued simultaneously, the interest rate and the deficit will still fall and real income may actually rise.
Graph for Problem 4(b)

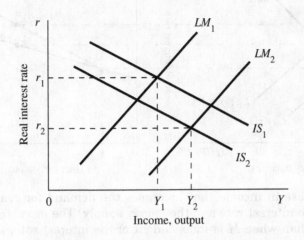

c. In part (a), the aggregate demand curve shifts left. In part (b), the aggregate demand curve shifts right if Y rises.

13. a. Graph for Problem 13(a)

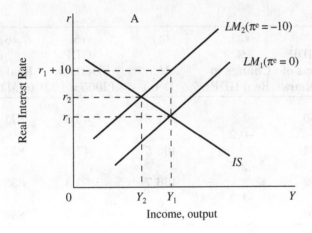

b. If r is on the vertical axis, the IS curve will not shift in response to a change in expected inflation, but the LM curve will shift upward by 10 percentage points. Consequently, i and Y fall and r rises. Although the graph is different from the one in the textbook because r is now on the vertical axis, the changes to Y, i, and r are the same.

14. If the money supply M increased as the interest rate increased, the money supply curve would be upward sloping.

Graph for Problem 14

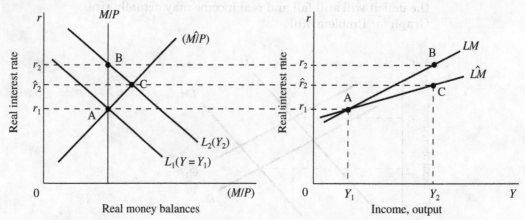

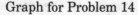

Consequently, an increase in income that increases the demand for real money balances would increase the interest rate and the money supply. The increase in the interest rate would be less than when M is independent of the interest rate, resulting in a flatter LM curve.

Data Questions

1. a. **Table 12-1**

(1) Year	(2) Real GDP in billions of 2005 dollars	(3) % Change in Real GDP	(4) M1 (Dec.)	(5) GDP Deflator (2005 = 100)	(6) Real M1 (= M1/P)	(7) % Change in Real M1
1979	5,850		381.8	43.8	871.7	
		−0.2				−2.0
1980	5,834		408.5	47.8	854.6	
		2.5				−2.3
1981	5,982		436.7	52.3	835.0	
		−1.9				2.5
1982	5,866		474.8	55.5	855.5	

b. The reduction in real GDP was much greater during the Great Depression, even though the reduction in real money balances from 1929 to 1933 was smaller than during the 1979–1981 period.

2. a. **Table 12-2**

(1) Year	(2) Real GDP in billions of 2000 dollars	(3) % Change in Real GDP	(4) Interest Rate on 10-Year U.S. Treasury Securities
1963	3,204		4.00
		12.6	
1965	3,607		4.28

b. Since the interest rate remained relatively constant while real GDP rose, it may be presumed that both the LM and the IS curves shifted to the right and that the horizontal shift was the same for both curves. Consequently, the Federal Reserve must have increased the money supply during this period.

CHAPTER **14**   **Aggregate Supply and the Short-Run Tradeoff Between Inflation and Unemployment**

Data Questions

1. a.   The three most recent years for which we have data are 2009, 2010, and 2011.

Table 14-1

(1)	(2)	(3)	(4)	(5)
Year	Unemployment Rate (%)	Average Unemployment Rate (%)	Consumer Price Index Excluding Food and Energy	Percentage Change in the CPI Excluding Food and Energy
2009	9.3		219.2	
		9.45		1.0
2010	9.6		221.3	
		9.25		1.7
2011	8.9		225.0	

b.   Graph for Data Question 1

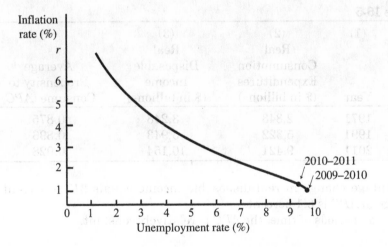

c.   Since the actual unemployment rate is substantially above the natural rate of unemployment, one can infer that the actual core inflation rate is below the expected core inflation rate. Consequently, over time the expected core inflation rate should fall. This will shift the Phillips curve down and, if there are no additional shocks, the actual inflation rate will fall.

CHAPTER 16   Understanding Consumer Behavior

Problems

4. a. $C_1 = 100; C_2 = 125; S = 20$

   b. $C_1 = 93.33; C_2 = 140; S = 26.67$

6. a.   A country with a rapidly increasing population will have a higher saving rate (and a lower aggregate *APC*) than a country with a steady population because each successive generation of workers, who do the saving, will be larger than the preceding generation of workers.

   b.   A country with a rapidly growing real GDP per capita will have a higher saving rate (and a lower aggregate *APC*) than a country with a stagnant economy. Each successive generation of workers in the growing economy earns more per person (and hence saves more per person) than what the current generation of retirees earned (and saved) when it was working and from which it is now dissaving.

10.   After the legislation was passed, all the future tax cuts became expected. According to this theory, people's permanent incomes rose (and, hence, their consumption rose) only in the first year, 1981, which would be the only year in which consumption changed as a result of the tax changes unless people had borrowing constraints.

Data Questions

1. a.   **Table 16-5**

(1) Year	(2) Real Consumption Expenditures ($ in billions)	(3) Real Disposable Income ($ in billions)	(4) Average Propensity to Consume (*APC*)
1971	2,843	3,248	0.875
1991	5,322	5,943	0.896
2011	9,421	10,154	0.928

   b.   Percentage change in real disposable income equals 212.6 percent; percentage change in *APC* is 6.1 percent.

   c.   Over long periods of time, the *APC* is relatively constant.

2. a.   **Table 16-6**

(1) Year	(2) Consumption Expenditures ($ in billions)	(3) Disposable Income ($ in billions)	(4) Average Propensity to Consume (*APC*)
1967	508	575	0.883
1968	558	625	0.893
1970	648	736	0.881

   b.   In 1968, Congress passed a temporary tax surcharge. This did not have a significant effect on people's permanent incomes, so they maintained their previous levels of consumption by reducing their current saving and temporarily increasing their *APC*.

CHAPTER **17** **The Theory of Investment**

Problems

9. a. An investment tax credit of 8 percent allows firms to deduct 8 percent of their investment expenditures from their taxes.

   b. The cost of capital declines at each real interest rate. Consequently, the *IS* curve shifts to the right. The *LM* curve does not shift.

   c. i. The *IS* curve shifts to the right for the same reason as in part (b). The *LM* curve does not shift.

      ii. As the real domestic interest rate rises, U.S. net capital outflow falls.

      iii. The U.S. trade surplus also falls. Consequently, the real foreign exchange rate rises.

Data Questions

1. a. **Table 17-3**

(1) Year	(2) Real Nonresidential Investment in Structures ($ in billions)	(3) Real Nonresidential Investment in Equipment and Software ($ in billions)	(4) Real Residential Investment ($ in billions)	(5) Real Change in Business Inventories ($ in billions)
2001	433	861	583	–41.8
2006	384	1,071	718	59.4
2011	322	1,124	326	35.6

   b. The percentage change between the highest and lowest values was 34.5 percent for investment in structures, 30.5 percent for investment in equipment and software, 120.2 percent for residential investment, and undefined for changes in business inventories. Inventory investment was relatively the most volatile, and investment in equipment and software was the least volatile during this period.

2.   **Table 17-14**

(1) Month	(2) Average Value of S&P 500 Index	(3) Percentage Change in S&P 500 Index	(4) Quarter and Year	(5) Real GDP (Billions of 2005 $)	(6) Percentage Change in Real GDP
August, 2008	1,281		2008: Q4	12,884	
		−31.1			−1.6
November, 2008	883		2009: Q1	12,663	
		−8.8			−0.2
February, 2009	805		2009: Q2	12,641	
		12.0			0.4
May, 2009	902		2009: Q3	12,695	
		12.0			0.9
August, 2009	1,010		2009: Q4	12,814	
		7.7			1.0
November, 2009	1,088		2010: Q1	12,938	

The fall in the stock market between August and November, 2008, and between November, 2008, and February, 2009, foretold the large subsequent declines in real GDP. The stock market rebound after February, 2009, foretold the subsequent economic recovery, but the latter was sluggish.

CHAPTER **18**   **Topics in Macroeconomic Policy**

Problems

6. a.   If capital gains taxes are reduced, the after-tax return to saving would increase. This might increase total saving, which would spur additional investment in a closed economy or a large open economy.
   b.   A capital gains tax reduction on past acquisitions will increase the after-tax returns on past saving rather than future saving. The wealth effect might even reduce new saving. Consequently, the revenue losses might not lead to additional saving and investment.
   c.   Although the concentration of tax reductions on new acquisitions would solve the problem in part b, it might not spur additional saving and investment as much as expected because individuals might expect the government to increase capital gains taxes again in the future once their projects become "past acquisitions."

Data Questions

1. a. **Table 18-1**

Year	(2) Real GDP Growth Forecast (%)	(3) Actual Real GDP Growth Rate (%)	(4) Unemployment Rate Forecast (%)	(5) Actual Unemployment Rate (%)
2012	2.3	_____	8.3	_____
2013	2.7	_____	7.9	_____

   b. The actual GDP growth rate and unemployment rate were not known when this *Study Guide* went to press.

CHAPTER **19** **Government Debt and Budget Deficits**

Problems

4. According to the traditional view, the future reduction in government spending would have no effect on the sum of current and expected future income, current consumption, or current private saving. According to the Ricardian view, a future reduction in government purchases will be accompanied by an expected future reduction in taxes. This will increase the sum of current and expected future disposable income, increase current consumption, and decrease current private saving.

5. a. Country A: $140 billion; Country B: $40 billion
   b. Country A: $0 Billion; Country B: –$100 billion
   c. Country A: $2,000 billion; Country B: $1,900 billion
   d. Country A: $2,000 billion; Country B: $1,900/0.95 = $2,000 billion
   e. $200 + 0.07($2,000) – $340 = $0 billion in both countries
   f. Understate; as the price level falls, the real value of outstanding government debt rises, but this increase is not included in the official deficit.

Data Questions

1. a.   **Table 19-3**   (Data in billions of $)

(1)	(2)	(3)	(4)	(5)
Fiscal Year	Total Federal Government Receipts	Total Federal Government Outlays	Official Federal Budget Surplus	Gross Federal Debt Held by Public (end of year)
2006	2,407	2,655	−248	4,829
2007	2,568	2,729	−161	5,035
2008	2,524	2,983	−459	5,803
2009	2,105	3,518	−1,413	7,545
2010	2,163	3,456	−1,293	9,019

b. and c.

Table 19-4

(1)	(2)	(3)	(4)	(5)
Calendar Year	Price Deflator for GDP (2005 = 100)	Percentage Change	Gross Federal Debt Held by Public (end of *preceding* fiscal year) ($ in billions)	Approximate "True" Federal Budget Surplus ($ in billions)
2007	106.2		4,829	−50
		2.3		
2008	108.6		5,035	−409
		1.0		
2009	109.7		5,803	−1,343
		1.2		
2010	111.0		7,545	−1,135
		2.1		
2011	113.3			

2. a. and b.

Table 19-5

(1)	(2)	(3)
Country	Ratio of Net federal debt in 2011 to GDP (%)	Standard and Poor's Feb. 2012 "Local Currency" Bond Rating
Greece	133.1	CC
Japan	127.6	AA−
Italy	100.2	BBB+
United States	73.8	AA+
Germany	51.5	AAA
Spain	45.6	A
Switzerland	0.4	AAA

c.   Countries with high net debt–GDP ratios in 2011 have worse current bond ratings.

d.   Countries with worse debt ratings must pay higher real interest rates on their bonds.